FERNDO
A LOOK

An aerial view of Ferndown in 1970
Photo courtesy of Kitchenham Ltd.

AUDREY
GREENHALGH

Researched by Audrey Greenhalgh during 1989/90

After a period of rapid social change such as Ferndown has experienced over the last seventy five years it is fitting that this record should be published to show how a village community has changed during the lifetime of its inhabitants.

In the cause of researching this book I consulted many people, the following list includes those to whom I am particularly indebted.

Sir Richard Trehane

Squadron Leader Percy Christopher

Members of the Ferndown Historical Society

Mrs Rosamond Mathews

Mrs Jean Rigler

Mrs Gwen Wells

Mr Henry Bolton

Miss Daphne Hills B.A.

The facts contained herein are, to the best of my knowledge, correct. However a lot of the information was obtained from the recollections of locals and can only be as accurate as the memories allow.

My thanks to my friend Audrey Craig for acting as my chauffeur and to Mike Power for preparing and making sense of my scribblings.

This book is dedicated to my brother Dennis Emerton, who shared my childhood adventures.

AUDREY GREEHALGH

First Published 1991

ISBN 0-9514502-5-5

1 Clayford Ave

Ferndown

Dorset

Typeset and printed by: Pardy & Son (Printers) Ltd., Parkside, Ringwood, Hampshire

Fiergen — Fyrne — Fern Down and eventually by the 1900's Ferndown. It began life as part of the Parish of Hampreston and grew up from the great heathland, with few cottages and even less shops but as time passed it changed until it is today a thriving town with its own Mayor.

In 1861 the population was just 1,115 most of whom were employed on the land. In general terms it stretched from Tricketts Cross, named after a family of small stature, along the Wimborne Road to Stapehill, and on the Ringwood Road from Tricketts Cross to Dudsbury Avenue. Victoria Road, Church Road, Dudsbury Avenue, Ameysford Road and New Road were all gravel roads with many pot holes which made for uncomfortable travelling. The boundary today though has moved south to include Longham and Dudsbury, and west to bring in Canford Bottom and Hayes. Whilst Ferndown has grown enormously its 'mother', Hampreston, has still retained its small village image.

Town Mayor Peter Gutteridge photographed with staff and fellow councillors 1990–1991.
Photograph courtesy of Photolink, Wimborne.

My Aunt Annie had a house in Ameysford Road named "Highfield", although at that time it was Ameysford Lane. My brother and I spent many happy holidays with her. I am pleased to say it is still there. In her younger days she was cook to a titled family. I will never forget the time she asked my brother and I if we would like a glass of lemonade, upon being told "yes please", instead of reaching for a bottle she reached instead for two lemons from the fruit bowl and, with other ingredients, she produced the most glorious glass of fizzy pop I have ever tasted, we thought she was wonderful.

Opposite my aunt's house lived my uncle, Jesse Revel, he had a smallholding. This has now unfortunately gone and a development of new houses are on the land. I can recall that my Aunt Sally, Jesse's wife, always had a big black stew pot hung over the open fire which was never allowed to empty constantly being replenished with rabbit and vegetables. They must have lived on the same diet for years but it obviously did them no harm as they both lived to a ripe old age. Another memory of those days was our wellington boots lined up in her outside porch ready for scrambling over the common behind the house; it was always very damp because I can remember collecting sundews and cotton grass that grew in abundance there. It is now a housing estate, I wonder if they suffer from damp?

Miss Annie Revel who lived in 'Highfield' with Audery and Dennis Emerton and her nephew 'Jumbo', father of Audrey and Dennis.

Eliza Hames and family.

A walk down Ameysford Road takes us past the home of Mr and Mrs Hames, mother of ten children; and on to the shops in Wimborne Road. When we were not with her, my aunt would go on her 'sit up and beg' bike. We would turn left and cross the main road. On the right hand side was a forest of pine trees, known locally as the 'plantation'. The first shop we would go into would be Ferndown Stores, which traded right up until 1990. At one time the store was called 'Creamers'. The adjoining shop, now a chinese takeaway, was part of the store selling wet fish and later becoming a bakery and after that a pet shop. And past the Central Stores run by a Mr A.G. Whittingham with his unusual Christian name of Antwerp. Besides being an agent for Dongola Tea and curing his own bacon he also would hire a horse and trap. If we had been good we went into the newsagents for a 'penneth' of sweets, and my aunt's Womans Weekly; it always had a story for children and, I believe, it still does.

Tying old shoes to the fender of the bridal car is an old custom. It originates from the days when the father of the bride gave the new husband his daughters old shoes as a symbol that he was now responsible for her.

When the couple cut the bridal cake it is so that they both share in the good luck.

We walk on past Goswell's Garage, past Manor Dairy as it was in 1912, by 1925 the Bolton family had taken it over. Mr Henry Bolton can recall the time when he used to help his father deliver the milk, twice a day then, no fridges of course, and very often he would find a pair of rabbits, cabbages, eggs or the like left on customers doorsteps in lieu of payment for milk. A farm workers wage in 1914 was only 14 shillings a week. By 1942 it had only gone up by 2 shillings to 16 shillings. Many had large families and money was often hard to come by and produce more readily available. He also recalls that on Christmas morning he would have to go and rescue his father who, due to the kindness of his customers with their offers of seasonal liquid refreshment, was incapable of making his own way back to the dairy.

On the opposite side of the road, just past the Plantation, is the Congregational Chapel, now the United Reform Church.

A. C. Whittingham's General Store.

COUNTRY SUPERSTITIONS

If a girl can walk un-harmed through a swarm of bees she is deemed to be a virgin.

Horses with four white feet are regarded as unlucky but one with a single white 'stocking' very lucky.

An early photograph of Wimborne Road, Goswell's Garage is in the centre of the picture.

Ferndown Congregational Chapel erected in 1905.

On we go until we reach the corner of Victoria Road. On the opposite corner is the post office and general stores. First run by Mrs Gould whose husband was a carpenter and coffin maker, the two jobs often going hand in hand. Later the store was taken over by Mr Galton and sold a variety of goods as well as being the post office. The store also provided the first home for Lloyds Bank, occupying his sitting room one day a week. Next door was the first Methodist Chapel. The building still remains although it is now a furniture and antique showroom. A new chapel was built at Ferndown crossroads which is now of course the fire station.

The first police station in Ferndown was situated in Victoria Road on the left hand side (before you reach Victoria Gardens) near the nursery. Vera Culley's father, an old 'Ferndownian', was the constable.

Galton's Stores.

COUNTRY SUPERSTITIONS

A warm January – a cold May.

See spiders in the morning is a sign of sorrow
See spiders in the noon brings worry the morrow.

See a spider in the afternoon, a sign of a gift
but a spider in the evening all hopes uplift.

Galton's Stores in 1920.

Wimborne Road showing the stores on the right taken in the 1930's.

Victoria Road taken in 1942.

Wimborne Road East taken from the end of Woodside Road around 1920.

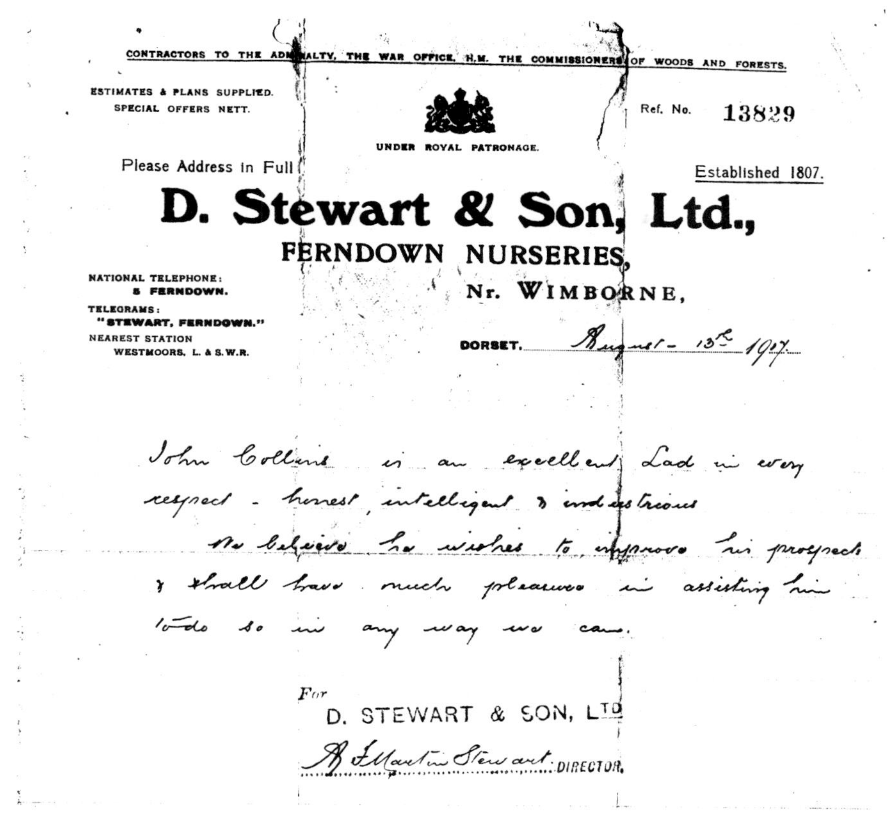

CONTRACTORS TO THE ADMIRALTY, THE WAR OFFICE, H.M. THE COMMISSIONERS OF WOODS AND FORESTS.

ESTIMATES & PLANS SUPPLIED.
SPECIAL OFFERS NETT.

UNDER ROYAL PATRONAGE.

Ref. No. 13829

Please Address in Full

Established 1807.

D. Stewart & Son, Ltd.,

FERNDOWN NURSERIES,

Nr. WIMBORNE,

NATIONAL TELEPHONE: 5 FERNDOWN.
TELEGRAMS: "STEWART, FERNDOWN."
NEAREST STATION WESTMOORS, L. & S.W.R.

DORSET. August – 13th 1917

John Collins is an excellent Lad in every respect – honest, intelligent & industrious
As he wishes to improve his prospects & shall have much pleasure in assisting him to do so in any way we can.

For
D. STEWART & SON, LTD
A. J. Martin Stewart. DIRECTOR.

John Collins Reference from Stewart's nursery.

A family of long standing in Ferndown are the Stewarts. They came from Scotland and, finding the soil to their liking, set up a market garden here in 1801. D. Stewart & Sons Ltd, were advertising on their letterheads as being 'contractors to the Admiralty, the War Office and H.M. Commissioners of Woods and Forests'. They had a nursery at the corner of Wimborne Road and West Moors Road going towards Tricketts Cross. They employed many local men, one of them John Collins whose reference, upon leaving their employ, is shown here. Another, Jim Prior lived in Victoria Road and it was his duty to ring the early morning bell at the nurseries, his neighbours could always tell the time in the morning by the clumping of his boots on the road as he passed by. Stewarts are still today in the forefront of market gardening with large garden centres at Somerford in Christchurch and God Blessings Lane at Holt. In the early days I believe they also had a rose nursery in a field at Parley Cross.

Miss Dora Prior with her chickens.

John Prior's Cottage in Victoria Road built in 1895 for £26.00.

It was Stewarts who were responsible for the laying out of the Ferndown Golf Course which was officially opened in 1922 with Ted Ray and Harry Varden playing the first round. The first club house was an old army hut; the present being built in 1937. The fees in 1825 were £3 a year and the professional in 1929 was a Mr Steadman, followed by a Mr Rendall and later Mr Percy Allis who in turn was followed by his well known son Peter. During the 30's the Ferndown Golf Club held every lady's and men's championship in Dorset, a great record. It is still a very popular club.

Our business concluded it was home again for lunch. We meet Uncle Jesse on our way, he is off to the 'Pure Drop' for a glass of something to 'whet his whistle'. The original Pure Drop was a thatched building but demolished in the 1920's. A new pub was built on the site and renamed 'The Ferndown Hotel' but I am glad to say it has reverted back to the original name. In 1911 when Fred Ellis was the licensee the pub was much frequented by the gypsy fraternity, fights were inevitable. In the 1930's they had a very good football team, they played on a field behind the pub.

The Pure Drop Inn before it was demolished in 1928.

The Pure Drop football team taken in the 1920's.

A longer walk up Victoria Road to the more populated part of Ferndown would have to be taken if we needed a greater variety of goods. We would pass John Capes nursery on the right. Mainly private houses on the left. And on to Street's Dairy, now owned by Unigates. They had two horses, one called Boxer and the other Adam. People were much more trusting in those days, they would leave their empty milk jugs on the draining boards ready to be filled, to keep out the insects they were always covered with a little muslin cloth with beads around the edge. If the children were home, an apple or carrot was left for the horse.

We then passed a house where Mr and Mrs Baker and their daughter, Mrs Trim lived. Next to them lived Mr Evans, the school attendance officer. Collins the second hand shop was always worth a browse and next door lived a Dutchman, Mr Pardy Cooper. He sold bulbs and earthenware containers, he must have been a very good nurseryman because he exhibited at Chelsea.

On the opposite side of the road was Wallace's the grocer, now a showroom.

Safeways occupies the site where a row of cottages once stood. In one of them lived Mrs Florence Hobbs who also owned the fields at the back. If she saw the children playing in them she would set her Alsatian dog on them.

Mrs. Trim.

Victoria Road in 1951.

Moving towards the village centre, on the corner of Albert Road, was a small garden shop owned by the Mays. Then more cottages; in one of them Dr Limbrey, the school doctor, held his surgery. Next was Morris's ironmongery store. He had a horse drawn delivery wagon for oil and similar items, Dolloways are there now but the shop still retains an old fashioned air about it with its wooden floors and variety of household and garden goods.

Still more cottages. In one of them lived Mr and Mrs Hurst. Mr Hurst was coachman and he took the last mail coach from Salisbury to Totton passing through the New Forest. Because of fears of being held up he was told that once he had started he was never to stop. He went on to be a driver for a Bournemouth doctor, and upon the doctor's demise he found he had been left his buggy and horse. He kept it in the back garden and took a great pride in its appearance and drove it daily around Ferndown. Next to the Hurst's, in a house named 'Marathon', lived Captain and Mrs Dacombe members of a very old Dorsetshire family who can trace their ancestors back to the fourteenth century and whose family home is an Elizabethan Manor House at Corfe. They had a large market garden with numerous green houses reaching almost back to Church Road. These were severely damaged from the blast of a bomb which fell near to them during the Second World War.

Next door to Captain Dacombe was a pair of cottages, now demolished, and a bungalow called Florin built by a retired publican and paid for by the florins that passed over his bar counter, he saved every one.

In later years Mr Stickland had an estate agent's next door. He was affectionately known as the Wessex Wizard. A fine magician and one time president of the Magic Circle, he often entertained the local people at concerts in the village hall.

On the opposite side of the road Captain Dacombe's brother owned a coal business that was later taken over by Tickles. On the same side was a fish and chip shop, a lending library and, on the corner with Ringwood Road, Cobbs Garage. It later became known as Victoria Garage. On the other corner was Turner's chemist, which is still a chemists today.

Ringwood Road in 1929. The second house on the right would now be where the White Heather stands.

We turn left into Ringwood Road and first come to an estate agents, then a paper shop, Jolliffe and Sons furniture store and an undertakers; he later moved round into Victoria Road where he still is today.

On the present site of The White Heather public house was R. Webb & Sons, butchers. The shop reached back almost into Spinneys Lane where Tesco's stores is now located. Later one of the sons had his own butchers shop, it was almost opposite, in the front of No 1, Ivy Cottage. It recently became an estate agents and is now a hairdressers.

In Spinneys Lane is a small row of cottages. In one of them lived Mrs Emma Penny with her daughters, they ran a laundry business and it was from this family that 'Pennys Hill' was derived. Also here lived Granny Foster who delivered the local babies.

The junction of Church Road and Dudsbury Avenue taken from Ringwood Road in the 1950's.

Coronation celebrations for George VI.

Further down Ringwood Road, past St Mary's Church and beyond Church Road, we come to a house now called 'Stile House'. It began life as 'Lawn Farm', and was a small holding and dairy but in 1914 it was the home of Dr Walter Johns. Dr Johns was a pioneer of open air treatment for T.B. patients and who, before moving to Lawn Farm, had a sanatorium at Alderney Manor and later at West Howe, just below the Shoulder of Mutton public house. Dr Johns was a church warden at All Saints Church Hampreston and held many fetes at his farm. He regarded his efforts at farming to be his contribution to the war effort. In later life he unfortunately became blind and had to move away from the area.

Lawn Farm home of Dr. Johns about 1935.

DORSET NAMES FOR BIRDS, INSECTS & ANIMALS

Biddle	=	Beetle
Bunkas	=	Rabbit
Butsie	=	Chicken
Dumbledore	=	Bumble Bee
Dunnock	=	Sparrow
Emmet	=	Ant
Hummock	=	Cow
Palmer	=	Caterpillar
Nestle Trip	=	Runt of a pig litter
Poly Washdish	=	Wagtail

Col. Atkinson raising the flag at Lawn Farm.

A later owner of Lawn Farm was Colonel Atkinson. The picture shows the colonel raising the flag pole in the grounds with the help of Maurice Wilcox.

Still later Mr & Mrs Sadler bought the farm, now renamed 'Sunnylands'. They had a tea rooms and pets corner which grew until it became a proper zoo. A male lion named Ajax and a female named Julia were mated, Ajax unfortunately killed Julia so a new mate was bought in, he obviously preferred her because they did eventually have cubs. The zoo was a great attraction and drew people from miles around. By now buses were running to Ferndown so access was available. The posters advertised lions, bears, monkeys, reptiles and even a miniature railway and a cafe. Admission was one and six (7½p) and 9d (4½p) for children. Eventually it had to close due to traffic congestion and neighbours complaining about the smell.

There is a story that after the zoo had been sold for building, contractors laying pipes came across the decaying corpse of a bear, the stench was so bad work had to stop until the remains were removed. The house still remains today.

Over the road, and opposite was Heath Farm, now a housing estate owned by the Husher family, Heath Farm Road retaining the name. Over Gypsy Lane, now Glenmoor Road, we come to Tice's duck farm. It opened in 1932 and closed in 1945. The ducks were only bred for their feathers which were then sent to London.

Heath Farm on Ringwood Road, home of Mr. Husher.

Ringwood Road in 1938.

Fancy dress parade in 1936 for the Coronation of George VI.

DORSET NAMES FOR FLOWERS

Willywind	=	Convolvulus
Bread and Cheese	=	Hawthorn Buds
Bulls Eyes	=	Marsh Marigolds
Bachelors Buttons	=	Marsh Marigolds
Birds on the bough	=	Common Fumitory
Beans Feast	=	Green Hellebore
Corn Rose	=	Poppy
Granny's Bonnet	=	Colombine
Jack go to bed at noon	=	Scarlet Pimpernel
Fireweed	=	Rosebay Willowherb
Gipsy Laces	=	Cow Parsley
Cow Queen Ann Lace	=	Cow Parsley
Lady in Bed	=	Wild Arum
Love Lies Bleeding	=	Wild Arum
Jack in the Pulpit	=	Wild Arum
Lords and Ladies	=	Wild Arum
Hearts Ease	=	Pansy

Moving back towards Ferndown we pass more cottages, in one of them lived Mr & Mrs Wilcox with their son Morris. Father Wilcox looks not too happy in this picture.

Frances Mary & Daniel Wilcox.

Morris Wilcox son of Francis Mary and Daniel Wilcox.

Frances Wilcox outside her cottage in Ringwood Road

For many years Mr Counter, an upholsterer, had a workshop on the corner of Dudsbury Avenue but before that it was very busy grocers shop owned by Mr Frampton. In Dudsbury Avenue itself there was once a mink farm.

Penny's Hill in the 1930's.

After passing more houses and cottages we reach Forge Parade, named after Neddie Cozens one time blacksmith at Longham. In the parade were a butchers shop, Higby radio, a cake shop, the Gas Company shop and 'Calico' Smith the drapers. Also a large gent's outfitters which could fit a man out from shoes to hat.

And on to the corner of Ringwood Road and New Road. The Post Office and grocers was run in 1920 by Mr Frank Stubbings. Before the post office was opened, stamps could be bought at a cottage on the other corner of New Road. Once there were four mud cottages known as 'The Barracks'. Later a Methodist Chapel was built on the site and that, in turn, was converted into the fire station. Some stones are set into the side wall, one of them bears the inscription Ebeneezer, and the other the letters W.D. I have not yet been able to find out the origin or significance of these stones.

In 1940 Cranborne Rural District Council set up a fire brigade committee to establish a fire service in Ferndown. Up until this time small local fires were put out by local volunteers, the larger fires being dealt with by Wimborne Fire Brigade. With the expansion of Ferndown a proper fire service was deemed necessary and as the chapel was up for sale it seemed a good opportunity to house it there.

Soffe's garage and cycle repair shop, shown in the picture, is where Kwik Save and the shopping parade now stand.

Dudsbury Avenue.

We turn our attention now to Church Road. Walking from Ringwood Road we pass St Mary's Church on the right. The first St Mary's was situated on the corner of St Mary's Road but due to the population growth a new church was built in 1901 on land left to the church in the Will of a Mrs Lyons. The church ran a scout troop, Dougie Cabe being the scout master, also evening classes during the winter months. In the Parish Magazine of 1905 it records that prizes of carving tools were presented to students from the carving class in the hope that they would make good use of them in their spare time. The church combined with 'All Saints' Hampreston to run an annual outing, usually to Weymouth or Swanage, and for this they hired a char-a-banc from Mr Robertson.

In this picture, taken in the 30's, we see the rector of 'All Saints', Mr Peverelle, the curate Mr Adams, the scoutmaster Mr Cabe, Mr Saunders, the verger, Miss Warren the organist and church members who include Miss Ada Dean, Miss Hewitt, Miss Lena Elton, Mr Charles Jones and Mr Reg King. Hats seemed to be the order of the day!

Hampreston and St. Mary's combined church outing to Weymouth in the 1930's.

Church Road opposite the school.

Daughters of Charlotte and Charles Elton outside their cottage in Church Road.

Continuing along the road we pass some large houses until we reach the corner of St Mary's Road, and the first St Mary's. Further along there is a house named 'Widgery' that is still standing.

'Widgery' Church Road.

Dean's family home in Church Road.

Old English Rhyme

Married when the year is new
He'll be loving and true
When February birds do mate
You wed nor dread your fate
If you wed when March winds blow
Joy and Sorrow both you'll know
Marry in April when you can
Joy for maiden and the man
Marry in the month of May
And you'll surely rue the day
Marry when June roses grow
Overland and sea you'll go
Those who in July do wed
Must labour for their daily bread
Whoever wed in August be
Many a change is sure to see
Marry in September's shine
Your loving will be rich and fine
If in October you do marry
Love will come but riches tarry
If you wed in bleak November
Only joys will come, remember
When December's snows fall fast
Marry and true love will last.

COUNTRY SUPERSTITIONS

Before barbed wire was invented hedgehog skins were nailed to gates and fences to prevent cattle rubbing against them.

Always start a journey with the right foot first.

When dressing, the right foot should always be shod before the left.

If a garment is put on inside out it is unlucky to alter it.

The girls who wears a daisy chain
Grow up pretty, never plain.

Crossing to the other side we reach the Village Hall. Erected in 1934, it was used for jumble sales, concerts, various causes and by, the still very active Women's Institute. There is a room at the back they call 'the noisy room' but I have been unable to ascertain why.

Next to the Village Hall is 'The British Legion' which started life in an old army hut donated by the Old Comrades. A more substantial one was built in the 30's on land given by Major Barden. It was always well attended on Saturday nights by the local youth, for that was the night of the 'sixpenny hop'. Miss Atkinson, daughter of Colonel Atkinson, one time owner of 'Sunnylands', started the first baby clinic in 1934.

Standing next to the British Legion, until 1990 was 'Ferndown Elementary School', built in 1901 for 60 infants, the mistress in charge was Mrs Teresa Trevett. In 1920 Mr Bowering was head and had amongst his staff Miss Bracher, a pupil teacher, Miss Keeping, Miss Hannay, Miss Patten and Mr Flower. School started at 9.00a.m., pupils assembled in the playground and marched into school in an orderly fashion with no talking. Assembly with hymns and prayers was held every morning in the hall after which the pupils dispersed to their classrooms for Bible study and the three R's. After lunch, which had to be eaten in the playground, the girls had needlework, domestic science, nature study and games classes, whilst the boys were taught woodwork, games and gardening. School finished at 4p.m. In those days most boys collected birds eggs and cigarette cards, helped with the gardening and outdoor chores at home, belonged to the scouts and joined in various church activities. With the girls it was the Guides, church activities and helping their mothers in the home especially when there were younger brothers and sisters. Empire Day was always celebrated at school so too was May Day with dancing round the maypole. Medals were given for good attendance.

The School.

V.E. party on a field by Penrose Road.

Miss Patten, Mr Flower, Miss Bracker, Miss Patten, Miss Hanney, Mr Bowering, Mrs Trevett and Miss Keeping. Taken in the late 1920's.

Ferndown First School 1904. Teacher Miss Nellie Sellors.

Ferndown First School in the early 1930's.
In this picture are a pair of Romany twins named Rueben and Caleb Wareham (2nd row from back).

The Middle year in the 1930's.

Pupils from the middle year taken in the 1930's.

Pupils from the middle year taken in the 1930's.

Pupils from the middle year taken in the 1930's.

Class VIII.

Ferndown School's production of Cinderella taken in 1948.

Cottage, now demolished, in Church Road. A similar one is still standing on the corner of Victoria Road.

Lots of cottages with lovely flower gardens were situated along Church Road, a few of the more substantial still remain on the eastern side but none on the opposite side.

This picture shows a cottage that met the same fate. One very similar can still be seen on the corner of Victoria and Wimborne Road. The double hedges that are still to be seen along Church Road were one way of keeping the cattle from straying when the land was still fields.

In the cottage on the corner of Church Road, and Westwood Avenue, lived Charlotte and Charles Elton, their cottage still remains. Charlotte was the daughter of another Charlotte and father James Hobbs who, in Kellys Directory 1895, was listed as a 'cow keeper'. Charlotte Hobbs' father was James Stone, game keeper at Hurn Court for Lord Malmesbury. He was also a travelling preacher and in 1852 preached at Longham, Witchampton and Horton Heath, and in 1854 at Colehill, Broomhill and Holtwood. His subject being, The Turbulent Priest, Having Fear, The Self Righteous Pharisee and The Mocking Soldier — all good stuff. Another member of the Hobbs family, Minnie, married Bill King, they lived in Albert Road. Bill and his brother Ray delivered milk for a local dairy.

Granny Elton mother of Charles Elton.

Charlotte and Charles Hobbs.

Minnie Hobbs wife of Bill King, Isabella wife of Charles Brown and Lillian Hobbs wife of Barlow Pitman.

Charles Elton.

Charlotte Hobbs.

Travelling Preacher James Stone.

The King brothers Ray and Bill outside Home Farm Dairy, Ringwood Road.

Turning left into Wimborne Road and on the opposite corner is a cottage, since demolished to make way for three new bungalows. We pass more fields, a copse and then the Common. There used to be cottages on either side of the road and in one of these mud cottages lived Mrs Amy Loveless who was born in 1887.

Maurice Wilcox, Barlow Pitman, Henry Barnes, Ted and Eliza Hames with their children and James Hobbs in a field off Wimborne Road backing on to the common.

We continue on past the Pure Drop public house behind which was Hilltop Farm and on towards Clayford Avenue. The common opposite is part of Lord Wimborne's Estate which at that time was a vast expanse of heath land. There used to exist a large pond. A true, but gruesome story is told by a local resident who, whilst walking there one day, came across the body of a man lying in the pond which was stained red with his own blood. Apparently he had slashed his wrists with a razor blade on the common and had managed to stagger, bleeding, only as far as the pond before collapsing into it. Subsequently that part of the common was bought by the Council to build the Upper School in 1972 and later the Sports Centre in 1976.

Continuing still further along the road we pass Hoares builders merchants, a very old Ferndown family, two pairs of cottages and a market garden on the opposite side of the Wimborne Road, a few more cottages this side, then a pair of cottages, just recently demolished, then Annie Brown's cottage.

A welcome break. Mark Brown, Maurice Wilcox, Sid Dean, George Thorne and Sid Kechington in Annie Brown's field.

The Browns are another old Ferndown family, they also farmed in a small way and it was Annie's job as a child to drive her father's cows home from the fields near Hampreston after school.

Two more cottages, one of which has been replaced by a new house and a market garden. At one time it was 'Kings the Baker', who boasted "anyones butter but Kings bread". Later it was bought by Poldens who supplied turf.

COUNTRY SUPERSTITIONS

Ash dry or ash green
Makes a fire fit for a queen.

Happy is the bride the sun shines on
Happy is the corpse the rain rains on.

Whenever the cat of the house is black
The lassies of lovers will have no lack.

Swallows fly high, a clean blue sky.

Walking down the hill, still on the righthand side, we come to a field where, at one time, stood an old cottage. One evening, in 1906, a tragic occurrence took place. Whilst in bed Mrs Harriet White and eleven year old Nellie Hinton were killed when the end of the cottage collapsed on to them. A slaughter house had stood against the wall of the cottage but one day it collapsed and, despite repeated pleas by Mrs White to get something done to protect the wall from the elements, nothing was, and so the tragedy happened.

The cottage in which Mrs. Harriet White and eleven year old Nellie Hinton were killed in 1906.

At the bottom of the hill is Brickyard Lane. As its name suggests, it led to the Brickyard and works. This was replaced by the Ferndown Industrial Estate.

The first bomb to fall on Ferndown happened in this area near Award Road opposite. A local resident, Mr Marchant, upon seeing the number of onlookers, took round a collecting box for charity.

Forge Cottage, on the corner of Cobham Road by the traffic lights, is all that remains of a once thriving smithy. Here worked 'Black Jack' as a wheelwright and 'Long John Brown' as the farrier but, with the advent of the motor car and traction engine, the horse and cart was less and less used and the smithy closed.

Continuing along the road we pass older type bungalows, originally holiday cottages, and on the other side a couple of thatched cottages that still remain today. They have the unusual names of 'Helde' and 'Leef', they sound almost Nordic!

On up the road we reach The Old Thatch public house. Once the lodge to Uddens House, then a tea room and finally a pub. It is reputed to be haunted!

Uddens Cross in 1925.

The Old Thatch 1990.

Uddens House.

Uddens House was built in 1747 and demolished in 1955. For a time it was the home of the Greathead family, Edward Greathead was born in 1777 and was a patron of All Saints. His wife, Mary Elizabeth, was born in 1786, she was the only daughter of Sir Richard Glyn. She gave her husband five sons and four daughters, her epitaph in All Saints Church, Hampreston reads 'she did what she could' — I should say so!

OLD MEASURES

3 Barley Corns	=	1 Inch
4 Inches	=	1 Hand
12 Inches	=	1 Foot
3 Feet	=	1 Yard
6 Feet	=	1 Fathom
5½ Yards	=	1 Rod Pole or Perch
1 Quarenten or		
40 Poles	=	1 Furlong
8 Furlongs	=	1 Mile
3 Miles	=	1 League
60 Miles	=	1 Degree
1 Domesday league	=	1½ Miles

A fathom in olden days was measured by the distance between two out stretched arms.

1913 } Uddens Estate   Mrs Old fees

Drs To C. J. Cutler

		£ s d
March 20th	For carting 1 horse load of Station pea Sticks put on Rail at Wimborne } Mrs O	4 . 0
April 29th	For carting 1 horse load of board from Uddens to R Jeans Newmans Lane and 1 load of spar wood same date to White Sheet	3 . 6
May 2nd	Carting Gravel from White Sheet to Uddens House 2 horses & man one day	11 . 0
9th	ditto to Uddens Park for widening road to the Garden 4 horses 2 carts 2 men 1 day	1 . 2 . 0
10th	ditto	1 . 2 . 0
13th	ditto for footpaths	1 . 2 . 0
Octr Novb	carting Gravel for Dolmans Lane bridges 1 day	7 . 0
~~15th~~	~~For Carting 2 horse load of split fir wood to Mr Gush Wimborne~~	~~7 . 0~~
		£ 4 . ~~18~~ 11 . 6

Paid C. J. Cutler December 1913

Estate	10 . 6
Mrs O Pole	4 . 0
Uddens Hse	3 17 . 0
	4 . 11 . 6

A BILL TO UDDENS HOUSE IN 1913.

Weather Lore

Jackdaws flying low, cows lying down and cats washing over their ears all mean it is going to rain.

If onions have an extra skin it will be a hard winter.

If there is ice in November that will bear a duck, they'll be nothing but sludge and muck.

A green Yule makes a full church yard.

Always hang horseshoes with the point uppermost or your luck will fall out.

The name Hampreston is described as 'Hame' in the Domesday Book of 1086, it became 'Hamme' in 1204, 'Hamme Preston' in 1244 and finally Hampreston in 1299. The word 'Hamme' means a river meadow and 'Preost' pertaining to priests, so we get the river meadows belonging to, or being lived on, by a priest or priests.

Apart from one or or two cottages falling into ruin, Hampreston rectory which suffered a direct hit from a bomb in the last war and Bingham's Farm, which was demolished, Hampreston village has changed little over the years. At the turn of the century Bingham's Farm was occupied by the Brent family. During the demolition of the building secret rooms were found in the roof. As the building was of seventeenth century origin, these could only indicate a hiding place for priests being hounded at the time.

Hampreston Village taken in the 1930's.

Weather Lore

A swarm of bees in May
Is worth a load of hay

A swarm of bees in June
Is worth a silver spoon

A swarm of bees in July
Is not worth a fly

Binghams Farm 1931.

Weather Lore

Cast not a clout till May is out

A dripping June keeps all in tune

If July 24th be fair and clear
There will be a prosperous Autumn that year

Oak before ash in for a splash
Ash before oak in for a soak

A wet January means a wet spring

February fills dyke, be it wet or be it white

A peck March dust is worth a kings ransom

March comes in a lion and goes out like a lamb

When April blows her horn, tis good for both hay and corn

Red sky at night, shepherd's delight
Red sky in the morning, shepherd's warning

Still standing in the village is Rose Cottage, originally two cottages and the one time home of the Stanton family. Henry Stanton was farm manager at Hampreston Manor Farm. Our picture shows Jack Stanton on his milk float outside the cottage. Also in the picture is Elizabeth his wife. Jack used to collect the seventeen gallon churns of milk from Hampreston Farm, Hillamsland Farm, Longham Farm and Kinson Manor Farm at 3a.m. and then drive to Bournemouth Square to the Stourvale Dairies. The milk would still be warm when he arrived. He would bring back newspapers and other goods that people had ordered at a charge of 6 pence a parcel. Members of the Stanton family still live in the village. The boards seen on the front of this picture are surrounding the village well.

Charles Stanton outside his home 'Rose Cottage' with Elizabeth his wife.

George Brent, son of James from Bingham Farm.

Hampreston Cottages built under the Elizabethan Poor Laws in 1938.

'Rose Cottage' in 1991.

Rick making in Hampreston in 1942.

'The Jolly Cowmen'
George Brent, Jim Pitman, Alec Pond, Len Cattle and Ted Thorne.

James Brent 1932.

A Harvest Home Toast

Horses strong
Sheep healthy
Barns full
Money plenty

In a cottage on one side of the Stanton's lived the Gurd Family. Fred was head carter on the Trehane Farm and George was second. Mrs Gurd was on the domestic staff and looked after Sir Richard Trehane when he was a bachelor. Hampreston Manor Farm was the home of the Pettey Family, they were well known locally and ran a milk delivery service. They sold out to James Trehane who had previously farmed at Charlton near Shaftesbury but, as his name suggests, was of Cornish origin. He had four sons, David, James, Richard and Jack. David went into horticulture and started the Camellia nursery at Stapehill, now run by his niece, Jennifer, who recently won a silver award at the Royal Horticulture Show. Richard following his father into farming and in 1967 was knighted for his services to agriculture. Sir Richard's son in turn, now runs the farm.

When the Rev. Peverelle and his family were bombed out of the rectory it was Sir Richard who came to their aid and let them live with him at The Manor. It was also Sir Richard who gave the nuns at Holy Cross Abbey much help and advice with their farming efforts.

Breaking the common in 1937, Fred Fanner ploughing, George Gurd leading.

Hampreston Lane looking towards the Manor in 1930's.

The same shot taken in 1991.

James Trehane, father of Jack, David, Jim and Richard.

Jack Trehane.

David Trehane.

Jim Trehane.

Richard Trehane
with Lavenham Welkin the bull.

Mrs. Gurd, housekeeper to Sir Richard when a bachelor.

Sir Richard Trehane in 1991.

All Saints Church dates from the fourteenth century although there are indications that a church stood on the site at an earlier date. The font and a small lancet window are of thirteenth century origin, whilst the round arch over the door is of an even earlier date. In the centre of the nave are two stones under which lie the bodies of two Jesuit priests believed to be cousins, one Richard Caryll who died in 1750 and Charles Caryll who died in 1745. Why were these catholic priests buried in a protestant church?

The parish registers date from 1617, patrons of the church included a William Earle, Thomas Corbyn in 1615, Thomas Reeks in 1775 and who, by 1786, had become a church warden.

In 1856 a Mrs Baldwin left £451 to the rector which was to be put into the Wimborne Savings Bank with instructions that 'the interest to be distributed to the poor of the parish, with the exception of Jonadab Troke so long as he lives'. Poor Jonadab, I wonder what he did to upset Mrs Baldwin.

Hampreston Church in 1945.

COUNTRY SUPERSTITIONS

A bloom on the tree when apples are ripe
Is a sure termination of somebody's life.

To meet a black cat is lucky, especially if it runs across your path.

Monument to Miles Bownes erected in 1630 in All Saints.

The enscribed church gates.

In 1823 Uddens House was owned by Mr John Ponton and it was he who paid for the vestry to be built. The church has a peel of seven bells, there were only three in 1737 but in 1738 these were recast and five more added at a cost of £53.17s.4d. On the treble was found the inscription **'Tho' I am little and small my voice is heard before you all'.** This inscription was lost when the bell was recast in 1927. The tenor bell was also inscribed it read 'At they departure will I sound and ring and bring thee to the ground'. Mr Percy Stanton who lived at 'Five Ash', the name of the crossroads at Hampreston, maintained that the bells for the church were recast in a field nearby, circles in the grass made by the heavy bells being clearly visible for many years.

In the church is a monument to Miles Bownes who was rector from 1614–30. On it are recorded the names of his two sons Francis and Miles and his five daughters Elianor, Agnes, Priscilla, Elizabeth and Mary. In the parish register is a translation of a former rector, Mr Matthews Place, of an excommunication issued by the Pope and pronounced by the priest in 1758 against one Henry Goldney 'for numerous crimes of sacrilege with the images of our Holy Saints aforsaken our most Holy Religion and continued in Heresy, Blaspheme and Corrupt lust', and it goes on to say 'he is cursed in all towns, cities, fields, houses and in all other places, be he standing, lying, riding, walking, running, eating, drinking etc, and what so ever he does beside'. I wonder what happened to the poor man?

'Bell, Book and Candle' is a form of excommunication in the Roman Catholic Church. When sentence is pronounced:

A bell is rung,
A book is closed,
A candle extinguished.

This indicates the spiritual darkness to which the person has just been condemned.

The pulpit in the church was put up in 1731 and made by Mr Bastard of Blandford for the sum of 12 guineas, erecting same cost 30 shillings.

Buried in the churchyard are many local inhabitants, the Rev. Peverelle, one time rector of 'All Saints' and the former head teacher of Hampreston School, Albert Henry Roberts. Also buried there is a lieutenant in Oliver Cromwell's army who had the misfortune to drown in the river, and some members of my family, namely my aunts, Annie and Sally and my Uncle Jessie. Also for some reason there is a recording of a priest being buried out side the church wall. There is an inscription on the entrance gates in the form of a small plaque which reads, 'given by Mrs Winifred Williams as a thank-offering for the safe return of her brother after interment in China in November 1945', Mrs Williams would be better known to many as Patience Strong.

Old Proverbs

A light heeled mother makes a heavy heeled daughter

A man must ask his wife if he is to get on in this world

A peck of worry wont pay a pound of date

A sighing heart will never break

A slut always carries her duster in her pocket

If you sing before breakfast, you'll cry before night

A whistling woman and a crowing hen
not much use to use to mice or men

An apple a day keeps the doctor away

Cats are like mothers-in-law, more attached to the house than the people in them

Never make a friend of a man until you've seen the smoke come from his chimney for twelve months

You'd spoil a new eighteen penny knife scraping an ounce of fat of a bone

Keep an old house dry and and old man wet

As much need as a toad of a side pocket

No more brains than a turnip

NO.2 HAMPRESTON REGISTER FROM 1678–1764 INCLUSIVE

THE POPES CURSE, BELL, BOOK & CANDLE ON A HERETICK OF HAMPRESTON

By the authority of the Blessed Virgin Mary of St Peter and Paul of the Holy Spirits, we excommunicate, we utterly curse & bar commit & deliver to the devil of hell Henry Goldney of Hampreston in the County of Dorset an infamous heretick that hath in spite of God & St Peter whose church this is in spite of all the Holy Saints & in spite of our Holy Father the Pope (Gods Vicar here on earth) & of the Revrd Worshipfull the Cannon, Masters, Priests, Jesuits, Clerks of the Holy Church, committed the numerous crimes of sacrilage with the images of our Holy Saints aforsaken our most holy religion and continued in heresy, blasphemy, corrupt lust, excommunicate be he finally and delivered over to the devil as a perpetual malefactor shesimatick, accursed be he & given soul & body to the devil to be buffeted, cursed, be he in all holy cities & towns, in fields, ways, in houses, out of houses, & in all other places, standing, lying, or riding, walking, running, waking, sleeping, eating, drinking & whatsoever he does besides we separate him from the threshold, from all the good prayes of the church from the participation of holy mass, from sacrements, chapels & alters, from holy bread, holy water , from all the merits of our holy priests, religious men, from all their cloysters, from all their pardons, privilages, grants and immunities, all the holy fathers (Popes of Rome) have granted to them & we give him over utterly to the power of the devil. We pray to our Lady, to St. Peter, Paul, and all the holy saints that all the senses of his body may fail him, that he have no feelings except he comes openly to our beloved priest at Stapehill, in time of Mass, within thirty days from the third time of pronouncing hereof by our dear priest, thereof confesses his henious, heretical & blasphimous crimes & by his repentance make satisfaction to our Lady, St. Peter and the worshipfull company of our Holy Church of Rome and suffer himself to be buffetted, scourged, spit upon, as our said dear priest in his goodness, hollines and sanctity shall direct, prescribe given under the Seal of our Holy Church of Rome the tenth day of August in the year of our Lord Christ, one thousand seven hundred, fifty eight. And in the first year of our Pontificate.

C.R.

8th OCT 1758	PRONOUNCED	THE FIRST TIME
15th Do Do	—	THE SECOND TIME
22nd Do Do	—	THE THIRD TIME

The above is a true copy taken from the original.
Translated by me Matt. Place
Rector of Hampreston
Dec 1811

Opposite the entrance to the church is Hampreston School. It was built in 1875 as an elementary mixed school and had been enlarged four times by 1920 to take in 180 children, most of whom came from quite some distance away. Annie Brown remembers her fellow pupils coming from Uddens, Stapehill, Longham and as far as Tricketts Cross, quite a walk for little legs. Minnie Brown was a school mistress there in the 1800's soon after the school was built. She was followed by teachers such as Miss Whitehead, Miss Gillette, Miss Etheridge, Miss Norris and Miss Hawkins. Mr Albert Henry Roberts was headmaster for a number of years, the children nicknamed him 'sligo' but just why Annie Brown cannot remember. He was also the organist at All Saints and after he retired went on to teach piano lessons. She went on to tell me that all the girls could sew before they left the infants, and if you have seen any samplers, they were usually impeccably done by very young girls.

Times change, lunch was eaten in the playground and usually consisted of jam sandwiches although bread pudding was a favourite. The toilets were buckets which had to be emptied at the end of the day. Mrs Vatcher had a cottage next to the school and she would sell the children sweets from her front room.

Hampreston School taken about 1910.

Early photograph of Hampreston school.

Early photograph taken with Mr Roberts the headmaster in 1905.

Early photograph taken in the 1920's.

Class 1 in 1924.

Going across the 'Five Ash' crossroads at Hampreston and along Stapehill Road there is a field on the left and, when it is ploughed, you can see the impression of where a pair of cottages once stood. Carry on along this country road with its hedges and wild flowers, past more fields, Jennifer Trehane's Camellia nursery and The Knoll Gardens, and you see the spire belonging to the Abbey of Holy Cross.

The Abbey was until 1990 home for Cistercian nuns. The story starts back in the 1700's at 'La Trappe' in Normandy, France. This was the origin of the Trappist Order of Cistercians. It was a silent order and Napoleon was very much against this way of life and began persecuting nuns and monks. The mother superior decided it would be prudent and safer to take the nuns to safer surroundings and so began their trek across Belgium, Switzerland and Germany, but still Napoleon's persecution went on, so they made once more for Belgium and the coast where they were lucky enough to find a boat which brought them to England.

Upon their arrival, in 1802, they were put in touch with two prominent catholic families who would help them, they were the Weld Family of Chideok and Lord Arundell of Wardour. They settled them at Stapehill in a farmhouse which had been a Jesuit site in the seventeenth century. The nuns immediately set about enlarging the building and tilling the fields rising to the sound of a bell at 3.45 a.m. Disaster struck in 1818 when a fire demolished most of the buildings that they had struggled so hard to achieve. Gradually things improved and for a while life moved at an even pace, but the gruelling hard work was taking its toll of the nuns, some of whom died from T.B. Those who remained worked much harder. They spent less time on the farm work and cultivating of fields and concentrated on vegetable growing and bee keeping. When the numbers eventually dwindled down to fifteen they realised that they would soon have to leave Stapehill permanently and this they did in 1990.

The Abbey was put up for sale but with one stipulation that the nuns' graves be exhumed from their present position and moved, in as reverent a manner as possible, to a new plot beside the cemetary at the entrance gates. This was subsequently carried out as requested. Workmen, employed to exhume the graves and re-inter them into a special plot donated by the new owners, came across a vault which, upon being opened, contained the remains of a large man 6 foot 7 inches in length and believed to be Father David Walsh.

In 1911, as stated in Hutchins Directory of Hampshire, the Lady Superior of the Convent of Our Lady of Dolours was Madame K. Sheen. Another lady superior was Madame de Charbannes who died in 1846 at the young age of thirty three, she was followed by Mother Mary Joseph Troy.

Stapehill Abbey.

A sad little story from Stapehill to end on was the death of Private Herbert Lush of the Dorset Regiment who was killed in action at Mons during the First World War, he was a married man and son of Mr and Mrs Silas Lush of Stapehill. After his death they found in his pocket a recent photograph of his wife and baby, on it were written the words, 'please daddy i'm come'.

Weather Lore

A cold wet May means a barn a full of hay

In October dung your field
And your lands, its wealth shall yield

Cut nettles in June, they come again soon
Cut nettles in July, they are sure to die

Rain Good Friday or Easter Day
Much good grass, but little good hay

COUNTRY SUPERSTITIONS

Bee keepers should always inform the bees of any deaths, births or marriages in the family.

Upon the death of a bee keeper, the widow or an eldest son should strike the hive three times with an iron key and say "the master is dead" Biscuits soaked in wine, should then be offered to the bees.

A stone with a hole in it is supposed to keep witches away especially if it is attached to an old iron key.

Goose fat spread on an old sock and wrapped round your neck will cure a sore throat, or spread on red flannel and placed on your chest to cure a bad cough or cold.

Upon the closing of an old graveyard, the last person buried there would be doomed to become the 'churchyard watcher' for ever.

A small piece of coal carried in the pocket is considered lucky especially if carried into battle.

The first butterfly to be seen should be killed otherwise misfortune will follow.

To see three butterflies together is unlucky.

To see a butterfly flying at night, a death will follow.

It is unlucky to pick blackberries after the 10th October because the devil has spat on them.

Sleep with dogs, rise with fleas.

Wash a blanket in May and wash a dear one away.

Stepping on a black beetle or a spider brings rain.

If you can see a hay wagon make a wish but count to thirteen first.

Cobwebs on the grass early in the morning means a fine day.

Always throw the first fish you catch back into the river or sea to ensure a good haul.

Always make a corn dolly from the last sheaf of corn cut to ensure a good crop the following year but you must never destroy the corn dolly until you have a new one to replace it.

I hope this book will have evoked some memories for the older generation of 'Ferndownians' and I hope they will forgive me for any mistakes I have made, for who is perfect? and will give the new Ferndownians a sense of history about the new area they have chosen for their home.

J.W. LEES

THIS IS HOW IT FEELS

'The maddest story of the Madchester era ... brilliantly told by Mike Keegan'

Daniel Taylor,
The Athletic

'A football fairy-tale. The story of Oldham's action-packed rise to the top tier of English football courtesy of the man who knows it best'

Tariq Panja,
New York Times

THIS IS HOW IT FEELS

AN ENGLISH FOOTBALL MIRACLE

MIKE KEEGAN

Reach Sport
www.reachsport.com

Reach Sport

www.reachsport.com

Published in Great Britain and Ireland in 2021 by
Reach Sport, a Reach PLC business,
5 St Paul's Square, Liverpool, L3 9SJ.

www.reachsport.com
@Reach_Sport

Reach Sport is a part of Reach PLC.
One Canada Square, Canary Wharf, London, E15 5AP.

Hardback ISBN: 978-1-914197-24-6
eBook ISBN: 978-1-914197-25-3

Photographic acknowledgements:
Reach PLC, Alamy/PA Images, YouTube.

Endpaper artwork:
Paul Town (Stadium Portraits)
and Andrew Mellor.

Book editing: Simon Monk and Nick Moreton.

Printed and bound by CPI Group (UK) Ltd,
Croydon, CR0 4YY.

CONTENTS

PART ONE: SLOW BURN – 1982-89

PART TWO: TELL ME MAM – 1989-90

To Joe Royle.
You made things we didn't dare dream a reality.

In memory of Dermot William Francis Butler
(17 September 1969 – 23 March 2021).
A fine man, wrenched from us far too early.

Ee, I'm allus glad to see a mon like thee,
That's as welcome, lad, as welcome as can be,
Fotch thee cheer up t'table,
Stop as long as thou art able,
For I'm allus glad to see a mon like thee

(The Oldham Tinkers, *A Mon Like Thee*, 1974)

PART ONE:

SLOW BURN
1982-89

CHAPTER ONE

The Manager Who Fell Off The Front Of A Lorry

Hard Shoulder, M62 Eastbound, June 1982.

IT is June, 1982. Britain is on the verge of taking the Falkland Islands back from the Argentine invaders and for the first time since the 1930s, three million people are unemployed. One of those is stood on the hard shoulder of the eastbound section of the M62, the motorway which links the north of England's east and west coasts.

Joe Royle, formerly of Everton and England, sticks his thumb out for a lift. He is meant to be at Boundary Park, for what he thinks is a second interview at Second Division Oldham Athletic. Behind him is a stationary Jaguar XJ6 Coupe, which has seen better days. Not only has it shuddered to a halt, it is now billowing smoke into the Lancashire air.

Royle's face is recognisable to millions thanks to a stellar career that earned him six caps for his country. Had it not been for injury it would have been more.

His fame means that he does not have to wait long. Salvation arrives in the shape of a lorry, whose Scouse driver recognises this stranded fellow man of Liverpool.

The driver pulls over, staggered at the sight of a football icon stood begging for a lift at the side of the road.

There is little time to explain. The driver listens to Royle's tale of woe and immediately invites him into the cab. Car abandoned, they head the short distance to the ground.

The recently retired footballer is grateful for the favour. He is 32, married to childhood sweetheart Janet and the pair have three young boys Darren, Lee and Mark, to feed. The smouldering car is on Hire Purchase, there is a mortgage to pay and, to put it bluntly, he needs a job. While his career has been glittering, retirement is not on the agenda. At his pomp – 29 goals in one top-flight season – he was earning more from selling cars on the side than he was for playing for one of the nation's biggest clubs. The most he has been paid was £25,000 a year.

He is an icon at Goodison Park, where he became Everton's youngest player at the age of just 16 in 1966. Twelve years ago, he played a starring role as manager Harry Catterick's all-conquering team sprinted to the First Division title. A tall, clever striker with an eye for goal, he has also played in the top flight for Manchester City, Bristol City and Norwich City. But it is now 1982, a knee injury has ended his playing career early, and memories will not pay the bills.

While he is the son of a Mancunian pianist, Royle was born and raised in Liverpool. He was educated at Quarry Bank High, where a decade earlier Beatles founder John Lennon had passed through the gates. The school has a reputation for sending entrepreneurial, artistic souls into the world and Royle is no exception.

Throughout his career, he supplemented his wage through buying and selling, and he is confident that he can transfer that eye for a bargain into football management.

For him, recruitment is the key to all success. His career has taught him that you can have the best coaches in the world but if the players are not good enough, success will not follow. He has picked up methods from each of the managers he has worked for bar one, Billy Bingham, the man who sold him from Everton – the club he had supported as a boy – to Manchester City in 1974.

Catterick, who was succeeded by Bingham in 1973, was a strict disciplinarian and has had a huge impact. He was an old-school operator who believed a manager's job was just that – to manage. He would only wear a tracksuit when he was due to see the club's chairman and was rarely seen on the training ground, Bellefield. However, his presence was always felt and his players were aware that, every now and then, the blinds in his office at the side of the practice facility would move. When that happened, the pace was immediately stepped up.

Catterick's hard line was the stuff of legend. On one occasion, he famously fined a group of players who were late for training on a Monday after getting stuck in traffic through little fault of their own. When they pleaded for leniency, he told them that they'd had since 4.40pm – the time of the final whistle on Saturday's match – to set off.

Catterick was also known for his skills in the transfer market, along with a commitment to develop homegrown talent. He ushered in an era of success that the long-suffering blue half of Merseyside had not witnessed in decades.

While his loyalties lay with Everton, Royle was also heavily influenced by Bill Shankly, the legendary manager of rivals Liverpool. Shankly, ironically, lived opposite Bellefield and would often venture on to enemy territory. On one of those occasions, he came across Royle, who was in the midst of a return from injury. The youngster, eager to impress, told Shankly that he had been running up sand dunes to strengthen his leg muscles and playing a lot of squash in an attempt to speed up his recovery. 'Son,' the Scot said, 'football is played on grass – not sand dunes or squash courts.'

Later in his playing career, with an eye on the future, Royle bought a record on the art of management released by Shankly, who took Liverpool to the First Division, three titles, two FA Cups and a UEFA Cup in a history-making 15 years. He would often listen to it as he contemplated a career in the dugout. One section stood out. In it, Shankly made the point that he always gave his players the best of everything for five days of the week. The best coaches, the best pitches to train on, the best facilities, the best food in the canteen and the best of his advice. Then, on a Saturday afternoon, he could expect them to go out onto the field and give him the best that they could. Royle knows that the message is a simple one but he believes it is effective.

He has also learned much about the art of man-management. Catterick had got the best out of him because he had shown faith in him. The same could be said of Alan Dicks at Bristol City. Dicks, who had taken the job at the age of 33, was another shrewd operator known for his dealings in the transfer market, which had propelled the Robins to the First Division. Under Ken Brown's guidance at Norwich, Royle had won player of the season in his first year. Brown's generosity in allowing him to head to the Caribbean earlier that summer on an end of season trip, despite knowing he would be leaving the club, was an act that stood out.

Royle is intelligent but he is also impatient. The knee injury ended his playing days early. Cruelly early. The London surgeon delivered the devastating news that he would not play again before the end of the previous season. In the time he had to plan for the rest of his career before his contract expired, he received knockbacks from Peterborough and from Blackpool, both in the depths of Division Four. The second interview which he is meant to be at, as he sits in the lorry driver's cab, is a big deal.

At Norwich they had been sorry to see him go. An indication of how well-liked he was came with Brown's invitation to join them in Jamaica. It was there, at the side of a hotel pool, that he saw the story in a two-day-old *Daily Mirror* the players were passing around. Oldham had sacked the long-serving Jimmy Frizzell and were looking for a player-manager. The quote which accompanied the story, from chairman Harry Wilde, made him laugh. 'Jimmy Frizzell has worked miracles at this club,' it read, 'but we are looking for something different'.

The job appealed. While they are firmly in the shadow of the two Manchester giants, Oldham had a reputation for being loyal to their managers and Frizzell departed after a dozen years at a club he had also served as a player. It is viewed as a safe seat and Royle, who knows he will be learning on the job, believes he will need time to succeed. Frizzell's sacking had come as a shock to all those in the football world who show an interest in the goings-on at the likes of Oldham.

The Scot had led the club from the Fourth Division to the Second, where the rise had inevitably stalled. They are a small outfit, and the perception is that Frizzell had them punching above their weight. In their history there has been no real silverware to speak of. Understandably, many of Oldham's fans are outraged at the move. The view in the town is that

Frizzell was a victim of cynical cost-cutting, rather than lofty ambition. Royle is under no illusions. He knows that Oldham are not looking for a player-manager – rather than a traditional manager – so they can redefine football and come up with an inventive way of getting promotion to the First Division, the promised land. The reality is simple. If they bring in a manager who can play, it means they can sell an existing member of the squad without having to pay for a replacement. They are a club existing on tiny gates which faces a constant battle to keep its head above water.

'Why don't you send in your CV? You've nothing to lose,' Norwich team-mate Martin O'Neill told him as they relaxed in the sunshine. Royle agreed. He wrote off to the club making no mention of his knee. His thought process was that by the time it gave way, as it inevitably would, it would be difficult for the club to sack him.

When he arrived home from Jamaica, three weeks passed before – to his surprise – he was called in for an interview.

It went well and, after staying overnight at his parents' home in Maghull, Merseyside, Royle got another phone call asking him to return for what he thought would be a second interview.

And then, with the Pennine hills in sight, the car broke down.

* * * * *

Royle has a chat with the lorry driver, who drops him off at the club's front door. Inside, chairman Harry Wilde tells him that this is actually not a second interview and that the job is his if he wants it.

The pay is a meagre £15,000-a-year – £10,000 less than he was on at Norwich – and there is no company car to replace the one he has just left on the hard shoulder. It is non-negotiable. He will also have to sell a player, almost immediately.

Royle accepts, in the process becoming the only manager in the history of football to come off the back of a lorry. Unsure of how things will play out, and if he is even cut out to manage a football club, he asks for a one-year contract. Mr Wilde is, unsurprisingly, happy to oblige. Royle is the new manager of Oldham Athletic Football Club.

It does not take him long to find an ally. Ian Stott, a bushy-browed, portly member of the board, tells his new manager that he runs a number of Jaguar garages and can sort him out with a part for his car.

Unbeknown to Royle, Stott has a fearsome reputation for driving a hard bargain. He is a privately-educated, successful businessman from a family of wealthy Oldham mill owners who knows almost as much about the value of a pound as he does about the characters of *Brass*, a soap opera around the lives of the rich and poor in a Lancashire mining town, which he watches religiously. Stott's dedication to making a few quid knows no bounds, as his club's new manager is about to discover.

For the time being, Royle cannot believe his luck. A new job and a new car part sorted in the space of an hour.

But things rapidly take a turn for the worse. After taking his first training session on Little Wembley, the often-flooded field at the side of Boundary Park jokingly named after the hallowed turf at the nation's home of football, Royle returns to his new office to find two strange faces in there, along with the club secretary.

He thinks they are members of staff he has not yet met. They are not. They are bailiffs – sizing up the furniture in return for an unpaid tax bill.

There is also a second issue that needs to be sorted before he can finally make arrangements to get home after what has not been a straightforward first day. The players he does not have to sell will need towels. The existing ones are, like the rest of the place, falling to bits.

Royle immediately turns to one of his old contacts and calls a business associate from Liverpool who has an unnerving knack of being able to get his hands on most things.

'Tony, I need about 40 towels,' he tells him. 'Two things – they must be cheap and they must be top quality because they have to last us for a season and they'll be washed every day.'

Tony, an ever-resourceful soul, does not pause for thought. 'I've got just the thing,' he says. 'They're really top quality and they'll be just the trick. For some reason they've not been a good seller – I've no idea why.'

'They'll do,' says Royle, immediately.

The towels retail at £8 but a price of £1 each is agreed and the deal is done. Days later, Royle has his first victory before a ball is kicked. There is a reason that the towels have not been great sellers, which quickly becomes apparent when they arrive. They are emblazoned with Page Three girls in all their semi-naked glory. The consensus among the delighted players in the dressing room is that this is a manager they can work with.

The first few weeks fly by. The to-do list is endless. Royle's paymasters are upset at the amount of training kit which has mysteriously vanished before his arrival. Their solution is to have it personalised, so the players can be held accountable, but there is no money to print initials on tops and shorts. Royle takes matters into his own hands. He buys a stencil and finds himself in the garage of his home into the early hours, painstakingly writing initials onto training gear.

The next challenge he faces is the most important. Royle is told that the board, in the latest of a raft of cost-cutting measures, are considering scrapping the club's youth system to save a precious £1,000 a year. This cannot happen.

While he may be young, Royle is not naive. For a club like Oldham, bringing through homegrown youngsters and selling them for a hefty profit to the big boys is going to be a vital resource which he knows cannot be dispensed with if he is going to be successful. Failing lucrative cup runs – and they are a rarity at Oldham – developing talent and selling it on is one of the few ways in which they can bring in decent money.

Royle faces opposition but he prevails. It is another victory and something to be celebrated. Any joy, however, is soon cut short when the bill for the replacement part arrives from Mr Stott's garage. 'I could have bought a new one for £20 less than that!' thinks Royle, but diplomacy is another of his skills and he keeps his views to himself.

CHAPTER TWO

The Chairman And The Scout

AT the time of Royle's arrival, Ian Stott is in need of a new challenge. He has a drive and a determination to succeed at all costs which can be traced back to his teenage years and he is ready for a new project. At one point, Oldham – thanks to its damp climate and willing workforce – was the cotton spinning capital of the world and, as a result, boasted more millionaires per capita than anywhere else on the planet.

Stott's family were among those to take advantage. At the peak of the boom, they owned five mills and, during the Second World War, turned production from cotton to canvas to help a British Army desperate for resources in its fight against Nazi Germany. As a thank you, they were later paid a visit by King George VI, a source of much family pride.

But those red-brick mills would soon turn into a source of frustration for the young man. Stott, born five years before the outbreak of that war, was sent to the prestigious Shrewsbury School, some 60 miles from home, where he excelled. A keen sportsman, he captained the cricket, hockey and football teams and performed well academically. When it came to next steps, Stott – already a colourful character who had developed sharp debating skills – wanted to go to Cambridge University to study law. However, his dreams were to be denied when a family member, heavily involved in the running of the mills, passed away suddenly. Much to his dismay, Stott was subsequently told in no uncertain terms that his academic career was at an end. He was needed in the business.

Dreams of taking on the biggest cases in the country's court rooms had to be put on hold, but things would change. The cotton trade plunged into terminal decline thanks to the emergence of competitors from abroad who could produce the same output at a fraction of the cost. The Stotts saw what was coming and acted accordingly. Showing valuable foresight, the family sold the mills in the late 1950s and suddenly, released from the shackles, the world was young Ian's oyster.

Only in his mid-20s, Stott set upon building a business empire with relish, adding a myriad of assets and investments. There was Bryn Cethin, a caravan park in Abersoch, North Wales, which proved to be lucrative – as did firelighter and shirt-making factories. The Sidings Night Club, in the plush Cheshire village of Alderley Edge, was also added to the portfolio. Stott would quaff champagne there with regulars such as George Best, the legendary Manchester United player and playboy. Having developed a taste for the high life, Stott fell in love with luxury cars. Dealerships were added. Those that sold Jaguars, his obsession, did well, although an investment in an Austin Rover garage was less successful, as the product was so poor. He learned the lesson and moved on.

There were plenty of big years and plenty of opportunities to expand but by the time Royle arrives, his feet are itchy. The majority of his businesses and interests had been sold for a hefty profit and Stott is keen on another adventure.

He is already on the board of his hometown football club thanks to his close relationship with their owners, the Lees family, who had a number of business interests of their own, alongside their JW Lees brewery, a couple of miles from Boundary Park.

While Oldham's continuous survival in Division Two since they arrived there in 1974 was admirable, there could be no doubt that the club was an afterthought for its owners. The Lees's had their own businesses to attend to. Stott believes that more can be done, and when Wilde departs not long after Royle's appointment, he puts forward his own case to take over as chairman. The club had been somewhat of a millstone around the neck for the Lees's and they are delighted to hand responsibility to a man with a proven track record of success who can give the role the attention it needs.

While there is a sense of civic duty, Stott takes on challenges because he thinks he can win them. There are financial barriers that make football an uneven playing field. There will be competitors with more money who can pay much higher wages. But, as there is in any business, there will always be room for creative solutions and opportunities to outmanoeuvre your rivals. And this is football, the nation's pastime, the best business of them all.

Stott immediately hits it off with Royle. The two are kindred souls. There is an acceptance that, at regular points, a player will be sold to keep the wolves from the door, but there is also humour, even in argument. Both men are ambitious, and are excited about where they can take this unfashionable football club.

After the big change in the boardroom, Royle sets about reshaping his own staff. It will have to be a gradual process. He knows that Oldham's first choice for the job was the West Brom defender John Wile, and that talks with him had collapsed because of his demand to bring in his own backroom team. A request for a new Volvo had not helped, either.

Scouting will be key. Oldham will rise or fall on the back of their recruitment and he needs a pair of eyes and ears that he can trust. Jim Cassell, who coaches Oldham's B Team, has impressed him in the early weeks. The pair have been to a few matches together to look for potential signings. Royle likes what he hears from Cassell. He is cool, calm and does not get carried away. There is little emotion in his judgement. He does not say anything that is irrational and he is impressed by his opinions. Initially, Royle gives him more assignments before deciding to ask him if he will become Oldham's scout.

* * * * *

Cassell is loving life and the extra assignments at the club have been welcome. He is a former footballer who was taken on by first love Manchester United but whose career eventually ended prematurely at lowly Bury thanks to a knee injury. He is now working for Trafford Council and is climbing the local authority ladder. It is a job for life – and he knows it – but he enjoyed coaching the 'B' team and is enjoying carrying out scouting missions for Oldham's new manager.

Cassell is a quick learner. He is also an intelligent, diligent and creative man who is keen to progress and develop. After joining the council he, unprompted, started organising activities for the area's children in their parks, ensuring they had plenty to do in the summer holidays. Every time someone in his department was ill, he offered to do their job. It was all about making himself better at his own job. His performance did not go unnoticed in those early days and eventually his boss, a war veteran named Louis Bell, pulled him into the office for a chat. Bell told his enterprising employee that he had outgrown his role and that he wanted him to become assistant parks manager.

Cassell's analytical skills have always been sound. He quickly assessed the situation and told Bell, who had the grand title of chief recreation and amenity officer, that he had little horticultural knowledge and was concerned he wouldn't be up to the job.

In an attempt to address his weak spot, he headed for a local bookshop and picked up two titles – *201 Indoor Plants* and *201 Trees and Shrubs*. Cassell spent months learning the Latin names and asked his wife, Moira, to test him every week. He quickly became knowledgeable to the extent he felt he could go anywhere on the planet and recognise the local greenery.

Soon, he was in charge of around 100 workers. What he did not know, he found out. He spent his mornings with grave diggers, afternoons with those who look after the bowling greens, teaching himself on the job. He did not think it was right to expect any of his staff to do anything he would not do himself. When the funeral registrar was off on holiday, he filled in and ensured everything worked like clockwork. There was considerable job satisfaction in that. Helping a family when they were most in need was a worthy act, and Cassell took pride in his role and was happy to perform such an important task.

Cassell knew Royle before he came to Oldham and felt the club had made a strong choice in making him manager. On more than one occasion he had the misfortune to play for Bury's

Reserves against Everton Reserves when Royle was returning from injury. Those games tended to be about keeping the score down. In one match nothing they tried would work. Royle was unstoppable and hit four.

Royle knows all about Cassell's background and makes his move, asking him to accompany him on a rare trip to Glasgow, where he is watching a fixture between the reserve teams of Scottish giants Celtic and Rangers. Royle has been at a meeting in London and arranges to meet Cassell when he boards the northbound train in Preston, not a million miles from Manchester.

Across the table, he tells his B Team coach that he wants him to get more involved in the scouting side of things. Just like he did with Mr Bell in his Trafford Council office, Cassell first raises his concerns. 'It's a big job this, Joe,' he says. 'And if I get you to bring in a load of rubbish, I can get you the sack.'

Royle nods in agreement. He knows that this is the most important aspect of management. Every penny counts and failures in the transfer market will come with a low tolerance level. But he trusts Cassell. They agree a small uplift in salary and the club has a new chief scout. The role will be part-time and Cassell is fine with that. He will spend his days looking after parks and funerals and his nights in his trusty Volkswagen Golf, travelling the country in the search for some hidden talents at Britain's footballing outposts.

Cassell jokes to friends that he goes from crems in the daytime to gems in the evenings.

CHAPTER THREE

The Number Two

ARGUABLY the worst place in Europe to live following the end of the Second World War was located a short walk down the River Clyde from the centre of Glasgow, Scotland.

The Gorbals was brutal – block upon block of tenements thrown up in 1840 providing rat-ridden accommodation amid a level of poverty that had to be seen to be believed.

Hastily built for the workers and immigrants from Ireland and Italy who fled to the city during the Industrial Revolution, the buildings were simply not big enough. Overcrowding – eight to a room, as many as 30 to a toilet – was commonplace. It was, in essence, a slum.

If you had the misfortune to live in a 'single end', it was even worse. A single end was the name given to the flat at either endof the rectangular blocks of squalor. The description was accurate – it consisted solely of one room. A whole home made up of one room.

That was the world into which Willie Donachie entered on October 5, 1951.

It was also a violent place, rife with Sectarianism. Donachie was born to a Protestant mother and a Catholic father in what was a relatively rare mixed marriage. On his first day at school, he and his friends had rocks thrown at them. When he asked the older kids in his group what was going on, he was told that the throwers were Protestant and that he, as a Catholic, should pick them up and throw them back.

It was accepted that there were two ways out from this often hostile melting pot. Football, or boxing.

Donachie would go to Parkhead, home of Glasgow Celtic, and would also head to Hampden Park, home of the Scottish national team. For matches against old enemy England he would be handed over the turnstiles. Official attendances for those games were given as north of 130,000. The reality was that, with thousands like Willie inside, the actual figure was much higher.

The youngster performed well on the football field. At one point Celtic, about to become the first British team to win the European Cup under the guidance of Jock Stein, were interested in signing him as a professional.

But Donachie was also academically gifted, and the club of his boyhood dreams thought he was bound for university. No offer was forthcoming and no explanation was offered.

The reality was that there was no money to pay for such higher education. A place at university was laughable, fanciful. Donachie, a bright boy, did land a prize job as a chartered accountant, but he had always wanted to play football.

The relationship with his father, a lorry driver, was not a good one. But Donachie senior did hand out two pieces of advice on his son's 16th birthday, which would stick. The first was to make his own decisions, the second was – if possible – to head to England.

The pearls of wisdom would stand him in good stead.

Manchester City had been scouting the Glasgow area at the time. This was fertile ground for young footballers and many of the English clubs sniffed around frantically. One of City's representatives spotted a 17-year-old Donachie, and he was invited down for a week's trial.

The suitors were undecided after the initial seven days and so they extended the try-out to a month. Donachie knew this was a chance he could not fail to take. He stuck at it and was given a professional contract. In 1968, he made it out.

While heavily industrial itself, Manchester was a different environment. Donachie's digs, in the rows of red-bricked terrace houses close to City's Maine Road, were not among the finest living spaces in the city. But they had an inside toilet and a garden, which was already a substantial upgrade on what he had been used to.

Even better, nobody asked him what school he went to – a common question used in Glasgow to ascertain what religion you were – because nobody really cared. It suited him down to the ground. 'Nobody wants to fight me,' he thought as he walked home from one of his first training sessions.

When Donachie arrived, City were being managed by Malcolm Allison, 'big Mal', a man of Essex who was widely viewed as a revolutionary.

Outspoken, charismatic and a dream for the media, Allison would do anything to gain a competitive edge. He treated his footballers like athletes. Professional runners were brought in to share techniques. There were regular visits to the nearby University of Salford, where there would be massages and talks with professors on fitness. His teams believed they were the fittest in the league. As they ran onto the field, they already had a mental and physical advantage on their opponents.

It was a tough start for the young Scot. In one reserve team match while playing wing-half – a kind of defensive midfield role – he was tasked with covering for his centre-half. During the game, the opponents played the ball over the defender's head. With Donachie nowhere to be seen, the visitors' striker pounced to smash the ball into the net.

His coach was not impressed. 'You were sleeping,' he told his player. Donachie agreed. He vowed never to be caught sleeping again and began to study alertness, and movement. It was a moment which would shape his life.

As part of his quest for marginal gains, Allison introduced his players to a man called Lennie Heppell. At first, there was much derision. Heppell was a professional ballroom dancer and it is safe to say that not everyone was impressed by his arrival on the scene. 'What the fuck can a dancer teach us?' asked one of the players. They soon found out.

Heppell was all about movement. A clever man with methods which at first seemed obscure. He had first come to the football world's notice via a striker by the name of Bryan 'Pop' Robson. Robson was dating Heppell's daughter, Maureen. With no previous experience, Lennie had spent endless hours teaching her how to play table tennis. The results were incredible. From a standing start, Maureen would go on to represent England at the sport.

Robson, a striker, had been struggling at his first club, Newcastle United. He turned to the man who would become his father-in-law for his advice. The reply was blunt. Heppell told him in no uncertain terms that his lifestyle was poor. He was lazy, he was sloppy and – crucially – everything he did was slow. Perhaps unsurprisingly, Robson was initially unreceptive. But he decided to move in with Heppell for a couple of weeks of intense coaching.

As they had been with Maureen, the results were incredible. Robson would end the following season as England's top goalscorer. The dramatic improvement prompted West Ham United to pay a club record £145,000 to Newcastle for his services. Word was out.

When in Manchester, Heppell found a willing student in Donachie. His methods were based around being alive. Emphasis was placed on anticipating rather than reacting. 'If you react, you're dead,' he would say. 'Be alive, be ready,'.

It was advice Donachie would heed and which would serve him well. After making his debut in 1970, he would eventually spend 12 years at Maine Road, developing a reputation as an athletic, tenacious left-back. He would also win 35 caps for his native Scotland, and play in the 1978 World Cup finals.

There was another key moment. In 1974, City made a move for Everton striker Joe Royle. Donachie immediately liked what he saw. For Royle's part, he remembered Donachie giving him a kick during a previous match and was quick to make a joke about it.

The pair became friends. While Donachie was the quieter of the two, he enjoyed Royle's sense of humour and the fact that he could take it, as well as give it out.

Royle almost instantly recognised his team-mate as a deep thinker. He admired his determination to win at all costs and knew from a very early stage that he would have a future in coaching. While some viewed his dedication to Buddhism and yoga as outlandish, Royle knew they were both tools Donachie used to better himself.

It is something he never forgot and – after he was handed the Oldham job – he knew that he wanted to bring him in as his number two. Royle liked the assistant he had inherited, Bill Urmson, who was a fine coach. But Urmson was all about the basics and fundamentals and Royle believed he would be ideal as a leader of the club's youth set-up. The more progressive Donachie was at Burnley after a stint in Norwich and the US and Royle, following his arrival at Boundary Park, asks his old pal to join him. Even better, he can get a few years out of him as a player, yet, which means he has filled two roles filled with one salary. Ian Stott is very pleased.

CHAPTER FOUR

Build, Knock Down, Build

THE early years are tough but, with Jim Cassell and Willie Donachie at his side, Joe Royle is well-equipped to deal with them. Aside from buying and selling cars, he also ran his own catalogue surplus business to supplement his wages during his playing career. When his team-mates finished training and headed for the golf course and then the nineteenth, he would be in his shop offering discount bloomers to grannies.

In short, his chairman is not the only one who knows the value of a pound. Royle is also an expert haggler and before long he is using those negotiating skills to buy and sell players.

That eye for a bargain extends to off the pitch, and Oldham's spartan gym is quickly restocked with second-hand equipment, cadged and borrowed.

Attendances before Royle's arrival, the club's consecutive eighth in the second tier, had plummeted as low as 3,000 and there had been a feeling of apathy among the Oldham public which played a part in Frizzell's departure, although many are outraged at his treatment and refuse to return.

It is a tough town and a tough crowd to win over for many reasons. At the time of the industrial revolution, cotton was king and Oldham hosted the throne. At one point, mill owners like the Stotts made hay while the jennys spun and the cash rolled in. The mills remain – this is the team from a town of chimneys – but for most the wealth is long gone. For decades now, mills have been closing with frightening regularity. For many of those brought in from far-flung corners of the Empire – predominantly Bangladesh and Pakistan – to go to work in them, there is now little employment opportunity.

Poverty is also widespread for large swathes of the white population, and parting with hard-earned cash to go and watch a team with no prospect of promotion is not as appealing as a few pints of Oldham Bitter in one of the pubs for every day of the year which the town can still boast.

Sport has provided little relief. The Roughyeds, Oldham's rugby league team, has never been to Wembley despite a period of sustained success in the 1950s. Neither has the football team. Both vie for the back page of the town's newspaper, the *Oldham Evening Chronicle*. The town has something of an east-west split. To the east of the town centre, towards the rolling foothills of the Pennines, rugby is king, whereas to the west it is football. Both sports are played in amateur leagues by hundreds of townsfolk at the weekend.

With a population of around 200,000, Oldham is a big town. But the glamorous draw of the Manchester clubs, 10 miles down the road, is considerable. As a result, there are at least as many shirts of United and City to be viewed in the town centre and in the schools as there are Oldham. Throw in all-conquering Liverpool and it is difficult for the local club to make a splash. Attendances are not as they should be, but Royle believes that there is potential, and a lot of no-showers to go at.

The football club is known by almost all Oldhamers as 'Latics' while the rugby team is referred to as just that – 'the rugby'. The 'Latics' name is believed to have stemmed from the club's early years, when education in the borough was so poor that the locals had difficulty pronouncing the word 'Athletic', although some claim it was part of the area's broad dialect, a shortened version of 'Athlatic'. Latics have not been in the top flight of English football since 1923, with their closest brush with success coming eight years prior, when they lost the First Division title to Everton by a single point. Then the First World War broke out and ruined everything.

Frizzell, appointed in 1970 with the club in Division Four, brought two promotions after years of re-election, when Oldham had to rely on votes from friendly clubs to avoid going out of the league altogether. Under his watch, crowds had risen, but these are thin times, despite a consistent stay in the second tier. There has been no sniff of promotion and the prospect of the First Division is a distant dream.

A man on a mission from the off, Royle heads out to the pubs, pushing over piles of pennies. He is often armed with free tickets to be used as raffle prizes. The joke he faces is an old one. 'If the first prize is two tickets, what's the second prize? Four?' Often, Royle is out five nights a week, spreading the word that there is a new man in town and that he needs their support. The responses are typically blunt, and delivered with the flat vowels of the townsfolk. 'Give us something to watch,' Royle is told, 'and we'll come and watch it'.

The JR PR campaign continues apace. One of the Oldham's directors owns a plumbing firm and pulls Royle to one side one afternoon. 'Can you get one of the players to a club in town?' he asks. 'We're promoting a new range of showers and are running a Miss Wet T-Shirt competition to launch it. We could do with a judge.'

'Well,' says Joe. 'It's a Thursday so we couldn't possibly send one of the players with a game on a Saturday. I'll tell you what – I'll have to come instead.'

Initially, things on the field in the first season go surprisingly well – well enough for the manager to attempt a bold move on his chairman. From Royle's arrival, it had been club policy to travel to most away matches on Saturday morning. The theory was that they would lose anyway, and so it was pointless heading down on a Friday and spending money on an overnight hotel stay. With a trip to Swindon next on the calendar and a slight improvement in form, Royle decides to present the case for some expenditure, telling his chairman that it would take five hours, thanks to roadworks on the M5, to get there.

'Nonsense,' is Stott's response. But he is not done there. The chairman promptly jumps into his prized E-Type Jaguar and hits the road for Wiltshire. With the suggestion of a smile on his face when he screeches to a halt back outside Boundary Park's main entrance later that day after a 445-mile round-trip, he tells his manager that the trip down to their opponent's ground took two hours and 45 minutes. Point proven.

At the end of that first year, an unlikely seventh-placed finish is secured and only nine points separate Oldham from promoted Leicester City. Many of the top clubs are beaten and there is genuine optimism. It is a decent start for the young manager – but the dreaded knock on the door from Mr Chairman is never far away.

'Mr Manager, we need to sell somebody,' Stott says, and that is that. Three of Royle's best players depart – raising much-needed funds but lowering expectation. It does not go down well with supporters but it is a necessity.

The following year, performance levels understandably drop and relegation is avoided in the penultimate match of the season. Average attendances fall from 6,962 to 6,036. Only a bumper 20,320, for the visit of neighbours Manchester City – and their huge following, which makes up more than half of the crowd – prevents them from falling to the low 5,000s. It does little to impress those within the town. A drop from seventh to 19th strengthens the widely-held view that this is a club on a downward spiral, despite Royle's efforts. Stott is apologetic. He assures his manager that he would not have been sacked, even if they had gone down. 'We sold a team from under you,' he says. 'We had to, but we believe in you.'

* * * * *

There are bright spots in the dark days. Signs of hope. Royle and Cassell speak regularly. Cassell recommends a player and, should the budget allow, Royle heads out to make his own mind up. One of those Cassell brings to his attention is Mark Ward, a diminutive winger at non-league Northwich Victoria.

Royle goes to watch Ward and sees enough to reach a verdict in 45 minutes. He makes a big show of leaving at half-time to try and put other scouts present off the scent. He wants them to think he is not interested. It works. The deal is done for just £7,500. Royle thinks Ward is the best non-league footballer he has ever seen. 'He's an arsey little bugger, too,' he tells friends. He likes arsey little buggers.

At their first meeting, Ward tells Royle that he will one day become his best player. He is not wrong. Two years later, the £7,500 will turn into £250,000 when he is sold to West Ham United.

With each passing episode, and there are many of them, Royle's rookie sheen rubs off. This feels to him like a real life game of snakes and ladders. One step forwards, two steps back. Sometimes three.

Transfer deadline days often see a hive of activity in the manager's tiny office, which backs onto Sheepfoot Lane, the long, slanted street outside Boundary Park.

At one point a deal is struck to sell a player to rivals Bradford City, whose chairman, Stafford Heginbotham, has a reputation for ferocious bargaining and an appetite for counting the pennies which almost rivals that of his Oldham counterpart.

When Royle tells Stott the fee he has agreed without his assistance, he is expecting praise, thinking he has secured a good price. Stott, however, is livid. He believes Heginbotham has paid around £5,000 less than he would have been able to get out of him and makes his feelings abundantly clear. It is a rare disagreement.

On another occasion, a fee is agreed for an incoming player but there is a minor disagreement over his weekly wage. It amounts to the grand sum total of an additional £25-a-week. Stott will not budge and neither will the player. The deal is in danger of collapsing when the player relents and signs on the dotted line. When he departs, an elated Stott performs a victory jig around the boardroom table.

But it is not all one-way traffic. Royle often jokes that if he wants to spend £10,000 on a player it has to go through five board meetings before approval comes back – but he knows he has seven magic words he can use that usually loosen the purse strings. 'Mr Chairman,' he will say with a wry smile, 'we will make money on this one'. With the job done, the cheque book is always opened.

The 1984-85 season – his third in charge – is another struggle and the winter months bring other issues. Elevated Oldham, whose ground is the third-highest above sea level in the country, gets its fair share of rainfall. The complex, if you can call it that, is on a slope. Little Wembley is at the bottom of it, on top of an old culvert. Often it is unplayable and a far cry from the hallowed turf at the nation's home of football it is named after.

On numerous occasions Royle has to ring around the borough's schools or head for the tops of the moors for somewhere to train. Close to his home, itself amid the town's many hills, a small football pitch sits next to an underused, windswept nine-hole golf course. For some strange reason, it is nearly always dry and Royle thinks he has cracked it, until an outraged local resident complains to the council, who own the land, and the town's professional football team is booted off.

There are other problems with Little Wembley. It is not fenced in properly and so bored local kids often trespass. Royle prompts laughter from his wife Jan when he takes to regularly driving past on days off to ensure all is well. On more than one occasion he spots juveniles on the grass, pulls over in a huff and tries to squeeze through the fence to give them a bollocking. They are often out of earshot by the time he manages to clamber through. 'On Saturday I'm the manager of a professional football club,' he thinks, 'and on Sunday I'm chasing kids off the fucking training pitch.'

A 14th-placed finish sees crowds fall further, to an average of just 4,713. On one particularly miserable afternoon, Stott is spat at by an irate supporter. This is life at Boundary Park but Royle is undeterred. He has seen early success from his transfer dealings. It has already become clear that the eye for a bargain that served him so well away from football can be translated to the buying and selling of players. It excites him. He knows that he will be permitted to re-invest some of the profit he makes back into his squad. He also knows his chairman is desperate to get one over on their rivals. On many occasions he will ask his manager if he had seen the previous night's episode of *Brass*. 'It was marvellous,' says Stott. Royle will not have watched the show, but knows if his chairman has enjoyed the episode it will have meant some poor soul had been done out of a penny.

The following season, 1985-86, starts well and in November, Oldham are in second place, but a horrendous run of 10 defeats in 11 matches follows. With a defence in desperate need of help at around Christmas time, Royle turns to Paul Jones, a veteran defender over the Pennines with Huddersfield.

Jones's knees have gone, but Royle believes that if the 32-year-old can be placed in cotton wool, his know-how will solve his side's problems. A fee of £10,000 is agreed, but when Jones turns up to sign his contract, the chairman has concerns. 'Can I have a word, manager?', he asks, and the two leave the player in the boardroom and head for the corridor. 'Joe,' Stott says when they are out of earshot, 'Are you sure he's OK? He stinks of alcohol.'

Royle knows that Jones likes a drink. He also knows he has to act quickly. 'Well, chairman,' he says, 'he's a very popular lad.

He's been on his Christmas do with Huddersfield, but they liked him so much at (former club) Bolton that he's been on theirs too. And he's got a lot of friends at Blackpool, so he's also been on theirs.'

Stott's fears are allayed, Jones arrives and before long is a calming influence at the side of Andy Linighan, a young centre-half he signs from Leeds.

Occasionally, on a Monday morning, Jones arrives looking like he may well have had a big weekend following Saturday's match. Royle has a quiet word and asks him if he would 'like to do the toast today'. The answer is nearly always in the affirmative and while the players head out for practice, Jones remains in the lounge where he fixes the toast and, no doubt, his sore head.

But on Saturday afternoons he is on it, and Royle believes the positives far outweigh the negatives.

Following Jones's arrival there is an upsurge in form, after things hit rock bottom. In January, a home defeat in the FA Cup Third Round to Fourth Division Orient, triggered audible anger. Royle's sons sit on the groundstaff bench, down from the dugout, and can hear the shouts from fans. 'Bring back Frizzell,' and 'Royle out' are among the less vitriolic. The boys are often upset. It is not nice to hear strange people calling for your dad to be sacked and, despite their tender years, they are wise enough to know what is going on.

With an arm around the shoulders, Royle reassures them that everything will be OK. And from winter despair there is spring optimism. With Jones in the ranks, Oldham recover and climb the table. But the sale of another asset is never far away. In March, another deadline day leads to another knock on the manager's door. Stott sticks his head around and has a sombre look on his face. It can only mean one thing. Cash is needed – and quickly.

Reluctant though he is, Royle thinks Mick Quinn, signed from neighbours Stockport County for £52,000, fits the bill. He recalls that Alan Ball, his old pal from Everton, England World Cup winner and current manager of Portsmouth, is after a striker but is close to signing former Manchester United man Andy Ritchie, who has fallen out of favour at Leeds United.

He calls Ball. 'Alan, the chairman needs some money in,' he tells him. 'I know you've got Ritchie down there so this may be a fruitless call but I know you've always liked Quinny. I'm telling you now that if you fancy him there will never be a better time, but it's got to be a hundred and fifty grand and it's got to be now.'

Ball agrees and the deal is done. Ritchie stays at Leeds, the wolves stay from Oldham's door. Crisis averted, investment tripled. There is an added bonus – Royle likes Ritchie and vows to bring him to Boundary Park further down the line if he can.

The sale of Quinn is greeted with more cynicism from the fans and the stay-aways. While Oldham finish eighth, a remarkable turnaround, they again fail to capture the town's attention. Only a cup run or real promotion push will do that. Attendances drop further, to 4,649.

CHAPTER FIVE

Leeds, Leeds, Leeds

PETE Gunby is a good man. So when he hears that another talented young player is being jettisoned by his employers he is aghast, but he also knows who to call to find them a new home. Joe Royle now looks forward to the calls, which always start the same way. 'Joe, it's Pete, you're not going to believe this…'

Gunby is a coach at Leeds United, the club of his hometown for whom he had also played. Leeds, a giant of the English game, have had an identity crisis. Following an unthinkable relegation from the top flight in 1982 they turned to one of the stars of manager Don Revie's all-conquering loved and hated team of the late 1960s and early 1970s.

On the broad, Scottish shoulders of Eddie Gray the responsibility of restoring the Yorkshire side to their rightful place was placed. To his credit, Gray placed a heavy emphasis on the recruitment and development of young talent. His youthful sides performed well and, in 1984-85, came close to promotion, only to miss out on the last day. Few thought Gray had done much wrong. But following a sluggish start to the following season he was sacked. This was Leeds. Leeds, which has no business being anything other than a First Division club. Leeds, which should not be in the Second Division with the likes of Oldham.

The club's directors turned to another of Revie's legends, Billy Bremner. The new man would not follow the same path of his former team-mate. Bremner believed his team needed experience, and needed it quickly. What followed was a cull.

Gunby was crestfallen at what he was seeing. The only consolation was that he knew Royle and was confident that when he called, the man on the other end of the line was usually happy to help out.

It had started the previous season with Andy Linighan, a towering young centre-half from Hartlepool, who became the first down what will become a well-trodden path westwards after a fee of £55,000 was agreed. Linighan came with the Jim Cassell seal of approval.

In the summer of 1986 Gunby picks up the phone again. 'You're not going to believe this, Joe,' Gunby starts, as normal, 'but they are letting Denis Irwin go'.

Royle knows Irwin, a two-footed, rapid Irish full-back very well. Cassell has seen him playing for Leeds in a Yorkshire derby against Sheffield United at Bramall Lane. Irwin got injured and was substituted at half-time, but he had done enough. Cassell's method is to take a team sheet and put a star against the name of a player who has stood out. Irwin's name had the asterisk against it before half an hour was out. On the Monday after the game, he called the manager to make him aware of what he had seen. 'Joe, he's got great pace, great feet,' says Cassell. 'He's alright.'

When Cassell hears Irwin is available he is back on the phone, almost pleading. 'Don't trial him,' he pleads. 'Just sign him. If you trial him, someone else will come in. Just take him.'

Royle has to move quickly. Gunby has also told him that

the youngster is already on his way to Chesterfield, who have acted first. This time there is no time to call Stott and ask for his permission. Even though Irwin is on a free, there still has to be a commitment to pay his wages.

The player is intercepted. He never sees Saltergate, the Third Division side's ramshackle ground, and is instead unveiled as Royle's latest recruit. He does not need much persuading. The money is actually a little less than it would be at Chesterfield, but the chance to remain in the Second Division is too much to pass up on. Irwin, who has already played close to 100 games for Leeds, backs himself and signs on the dotted line. When he finds out, Stott is perplexed, but the magic words do the trick again. 'We'll make money on this one, Mr Chairman,' says Royle.

The new recruits see an unfamiliar air of optimism around the club and in Royle's office. The recruitment model, and the time given to build cash reserves, means that the squad appears to be the strongest it has been since his arrival. Stott senses the opportunity – so much so that he also agrees to spend the sum of £100,000, unheard of for Oldham, on highly-rated Grimbsy Town centre-half Kevin Moore. Moore was destined for a career in the First Division and there is a belief he can get there with Royle's team. If they are not promoted that season, a clause in his contract dictates he can go elsewhere for the same price. It is an example of the creativity that exists with the club. Royle and Stott are learning as they go along. They know Moore is unlikely to come to Oldham amid interest from clubs in the top tier so they come up with what is an unorthodox idea, which works.

The optimism is, however, somewhat tempered by the arrival of a new plastic pitch. Eternally-enterprising Stott has done a deal with a manufacturer and Oldham Council which will see the grass ripped up and a £385,000-surface laid at no cost to the club. The pitch will become a community asset. In the evenings, the good folk of the town will be allowed to come and play their own matches at Boundary Park for a fee, as will local schools. The council and the club will split the takings.

It feels like a win-win. But Royle is concerned about the surface. He has seen how the notorious plastic pitch at QPR's Loftus Road has prompted ridicule, with balls bouncing off its rock-hard surface and over the heads of bemused players on a regular basis. There is another at Luton, which has also been panned in the press. The nation is not convinced. The widely-held view is that plastic pitches are for American Football, not for the English game. Stott assures Royle that the surface Oldham are getting will be state-of-the-art and will not be a laughing stock. It will provide a true bounce and will suit a side that has a passing game.

Royle need not have worried. He has always recruited footballers who can play football and his players can adapt. They quickly get to grips with the alien surface, which they can train on, and in October their ranks are strengthened further after another call from Gunby. This time, he tells Royle that Tommy Wright, a quick-footed young Scottish winger, is available for £80,000. Wright is another whom Cassell likes, but the figure was clearly going to be an issue.

Stott is accommodating but only to a certain extent. He will not sanction moves that he believes the club cannot afford and he tells the manager that the fee is out of the question.

Royle knows that Wright is a safe bet and – even at that price – a snip. So he does what he has developed a knack for. He gets creative and begins to think about a way to get the deal done. When Mick Quinn had been sold to Portsmouth, triggering a £100,000 profit for the club, Royle had been approached by a local businessman and club sponsor by the name of Norman Holden. Holden had told him that a six-figure sum was a staggering return on investment and had loathed the fact that he could never expect such a yield from his own shares or from a bank. Royle had told Holden that, in future, he could buy a player for the club and take a return on his loan when the player was sold. He now remembers that conversation. Wright is the man. Holden hands over the cash and the winger becomes an Oldham player, with the initial £80,000 and half of any profit promised to head back to the businessman when he is sold.

* * * * *

A fine home record along with nine wins on their travels leaves Oldham in third place which, in any other year, would be enough to secure them promotion to the top flight for the first time since 1923.

But not this year. Not this season. For the first time, the Football League has introduced a new play-off competition. Instead of the old system, which saw the top three teams from the Second Division promoted in place of the bottom three in the First Division, they decide to create an end of season contest in which the team which finished third would play that which finished fourth over two legs, while the team which finished third bottom of the First Division does likewise against the fifth-placed team from Division Two. The winners of each clash then face each other in a two-legged final to determine who wins promotion. Oldham, then, will face none other than Leeds, the team they are now routinely pilfering for cast-offs. Despite annoyance at the new system robbing them of their rightful place in the top flight, there is a confidence that Bremner's side will be dealt with. During the season, a fired-up Oldham had cruised to a 2-0 win at Elland Road and the lessons from a narrow 1-0 home defeat have been learned.

The first leg, in Yorkshire, is a tight affair. Latics look to be heading for a valuable 0-0 draw when substitute Keith Edwards heads a last-minute goal that the hosts' efforts barely deserve.

Still, 1-0 is not the end of the world and that deficit is quickly wiped out at Boundary Park when midfielder Gary Williams equalises. With close to 20,000 present, as many as half of those from Yorkshire, there is euphoria on the home terraces when young striker Mike Cecere then scores what appears to be the winner in the final minute.

Three sides of the old stadium are celebrating wildly. The scenes are replicated on the plastic. On the touchline Royle screams at his men to focus and switch back on. They do not hear him. From the kick-off the ball is hopefully launched forwards and Leeds are in the penalty area for one of the few times in the match. When it drops, Edwards strikes again, his low shot hitting the legs of Oldham keeper Andy Goram. It ricochets into the air, goalbound and clips a post. There is an agonising wait. It drops into the net. Disaster. In the stands, some – still celebrating – do not even see the goal and have to be told what has happened. It is something which has to be seen to be believed.

Many, including the players, are unsure of the rules. Does this mean Leeds go through on away goals? It does not. Away goals only count after extra-time. Oldham have half an hour to get over the shock and try and find another winner.

It is not long enough. Oldham grow increasingly frantic and cannot repeat the trick. The chance does not arrive and the final whistle abruptly signals the end of a season. Almost immediately there are tears, while the vast away end is a white sea of celebration. In the dressing room there is absolute silence. Royle cannot think of anything to say to lift his players. Oldham had finished seven points clear of those currently celebrating noisily on the other side of the thin wall. Eventually he tells them that they should be proud of themselves.

That night, Royle's phone rings at 5am. It is the pregnant partner of one of his players. He has not come home, she tells him, and she is worried. By now, Royle knows much about what goes on in Oldham and much about his players. He gets out of bed, puts on some clothes and goes off to find the errant player, who has taken the defeat worse than most. He knows where to go and he finds him. The man in question is inconsolable but Royle puts his arm around him and takes him home.

Weeks later there is an end-of-season trip to a Greek flea pit. There are loud cheers around the hotel bar when news filters through from home that Leeds, who had drawn with Charlton Athletic in the final over two legs, have lost the third match to the First Division side, who will retain their top-flight status.

Royle smiles as he nurses his beer, but he knows that this is an opportunity lost. 'A touch away from paradise,' he thinks to himself but he knows that he will soon be rebuilding again as the club takes another few steps backwards before moving forwards. Gates had risen to an average of 6,883, but nowhere near as much as he and his chairman had hoped. No other side in the top 10 had a smaller figure. The town remains sceptical and players will have to be sold.

As agreed via the clause in his contract, Moore departs, to Southampton. One of the first to follow him out of the door is Andy Goram, an athletic goalkeeper who has risen through the club's youth ranks after being released by West Bromwich Albion. The local-born youngster is not tall but his agility and reading of the game are stunning. As things transpire the move comes not long after an away defeat at Carlisle in a frustrating start to 1987-88, which sparked tempers.

At the front of the coach, physio Ian Liversedge was being pestered for beers by the players. He thought it would be funny to throw one over his head, which he did. It hit Goram on the head. The goalkeeper, understandably, did not take it well. He raced down to the front of the coach and punched the physio, injuring his hand in the process. Telling the board that your goalkeeper is struggling to be fit because he's walloped the medic on the way back from an away game is not the best course of action. Royle managed to keep it quiet but not long after, following another knock on the door from Stott, he identified Goram as the latest saleable asset.

Again, he went into sale mode. Royle had seen it spread all over the papers that Hibernian, a Scottish Premier League club, were signing a keeper by the name of Ian Andrews, from Southampton. Royle knew Pete Cormack, the Edinburgh side's assistant manager, as they had played together at Bristol City. He also knew that Cormack would know all about Goram because Hibs and Oldham had been together in a pre-season tournament on the Isle of Man.

Royle picked up the phone. 'Pete,' he said. 'I know you saw us in the Isle of Man and I know you saw our keeper.'

'He's the wee lad?' Cormack responded, using the Scottish term for 'small'.

'Well, Pete,' said Royle, 'he's not that wee – he's a fraction under six foot, but he is quite honestly the best young goalkeeper in England. I'm not calling Andrews, but if you like Goram you can have him.' Sensing uncertainty, he paused. Time to get creative again. 'I'll tell you what – give us £325,000 and he's yours. If, after a month, you don't like him then we'll take him back.'

'Fair enough,' said Cormack, and the deal is done.

A month later, Cormack called, almost breathless. 'Joe,' he said, 'we can't believe how good he is.'

Vultures are now circling around the others who have performed well. A good season can do that. Another rebuild is around the corner.

CHAPTER SIX

Forward Planning

ANDY Ritchie is a resourceful soul. So when he falls out with Leeds he decides to take matters into his own hands. The CV he subsequently sends out to every club he can think of – in England and in Europe – is impressive.

Coming through the youth ranks after signing straight from school at Manchester United, the club he had supported as a boy, Ritchie, who scored a hat-trick for England schoolboys against West Germany, made his first-team debut at the age of 17. A striker, he announced his arrival with a hat-trick against Leeds at 18 and another at 19 against Spurs.

Ritchie, a Mancunian and United fan, was in his element at Old Trafford. But with the club hurling money at a barren spell that had stubbornly persevered since the departure of Sir Matt Busby, he realised that the writing was on the wall, especially after he had been allowed to speak to Aston Villa, Chelsea and Newcastle. On each occasion, a move failed to materialise. But when Brighton, in the top flight and managed by England great Alan Mullery, came in for him he listened to what they had to say. First-team appearances in the famous red shirt were beginning to become few and far between.

He wanted to develop as a player and was a smart, grammar school boy. Suddenly, he was off to the South Coast after 13 league goals in 26 starts for United. Leeds would be the next stop. At Elland Road, under Eddie Gray, he would become the club's top scorer. But with Gray gone and Bremner in, Ritchie, like so many others, finds himself surplus to requirements and – following an impasse over a new deal – on a week-to-week contract.

It is no life for a married man with a young child. Security is needed and he waits to see what kind of response the CV garners. It should not be as difficult as this. Ritchie has a reputation as an intelligent striker with a keen eye for goal. His early debut, which gives the impression he has been around for some time, coupled with his thinning hair, may give the wrong impression. There is life in the old dog yet.

But the phone does not ring. There had been some early interest from Brest, in the north-west of France, and he is due to go over and see what they have to say when Joe Royle calls. 'I've tried to sign you before,' he says. 'I've got your CV – come for a chat.'

The journey from Wetherby to Oldham takes around 90 minutes. Ritchie is met at Boundary Park by Royle, who launches a charm offensive. The 27-year-old likes what he sees. Over that four hours he feels as though he has met every member of staff. The place has a homely feel. There has not been much love of late at Leeds, and Ritchie is ready to be liked again.

He knows that Oldham are on a rebuild – and he also knows that his Leeds team was lucky to dump them out of the play-offs three months earlier. 'I want to build something special,' says Royle. 'We've got some good young players.'

He need say little more. A tribunal later sets the fee at £50,000. The first block of the rebuild is in place.

While Ritchie's arrival is welcome, the hangover from the previous season is inevitable. As December arrives, prior to a long trip to the South Coast to Bournemouth, Royle's men have won just four of their opening 19 games. Relegation, rather than promotion, is what is on the cards. Action is needed.

Royle knew from the minute he walked into the Cedar Court Hotel, on a roundabout at Ainley Top, next to the M62 above Huddersfield, that he had made the right move.

The striker he was about to speak to was already there, early, in a suit and tie.

Frank Bunn wants to impress. He sees the meeting as an interview and has dressed accordingly. The tall striker is a product of his upbringing. They may not have had money to burn in Birmingham's rough and tumble Chemsley Wood, an overspill estate eight miles to the east of the city centre built in 1966 and known for its 51 high-rise tower blocks, but they did things properly. Bunn's father, an assembler for British Leyland, home of the Mini and producer of more vehicles than anywhere else in Britain at its enormous Longbridge plant, is a strict disciplinarian and raised his son accordingly.

The men order coffee. Royle is eloquent, outlining his vision for the club. Bunn, like Ritchie, is a willing listener. He had started life at Luton Town before moving to Hull City, also of the Second Division. Life at the side of the River Humber had gone well initially but things had taken a downturn of late. So when his manager, Brian Horton, told him that Royle was interested, he was keen to speak.

It takes less than an hour to iron out personal terms. Bunn's girlfriend has just landed a job in Hull but she works for a large medical firm who also have a presence in the north-west, so two transfers take place at once.

Two days later, on the Thursday, Bunn trains with his new team-mates for the first time. On the Friday, he gets on the coach for Bournemouth not knowing who he will be rooming with. It ends up being his fellow strike partner, Andy Ritchie.

The scoreline – a 2-2 draw – is unremarkable. But on the bench, when he sees his two new players develop an almost instantly telepathic understanding, Royle can barely contain his excitement. His mantra, unsurprisingly for a former striker, is that you are only as good as your frontmen. It quickly becomes apparent that he has two very good frontmen.

He smiles to himself on the bench, almost glowing, and thinks 'we've got something here'. 'They loved playing alongside each other,' he tells Willie Donachie on the coach on the way home. 'They are so comfortable with the ball.'

Royle goes to bed that night a happy man. He feels like he has taken a big step forward. For the players themselves, it is almost telepathic. Bunn is the target man, while Ritchie is always in and around. At times, the ball looks like it sticks. It feels like it may be the start of something beautiful.

With Ritchie and Bunn continuing to gel, the last 25 league games see just four defeats. While the tenth-placed finish is a drop from the previous season, the losses of some big players have been absorbed by Royle's recruitment strategy. The sales that followed at the end of his first season have been repeated but this time his squad is stronger and better-equipped to deal with the losses. There was no drop to the bottom of the table. Even more encouragingly, attendances have shown a small increase. People are beginning to sit up and take notice of the project that is unfolding down at Boundary Park. There is a belief, among some, that Royle's seventh season in charge may be the lucky one. It is, however, unfounded. Royle had targeted 20 clean sheets but as things transpired, only bottom two Birmingham and Walsall end up conceding more in the 1988-89 campaign. Fortunately, with Bunn and Ritchie continuing where they left off, only promoted Chelsea and Manchester City score more.

While the 16th-placed finish is disappointing, there are more grounds for optimism. Earl Barrett, a young defender plucked from City's reserves, has excelled. Ian Marshall, a defender who can also play as a striker, taken from Everton's second string, has also impressed. In January, the arrival of the no-nonsense Welsh centre-half Andy Holden, from Wigan Athletic, shored things up at the back. The success rate on signings is remarkable.

There is a feeling, as 1989-90 approaches, that if they can carry their form into the new season they may well be ready for another shot at promotion. First, there will be the annual end-of-season jaunt to Majorca, and then it will be down to business. Royle is now seven years into the job. He is already far-removed from the man who arrived on the back of a lorry. He feels he has a group of players who, with some luck on the injury front, can do something special. There are others in the league who will have spent much more money, whose players earn wages his group of cast-offs can only dream of. But Royle senses something, and history has already taught him that his judgement is sound.

PART TWO:

TELL ME MAM 1989-90

This is how it feels to be lonely,
This is how it feels to be small,
This is how it feels when your word means nothing at all.

(The Inspiral Carpets, *This Is How It Feels*, 1990)

[SPANISH INTERLUDE]

Sentido Cala Vinas Hotel, Majorca, May 1989, 6pm.

JOE Royle strides into the foyer of the Sentido Cala Vinas Hotel. He is in a good mood. His players and staff flew out a day earlier for their end of season trip but he stayed behind to attend a gala dinner held by the north-west's football journalists. It is always good to keep the gentlemen and ladies of the press onside, but he is now looking forward to a week under the Majorcan sun with his charges.

Assistant manager Willie Donachie is waiting for him at reception. Concern is etched on his face.

'Everything all right, Willie?' Royle asks.

'Not really, boss, no,' comes the reply in thick Glaswegian.

Royle knows his players can be a handful, but he also knows that they often get close to the line before retreating, and so is not too concerned.

'Come on Willie – they've only been here a day,' he says, 'how bad can it be?'

'Well, boss,' says Donachie, 'they're all in prison.'

Coach and Horses, Magaluf, Majorca, May 1989, 2pm.

The sun is shining, the San Miguel is flowing and the Oldham players are sat around a table outside a British pub at the bottom of a popular strip, enjoying themselves.

It has been an average year, with a 16th-placed finish, but they ended the campaign strongly and there are hopes that the next year may be a good one. Now is their chance to let their hair down on the annual jaunt, before heading away with their families ahead of an all-too-sudden return to pre-season training in the no-doubt relentless rain. All is well with the world until Phil Black, a Manchester boutique-owner and friend of the manager who has come along for the trip, spots a delivery van turn up outside a tourist shop next door.

Blacky, who was famously the first to bring Armani and Versace threads to the northern city, sees the lorry's driver grab a box from the back and head into a nearby shop. A high-spirited soul, he sees his chance and springs into action. Within minutes, he is back, with a box under his arm. He hides it under the table. There is much laughter. Many of the players see Blacky as one of them. It is, in effect, a harmless prank.

When the lorry has gone, Blacky opens the box to find dozens of bottles of sun cream. He takes one out, squirts it all over his face and then showers some of the players sat close to him, sending them scattering for cover.

The scene has not gone unnoticed by some nearby locals. It takes about 15 minutes for the police cars to arrive – and they do so in a blaze of sirens. It does not take the officers – jabbering instructions in Spanish – long to spot the box. Through the boozy haze, Blacky immediately sees sense and owns up. Despite his protestations that it was only a joke and that he was always going to take the box back to the shop, he is bundled into the back of a car and taken away.

At first, the players see the funny side. But after a while, fuelled by the booze, anger rises. A couple of hours have passed and there is still no sign of Blacky. Some feel a sense of obligation. Some do not. A debate ensues. 'Fuck him,' Ian Marshall declares in squeaky-voiced Scouse. 'He's the gaffer's mate, not ours.'

Frank Bunn, who is known for his diplomacy skills, decides to act. 'I'll sort it,' he says, and heads for the police station.

An hour passes and there is no sign of Bunn. There is another crisis meeting and the decision is made to send Jon Hallworth, a self-assured, well-spoken goalkeeper known to his team-mates as 'Captain', after the stiff-upper lip Blackadder character Captain Darling, on a mercy mission.

When Hallworth arrives he finds that things have not gone according to plan. Both Bunn and Black have been arrested and are in a cell. Hallworth cannot speak Spanish, the officers cannot speak English and after failing to come to an understanding, he joins the others behind bars.

A short time later, four police cars turn up back outside the bar where the drinks are still flowing. The remainder of the group is rounded up and taken to the station.

When they arrive, there are more shenanigans. While trying to diffuse the situation, Ian Liversedge – the club physiotherapist affectionately known to all as 'Soss' – gets involved in a row with the most volatile of the police officers. A short man with an even shorter temper when drunk, he ends up aiming a headbutt at the peevish jabberer and gets punched for his troubles.

The players are put into three cells, all in a row. One of them starts singing *Always Look on the Bright Side of Life* from *Monty Python's Life of Brian*, and there is laughter. Eventually, the group is told that if they sign a piece of paper and pay a fine they can go. Reluctantly, they agree to do so, sore that they have been turned over by the local constabulary. All, that is, apart from Hallworth and Marshall.

For Hallworth it is simple. He has not done anything wrong and does not want to sign what is effectively a confession. Marshall, who had joined the previous year after failing to cement a place in First Division Everton's talented team, has other reasons for his reluctance. He is the son of a sailor from Bootle and when asked to sign the paper his thoughts immediately go to his father, and a story he had often told about his own youth. Marshall senior was in Cuba when there was some sort of a kerfuffle at the port. He was asked to sign a piece of paper by the local police and assured that when he had done so, he would be free to leave. He did as asked and subsequently ended up spending the next 12 months in a Communist prison.

'Fuck that,' says Marshall, thinking the fate of the father may now befall the son. 'I ain't fucking signing anything.'

The big man will not listen to the pleas of his team-mates. He is stubborn and he is pissed. He holds out for another hour, as does Hallworth. Eventually, with the police growing as tired of the situation as their prisoners, a solution is reached. Blacky will pay the fine on behalf of all the players as long as there is no signing of the papers.

Finally, the doors are unlocked and the players head back to the hotel. Their relief does not last long. When they arrive, an angry manager is waiting for them. 'What the fuck have you lot been doing?' is Royle's opening line.

CHAPTER SEVEN

Oldham, 1989

IT should have been £367 per year, but John Battye is quick to see an opportunity to get Oldham's plight into the pages of the national newspapers. The Oldham Council leader, a staunch Labour Party man whose family ties to the party stretch back more than 100 years, calls his chief executive to tell him that the controversial new Poll Tax, introduced by Margaret Thatcher's Conservative Party, will be fixed at £365. That way, they can call it the Tory Tax, 'costing Oldhamers a pound a day'.

It does the trick. The headlines are grabbed, which helps draw attention to the borough, but Battye is in charge of a town which, economically, is not in good shape.

The Poll Tax, a new tariff based on house size, will see many of those in Oldham pay the same rates as those in some of the most affluent areas of the country. It is viewed by many in Labour's working-class heartlands as an attack on the poor by a right-wing, capitalist Prime Minister, who has previous in that department.

It could not have come at a worse time. Battye, from Saddleworth, one of Oldham's few affluent areas, was educated at Hulme Grammar, the town's top fee-paying school, and has long been on a mission to ensure that those less fortunate than himself are given the tools they need to be successful in life.

It stemmed from a lecture given by a former headmaster, Sid Johnson. The teacher told his captive audience that he failed to understand why the country had universal suffrage – the right to vote for all – given it meant that 'my vote for the Conservative Party is being cancelled out by some layabout in Limeside (one of Oldham's poorer areas), who's no job and who is an alcoholic'.

Despite his tender years, Battye was appalled at his master's comment. He thinks of the 'Limeside layabout' in different terms. The man has no job, has a drink problem, and as if that was not bad enough, here is his own headmaster trying to take the vote off him. That night he joined the Labour Party and immediately went out to canvass for them.

In 1970, he became a councillor and has since risen up the town's political ladder. Battye is a proud Oldhamer from a small village called Delph, which locals fondly referred to as 'Little Russia' given its tradition since the 1890s of almost always electing at least one Labour councillor, despite being in a relatively well-to-do area. At the weekends he would watch Latics on Saturday and the rugby on Sunday. He is saddened at the town's plight. The landscape is blotted with dozens of now-empty mills and there had been considerable pressure to turn them into museums and apartments. His view was that this would be a waste of time. There was no appetite for either and the real issue – that of a new employment stream to replace the mills – needed to be tackled.

He set about bringing fresh industry to the town, with some success. In 1989, the *Daily Mirror* had moved its northern printing operation to Chadderton. Battye and his colleagues were finding that there was a demand for former mill workers from computer firms, especially the female machine-operators, who could turn their threading skills from cotton to microchips. But the arrival of Thatcher, at the end of the 1970s, had not helped large swathes of the town's population. Austerity had brought the end of vital grant aid. Instead, Battye had turned to the European Union and had managed to pilfer around £5m of a £9m 'textile fund' that was meant to be split among the many towns of Greater Manchester.

As he told reporters, when the economy caught a cold, Oldham caught pneumonia. There was a low skill base in the town and when the remainder of the textile industries departed in the 70s and 80s, it left Oldham with a much higher than average unemployment rate. Next to the M62, the sprawling borough should have been a prime location for businesses but there was nowhere to put them, and Battye set about building business parks to ensure that would not be the case in the future.

One of the few things the town can boast is a strong night-time economy. In the 1950s and 1960s, it had been something of a destination for coach tours from across the region. While that cannot be said of 1989, the town centre comes to life when the sun drops. Yorkshire Street, the main drag, is lined with bars, clubs and takeaways. The same can be said of Union Street, which runs parallel at the bottom of the hill that separates the thoroughfares. Both streets are often packed, especially at weekends, as the town's youth attempts to party away the mundane monotony of the working week.

There are more than a dozen nightclubs, for all tastes and for all ages, and more pubs than it would be possible to visit in one night. And while Oldham is not Manchester, the cultural explosion down the road – fuelled by an influx of the party drug ecstasy and bands such as The Stone Roses and Happy Mondays – has had a seismic impact. Clothes have become baggier, haircuts shaggier. There is even an Oldham band which has become part of the Madchester scene.

In 1988, Royle's son Darren opened the door of the family home to the unfamiliar face and bowl haircut of a man 10 years his senior. The stranger introduced himself as 'Clint', told him that he was in a local band called The Inspiral Carpets and that the group wondered if his dad could have a listen to their album and provide a quote for their press release.

Royle, with music in his blood, was happy to do so, although he had little idea that his subsequent words would soon end up on national radio.

John Peel, the legendary BBC Radio One DJ, had taken a shine to the four–piece. A northerner, he had worked as a mill operative in nearby Rochdale after leaving public school and was a champion of working-class artists. He admired the grittiness of the Carpets, who had been around in various formats since guitarist Graham Lambert and his pal and fellow Oldham Schoolboys footballer Stephen Holt decided to set up a band way back in 1980. At a time when hip outfits from Manchester, loaded with big-city swagger, were dominating the airwaves, they seemed a bit like an earthy, 1960s throwback. Boon's skills on the Hammond organ and a logo which featured a cow smoking a joint and the slogan 'Cool as Fuck' added a quirkiness which struck a chord with the DJ, whose showcasing *Sessions* show started in 1967 and had helped launch the career of the likes of Pink Floyd, David Bowie and The Sex Pistols.

On July 6, 1988 Peel told his army of listeners: 'This is a band that has the Royle seal of approval,' before referring to the manager's words. 'He says he "enjoyed the strong organ influence and slight Buzzcock tendencies".' Royle's eye for artistry clearly stretched beyond the field of play. Peel then played all five tracks of the demo album, *Dung 4*.

More appearances on Peel's show followed, and word began to spread. By August 1989 the band had moved out of Oldham to Manchester and were touring, with a single called *Find Out Why* whose video had appeared on ITV staple *The Chart Show*.

Battye believes sport and music can help raise the profile as the 90s approach. He is impressed by Royle as both a person and a manager. Only the previous year, Battye had received a panicked call from a pub in Failsworth, on Oldham's border with Manchester. The landlord has called the council leader because he did not know where to turn. The pub had been collecting pennies for charity for months, and they were piled high on the bar. They had asked for an Oldham player to come and push them over when they had hit the target they were looking for in a grand ceremony, but the day had arrived and when they had called the club the person they had spoken to said they knew nothing about it. Battye called Royle to explain the situation. At 7.30pm, not one, but three Oldham players turned up under manager's instructions. They stayed until closing time and the evening was a rousing success.

On another occasion, Royle had been asked to come to the opening of a batch of specially-adapted bungalows for those with disabilities. The manager was supposed to be there for half an hour, and a couple of residents had been chosen to meet him. After spending time with them, Royle asked the council leader how many residents were in the new houses in total. The answer was 20. Royle then proceeded to go to every house on the complex and meet all of them. He was there all afternoon. Battye knows that the impact of sport can be huge. He has seen it elsewhere in the north-west, but not in Oldham. Neither Latics or the rugby have ever been to Wembley and he is not holding his breath that the sad statistic will change this year.

CHAPTER EIGHT

Ready For War

IT starts with a bollocking. 'First things first,' Joe Royle tells his players in the first training session of the 1989-90 season. 'Any of you lot who haven't told your families that you were in the nick in Spain had better do soon because you're all going to be in the papers this weekend.'

It is not the best welcome back – and things are about to get worse. The group are taken to a running track, which belongs to a nearby school, and introduced to Willie Donachie's latest idea – a professional athletics coach who is going to put them through their paces and find out who has enjoyed the summer a little too much.

There is muttering and cursing as the group assemble to be introduced to what is known as 'Fartlek'. It is, in essence, a simple form of interval running, which originated in Sweden. Short bursts of speed are followed by slower jogs and an eventual long-distance race.

Royle has assembled a quick bunch of players, Ian Marshall, Denis Irwin and Earl Barrett to name three. But there is one who is absolutely cruising, gliding past his team-mates as though they are running in treacle, destroying the field. It is no contest. An embarrassment.

Royle, stood on the side of the track with Donachie, cannot

believe what he is seeing. He does not recognise the star man and turns to his assistant. He is not a man for excessive swearing but in this case he cannot help himself.

'Willie,' Royle says. 'Excuse my French, but what the fuck is that?'

'That' is the man Manchester City have christened 'Barrett's Revenge' and, for some time, Royle had been thinking they may have been right.

The previous season, City had forced him and Ian Stott to part with £10,000 for a young defender called Paul Warhurst. Warhurst was another whom both Royle and Jim Cassell liked the look of. He had pace and balance – two of what they had quickly identified as the key ingredients on the plastic – and given he was not getting anywhere near City's first team, he was likely to be cheap.

After one reserves match, Royle went for a cup of tea with Mel Machin, the City manager and an old friend from his days at Norwich. 'What happened to the kid who came off at half-time?' he asked. 'He's going on a free to Chesterfield tomorrow,' was the response. 'He's driving me mad, Joe, he's always injured.' Royle saw his chance. 'If he's free, we'll take him – he's better than what we have in the Reserves,' he said, before calling his chairman to get the green light.

Peter Swales, however, was having none of it. The City chairman had been burned by the Earl Barrett experience. The £35,000 Royle had paid for the defender two years previously, who had won nothing but rave reviews since the move, was beginning to look laughable.

When Royle called back to seal the deal, Machin was embarrassed. 'I've spoken to the chairman,' he said, 'and he's told me that he's free to anyone else but if he's going to you lot it's got to be 10 grand'.

Royle went back to Stott and delivered the bad news. But by now there was trust, and Stott was not dismayed. 'Are you sure?' he asked Royle.

Royle was sure. 'We'll make money on this one,' he told Stott, and the deal was done. At a subsequent board meeting a delighted Swales crowed to his fellow directors that they would call Warhurst 'Barrett's Revenge', thinking they had finally got one back on the little runts up the road. 'We've done it, chaps,' he said. 'We've got Barrett's revenge.'

While more of a long-term project, injuries dictated that Warhurst make his first-team debut not long after his move down at Portsmouth. During the first half, Royle noticed that the youngster was struggling for breath and, all of a sudden, Ian Liversedge launched something out of the dugout and onto the pitch like a grenade.

'What's that?' he asked his physio.

'It's an inhaler,' said the physio. 'He's asthmatic – did you not know?'

'No!' was Royle's incredulous response.

At half-time in the dressing room, the new boy was gasping for breath. The initial signs were not good.

Not long after, Warhurst picked up a hernia injury. Royle saw the prolonged absence as an opportunity. He called Dr John Kelso, the club medic, and asked him for advice. Kelso, who had a practice in the Lees area of Oldham for many years and who was widely respected in the town, performed the role for the love of the club but his advice was often invaluable. He knew of a specialist in asthma and, while recovering, Warhurst was sent to see him. The defender, from nearby Stockport, had always had issues with his breathing. Not long after birth, he spent hours in an oxygen tent at Cherry Tree Hospital, with his worried mother at his bedside.

A City fan from childhood, he was elated when he signed for the club as a schoolboy at 11, but always knew something was not right. In training he could never run more than 400-500 metres. In the sprints he always finished first, against some seriously quick team-mates, but the long distances were a nightmare for him.

And here he was, as the team reported back for 1989-90, at the front of the pack. Medication changed, asthma dealt with, hernia gone.

What the fuck is that? Paul Warhurst.

Following a week of fitness work, with Warhurst continuing to astonish, the group heads to the Isle of Man for their pre-season trip. With them, for the week away, is Lennie Heppell, who is now something of a star within the world of sport. Word of his arrival has spread on the little island in the Irish Sea, and a young table tennis player asks to come and see him at the team hotel.

Heppell is happy to agree and the two begin to play in the games room, watched by Donachie and a group of the players. It is fascinating. The youngster is a fine player, but he is defensive, and focuses all of his efforts on getting the ball back over the net. Heppell is not impressed and immediately raises his game, flying towards the net and forcing the pace. When the ball drops to the floor on his side of the table Heppell, well into his 60s, races around to pick it up and get started again. The youngster is getting further and further back, away from the table. Everything the dancer-turned-coach does is razor sharp. 'If you're going to be great, you have to be aggressive,' he tells the visitor. It is a message not lost on those watching.

Donachie is delighted with Heppell's impact. He wants the players to take note. They want to grab this season by the scruff of the neck. Start on the front foot. Ensure they are ready to go at the referee's whistle. Be relentless. If Heppell, in his 60s, can live by that mantra there is no reason his players cannot.

Heppell looks after himself, and part of that is down to his diet. Getting players to eat the right foods has often been difficult for Donachie, who accepts that there is little he can do about the drinking. It has been a constant battle but things are improving and the group is listening. Donachie is impressed. They have come far. His mind returns to a previous season, when the club signed a player and found that when he arrived he was overweight. Donachie had asked the man in question if he could keep a weekly diary of what he was eating with a view to making a few adjustments. The player gave his consent and so they went to see his wife in the players' lounge to see if she would assist.

Her response when Donachie told her his plan? 'You haven't got a diary fucking big enough.' Those days are a thing of the past. This is a squad that takes onboard most of what he tells them. That wants to succeed.

* * * * *

Things are stepped up when they return to England. The training ground is Donachie's domain, and Royle, as he does, gives him a lot of freedom. The sessions play out to the noise of his Scottish accent echoing around the empty stands. 'Quicker, faster, stronger!'

When it comes to the difficult stuff – telling players they are going, signing players, bringing in staff, letting them go – Royle steps up. He is also responsible for the management of the team. He is the disciplinarian, but works on a basis of trust. Instead of the traditional fines system, he sometimes has those who step out of line doing lines, as though they were back at school.

A comment of 'listen, bollocks, behave yourself,' usually does the trick. He has a sharp wit and can tie his players in knots, instantly bringing them down to earth should they get carried away. But flashpoints are few and far between. The respect he commands from his group is huge and it is a club which often has a smile on its face, although the mood swings of Ian Marshall are already becoming the stuff of legend. Earlier in the week he was all smiles, larking around with goalkeeper Jon Hallworth. The next day, Hallworth came in and said hello. 'Fuck off, will ya?' was the response. Royle smiled. There is a camaraderie.

This is a largely northern group from working-class backgrounds. Royle notices an edge about them, a mischief, and he believes it can do them no harm. One of his fundamentals is honesty. He is still not long retired, relatively young for a manager and his players can relate to him. He played under one manager who lied to him and he has never forgotten how that felt. His players are never in the dark over how he feels towards them and there is no silent treatment. When he subsequently calls in a favour and has a quiet word with a member of the press he knows, he is quick to tell his players that the Magaluf story has been pulled. He looks out for them.

With regards to tactics, Royle and Donachie have always

tailored the system around the players they have. This year is going to be a simple 4-4-2, with two wingers. In midfield, Mike Milligan and Nick Henry are told to win the ball and get it out wide. The full-backs, Denis Irwin and local lad Andy Barlow, are told to get forward and support them. The wingers need to get the crosses in and the strikers – always two of them – will do the rest. There needs to be bodies in the box. Because of the pace of the defence, they will press and keep a high line, especially at home. There is little chance of being caught on the break. It is a passing game, and the plastic is embraced. It is better than a muddy grass pitch and they feel they have a team who have the ability to play on it.

The 4-4-2 fits with Royle's philosophy. He thinks it works at Second Division level. He believes in it, Donachie believes in it and, most importantly, the players believe in it. For a long time, this has been an offensive team. Nothing is going to change on that front this year.

As pre-season progresses the fitness sessions become brutal. Around a mile up a substantial hill from Boundary Park is one of Oldham's green spots, Tandle Hill Country Park. The squad runs from the stadium to the park and then across its hilly trails. When they have finished they run back to the stadium. Passing motorists on busy Rochdale Road do double takes as a squadron of blue tracksuits makes its way back towards Boundary Park.

It is worse for those carrying injuries. For them, it is an 8am meeting with Ian Liversedge and his assistant physio and kit man Ronnie Evans at Royton Baths before joining in with the fun and games at the club. There are no days off.

Preparations, however, take a turn when the financial reality of where the club remains are reinforced. If a big offer comes in, it cannot be turned down. Just before the start of the season there is movement on Tommy Wright, who has refused to sign a new contract in the belief he can get a better deal elsewhere. He is right. A call comes in from Leicester City, who are also in the Second Division but whose budget is substantially higher than Oldham's.

A deal is struck at £300,000 – not bad for a man who cost £80,000. It is good news for the club's bank manager but also for Norman Holden, who reaps a stunning return on his original loan from three years earlier.

Royle, by now, is relaxed about things. It is hardly ideal to lose one of your star men at the end of the summer, just before the big kick-off, but he knows exactly where to go for a replacement if needed. For years, he and Cassell have made regular Friday night trips over the beautifully bleak Saddleworth Moors to watch Fourth Division Halifax Town as part of their eternal hunt for hidden gems. They had quickly become fans of a scruffy-looking, skilful winger by the name of Richard Holden. 'He's borderline genius, borderline insane,' Royle had been told when he made inquiries about the young lad from Skipton known as Rick, who had previously ended a career at Burnley after one match to continue his studies at Carnegie College, in Leeds, where he picked up a BA (Hons) in Sports Science.

Holden also has the Cassell seal of approval. On one occasion, he travelled to Scarborough for a midweek match to watch the young winger. As he tended to do, Cassell shunned the directors' box for the away end. His belief was that if you are crazy enough to go and watch Halifax play in the freezing cold at Scarborough on a Wednesday night then chances are you know a lot about your football club. He liked what he heard from the Halifax fans of Holden, and he liked what he saw on the pitch even more. Stood on the terrace with a cone of chips and a Styrofoam cup of Oxo, Cassell immediately recognised that he was witnessing a fine player. Holden may not have been the quickest, but his feet and body movement, not to mention his deceptive turn of pace, were unbelievable.

There is interest from elsewhere. Rivals Barnsley like what they see, but manager Allan Clarke is put off by his reputation as not being the most hygienic of footballers. 'I've heard he doesn't clean his teeth so we won't be signing him,' Clarke told the board.

Oldham were not interested in dental care, but could not afford the asking price and instead Watford, then battling relegation from the First Division, came in. Upon arrival at Vicarage Road, following a long trip down the M1 in a clapped-out old motor, manager Steve Harrison took one look at Holden, in a t-shirt and with long hair, and brought him a razor, a shirt and tie and some trousers.

Watford were relegated and failed to make it back at the first attempt. Things have not gone well. Royle has kept tabs on the situation and knows, through his network of contacts within the game, that there are rumours Holden is unsettled.

The rumours are right. Holden is far from impressed with the direct style of play deployed by the Hornets, complaining that the ball is always going over his head. He needs to get to a club where they play football properly, where he can get the ball at his feet and where he can display his talents.

Holden, whose shoulder-length wavy hair is a nod to his hero, the Argentina legend Mario Kempes, is the best crosser of the ball Royle has ever seen. He knows he has to act following Wright's departure and he does just that. A fee of £165,000 is agreed, the most Royle has spent on a player. Regardless, it is close to just half of what has been banked by the sale of Wright. He believes Holden is worth it, and will provide his side with more quality balls into the box than they have ever had. Balls Ritchie and Bunn will thrive on.

The following day, Holden enters Royle's office to discuss terms, accompanied by his girlfriend who, helpfully, is from Oldham. Not one for unnecessary pleasantries, Holden tells his prospective new boss how much he is on a year at Watford. 'I need the same,' he says. 'That's my mortgage.'

The answer is not what he is expecting. 'I'm not giving you that,' says Royle. There is an awkward silence, but before Holden can protest, Royle continues. 'I'm giving you five grand a year more,' he adds. Holden smiles.

Royle knows his new boy is cut from a slightly different cloth. But he also thinks he may have just made the most important signing of his managerial career.

With Holden in the ranks, as kick-off approaches he feels quietly confident. The quality on display in Donachie's training sessions has elevated. The players are clearly desperate to play. They, to be frank, are kicking lumps out of each other in an attempt to catch the manager's eye and make the squad. The way that the wage system has been devised means that large chunks of cash are dependent on being selected for the first team.

While Royle jokes that 'bonus' is a four-letter word to his chairman, the players know that if they win, then they will be a lot better off come Saturday night. The final session is a good one. Balls ping across the astroturf with accuracy. There is intensity and there is fitness. 'For fuck's sake,' shouts Hallworth as another shot hurtles past him.

Rick Holden, the scorer, has quickly made himself at home and has found a like-minded character in the goalkeeper.

After an earlier session the winger could not start his battered old car. His new team-mate told him that he had nothing on that afternoon and would happily drive him the 30 miles to Skipton. Holden, a cynical soul, was stunned by the gesture. The pair ended up heading to the town's hostelries and a great friendship was born. But Holden knows Hallworth hates shooting practice and so he is now peppering him at every opportunity. Shots continue to fly into the net. Royle nods approvingly.

CHAPTER NINE

Latique Style

FOR a short time they were the talk of the football world. Mossley, a non-league team from a tiny, hillside town in between Oldham and neighbouring Ashton-under-Lyne, were somehow banking £100,000-a-year from selling a product that had nothing to do with football – and that the public could not get enough of.

It was all down to a young, enterprising local who had been a ballboy for the club at the age of 10. Alan Hardy, who by the age of 16 was on the committee, was the first to spot the potential of something they were calling scratchcards. They were, in essence, a raffle ticket. A piece of card covered in a silver film which purchasers would scratch off with a coin, or a fingernail, to reveal whether they had won a prize.

Hardy had left school and was working as a salesman for Lyon's Tetley, persuading companies to buy thousands of tea bags among other products, when he spotted the potential.

He persuaded the board of the club to order scratchcards, complete with Mossley branding, and put a booth in the centre of Ashton, a market town which could boast significant footfall. To say it had taken off was an understatement. Queues began to form outside the booth. The public could not get enough. Before long, little Mossley were banking six figures and had become the envy of non-league football. Such was the success of the initiative that Hardy was asked to become Mossley's first full-time employee. A football obsessive, he readily accepted.

The situation at their neighbours had not gone unnoticed at Boundary Park and in 1981 Hardy was invited to attend an interview for the post of assistant to the commercial manager at Oldham Athletic. Not long after, the commercial manager role was his.

At the time, Hardy knew that Oldham would have to diversify to bring in revenue. They had a lottery scheme of their own, but they simply could not rely on that alone to bring in the funds they needed. As the 1980s progressed, he got more and more adventurous. A 10k road race was introduced, which ended next to the ground and attracted thousands – each paying an entry fee. A trophy room was added, which proved to be lucrative given the size of the amateur football and rugby league scene in the town.

But what Hardy really wanted was a club shop. Time and time again he had made his case to Ian Stott and the board. Time and time again he was told that there was no money.

His 10k race was sponsored by the TSB Bank and he mentioned the club shop situation to one of their managers. The manager asked him to present a business plan, based on a loan of £40,000. Hardy went away and came back with the details, which included a promise to have the loan repaid in five years thanks to anticipated profits from the shop.

All was agreed and, in the summer of 1989, the builders arrived. The result is the arrival of the imaginatively titled Latique, and finally Oldham have a club shop worthy of the name. It is only one-storey, but the potential, Hardy thinks, is huge.

Another revenue stream is the pitch itself, which is proving to be useful. Over the summer months, it hosts the Sondico International Oldham Athletic cricket knock-out, bringing local teams to Boundary Park.

Before the start of the season there is another new arrival aimed at generating more cash. After much prompting from Hardy, £12,000 has been found for a giant electric scoreboard – which the *Oldham Chronicle* gushes is 'the third biggest in the country behind Wembley and Newcastle United'. Fans will be charged to post birthday messages, while local firms are told they can put up adverts for a small fee.

A local young IT enthusiast, Mark Gorey, is brought in to operate it. Room is made for a computer room in a small box at the back of the main stand, next to the PA announcer. Gorey, from nearby Chadderton, is a huge NFL fan and plays quarterback for the Manchester Allstars team. He immediately sets to work creating American-style graphics of referees lecturing crying players, balls hitting the back of nets and clapping hands along with the cry: 'Come on Oldham'. The spirit of creativity runs throughout the club.

The new season will also see a new name on the front of Oldham's shirts. Since Joe Royle's arrival, JW Lees have been the club's main shirt sponsors. But it has always been more of an act of generosity than a genuine business deal. In the build-up to the season, it looks like a giant Marks & Spencer department store is going to be built on Clayton Playing Fields, a series of amateur football pitches behind the Chaddy End, the cowshed-style stand behind one of the goals where the most raucous element of Oldham's support gathered for matches. As part of the deal for the land, construction giants Bovis agree to do something for the neighbouring club and sign a three-year, £120,000 shirt sponsorship.

Ian Stott is delighted, as his face shows when pictured in the *Chron* after the firm's managing director lands on the centre circle in a helicopter with a giant cheque.

Hardy has a helping hand in Royle. Ahead of the new season, 1,300 supporters gather at the Queen Elizabeth Hall in the centre of the town for a surprise announcement. Hundreds are turned away at the door. The event is to launch Starline, a new members' draw scheme. After an impassioned speech by Royle, fans flock to the picnic tables arranged at the front of the hall to sign up.

CHAPTER TEN

Six-Shooter

THE natives are restless and can withhold their frustration no longer. 'What the fuck, what the fuck, what the fuck is going on?' is the chant that booms out of a seething North Stand at a furious Elland Road.

On the bench, a smiling Joe Royle turns to Willie Donachie. 'You'd think they would be used to it by now,' he says.

Used to little Oldham coming to their illustrious home and turning them over once again. Twice in the first-half, Latics – in their all-red away kit – have beaten their hosts' offside trap and twice they have scored, to take a 4-1 aggregate lead and effectively kill this Littlewoods Cup tie after triumphing 2-1 in the first leg at Boundary Park. Within the space of four minutes, Frank Bunn and Andy Ritchie have capitalised on some horrendous defending by the favourites for the Second Division title. For the first, Mike Milligan got behind the defence from a goal kick, nodded it beyond Mervyn Day and Bunn tapped in. For the second, Earl Barrett expertly controlled a high ball, went on a weaving run and put Ritchie through on goal. Against his former club, the striker expertly finished with a low drive into the bottom corner.

Leeds pull one back on 59 minutes but they do little else. Following the final whistle manager Howard Wilkinson is furious and claims both goals were offside. The reality, as replays show, is that they were not, and that his side have been outplayed over two legs by a team whose wage bill is a fraction of their own. A team that now goes into the hat for the next round and who, as the *Oldham Chronicle*'s Bob Young states, will be a serious shot at promotion if they can replicate that type of performance regularly in the league.

Victory in Yorkshire has turned an average start to the season into a good one. In the *Chron*'s preview of the forthcoming campaign, Young had declared that Royle – now second only to First Division Nottingham Forest's Brian Clough in terms of time of service – had assembled his best squad yet. Odds of 33-1 on promotion suggested that the bookmakers did not share such optimism. This remained a side built on a shoestring. There are some big hitters in the league and Oldham's budget is well below the halfway mark. But Royle had told Young that should they have better luck with injuries – something that had crippled them the previous season – he felt they were as good as anything in the division.

The opening day, however, brought a forgettable 1-0 defeat at Ewood Park, home of Lancashire rivals Blackburn Rovers. Swindon and Watford then left Boundary Park with a point.

In Berlin, the wall came down, ending decades of misery and uniting east with west. But there appeared to be no wind of change sweeping through Oldham. A trip to promotion favourites Newcastle United ended in a 2-1 defeat. However, the St James' Park outing was memorable thanks to a stunning overhead kick from Rick Holden, in front of the away end. Despite the club's sluggish start, the winger was rapidly becoming a fans' favourite, and his eccentric celebration was fitting of the strike.

Royle was relaxed. He had seen enough from the group to reassure him that things would quickly change. He was right. Victory finally arrived in the shape of a 3-2 victory over a Plymouth Argyle side tipped to struggle. Then Leeds were defeated under the Boundary Park lights on what felt like a breakthrough evening. Despite the visitors taking the lead through former Manchester United winger Gordon Strachan, one of many big-money names, Oldham started to show what Royle and Donachie had seen on the training ground in a real match.

Ritchie, enjoying fixtures with his former club, quickly equalised and then Holden seized the moment. Picking up the ball 35 yards from goal, he had weaved one way and the other, leaving white-shirted defenders trailing in his wake. The close control was a sight to behold. On and on he had gone, into the area where Leeds defender Noel Blake had stuck out a boot in desperation. Holden had felt the contact, and could have easily gone down and won a penalty, but he kept his balance and somehow touched the ball delicately beyond advancing goalkeeper Mervyn Day. It had sent the Chaddy End into raptures. Sensing the moment, and the drama, Holden did not celebrate as the ball rolled into the net. Instead he remained face down on the turf as those of a home persuasion in what was an encouraging crowd of 8,415 went wild and his team-mates piled on top of him. It was another fine goal for the new boy.

More than that, it capped a performance that confirmed the manager and his assistant's suspicions that this team of theirs was capable of doing something special.

A couple of weeks after victory was secured at Elland Road, Donachie is in a nervous mood. Oldham have been drawn to play Fourth Division Scarborough in the next round, at Boundary Park, which should be a relatively straightforward night. But the minnows from the Yorkshire coast pulled off a stunning comeback in the previous round, scoring three goals in quick succession to defeat Chelsea – second-placed in the First Division – 4-3 on aggregate after a tremendous 1-1 draw at Stamford Bridge.

The training session starts on the halfway line, where the players gather, with yoga. The silence is broken by the clatter of bottles from elsewhere in the ground. 'Milk's here,' jokes full-back Andy Barlow, and there is laughter.

But Donachie is not smiling. If Scarborough can knock out Chelsea they can do the same to Oldham, unless they are focussed. He can sense a feeling of complacency in the squad and the laughter underlines it.

Spirits are high. The triumph over Leeds has been backed up by an upsurge in league form. There has also been victory at Stoke City while West Brom, Leicester City – with Tommy Wright – and Barnsley have also been seen off, with a 2-1 defeat at promotion-chasing Sheffield United and a miserable 2-0 reverse at lonely Bournemouth the only dark spots. Saturday's 2-0 defeat of Middlesbrough has put the stuttering start behind them. They are now, incredibly, nine months unbeaten at home.

But Donachie knows he must keep their feet on the ground. As a player, he would often go and watch his forthcoming opponent, so he would be prepared when he faced them. His coach at City, Ken Barnes, used to criticise him for it. 'Concentrate on your own game,' he would tell him, 'don't worry about them.' But while Donachie could see the merit in that, there is nothing that gives him more apprehension than not knowing what you are in for. It is one of the controllables, and it would be folly not to ensure you give yourself every chance. That view, part of his marginal gains mantra, has followed him into coaching. He has seen Scarborough several times and thinks he has identified a weakness.

'They play a high line in defence,' he tells his players. 'So if we can time our runs and get in behind them, we should have some joy.'

Much of the session is based on doing just that.

Sensing another upset, the TV cameras descend on Boundary Park. The match will take centre stage on ITV's *Midweek Sports Special*. Close to 8,000 gather for the fixture under the lights, further evidence that the public of Oldham is gaining interest. They have to wait less than 10 minutes for the first goal. Holden, on the left, sends in a cross with the outside of this left boot. It is not his best, and is heading straight to Ian Ironside, in the Scarborough goal. Ironside overestimates the bounce of a plastic pitch and dives over the top of the ball to leave Frank Bunn a tap-in to an empty net from all of around two yards.

The second, eight minutes later, is more straightforward. Neil Adams clips an inswinging corner from the left and Bunn steals a march on his marker to head into the ground and beyond Ironside.

Two minutes later and the same man completes his hat-trick. With the visitors persisting with their high line, Barlow volleys a booming pass forwards and Ritchie gets in behind his marker. Ironside races off his line and blocks his shot, but the ball falls to

Holden. He scuffs his cross but it finds Bunn who hits a superb low shot on the turn with his left foot into the bottom corner for his third.

The wait for his fourth lasts a full 15 minutes. This time Mike Milligan drops the ball behind the Scarborough defenders and Bunn latches onto it. Ignoring Ritchie, to his side, he casually slots beyond a stranded Ironside and into the same corner for his fourth.

'Bunn decides to go it alone,' commentator Tony Gubba tells viewers when the highlights are screened later that night, 'and it wasn't a bad idea, was it?'

Bunn, a modest man, is almost embarrassed. Adams jogs over as they trot back to the halfway line and jokes that a £1m move may not be far way.

Three minutes before half-time he has his fifth, which equals the tournament record. This time it comes following a surging run and pinpoint cross from Denis Irwin, on the right. Again, Bunn just has to tap it in. He does so and climbs the fence at the front of the Chaddy End to celebrate with his adoring public.

On the terraces, they believe they are seeing something special. Word spreads that if Bunn gets one more, he will have performed a feat unmatched in the tournament's 29-year history.

The next goal – and the best of the night – belongs to Ritchie, who latches on to a Bunn flick from a goal kick and wallops a volley over Ironside in front of the visiting supporters, who may have been wondering whether their trip was a worthwhile one.

At 6-0, it becomes a training ground exercise, and there is little action of note. That is until a minute from the end, when, for the umpteenth time that night, Oldham get behind the visitors' defence. This time it is Barlow, unmarked in acres of space on the left, who dinks over a cross. It is headed straight into the air by a Scarborough defender but when it drops Bunn lashes it in on the volley for his sixth.

Bunn raises his right arm, almost apologetic. He knows Steve Richards, one of the centre-backs, from his time at Hull. Another Scarborough player, Paul Olsen, was also at Boothferry Park. The visitors' left-back is from the same part of Birmingham and his relatives drink in the same pub as Bunn's father.

The final whistle blows and the players leave the pitch to chants of 'Frankie Bunn, Frankie Bunn, Frankie Bunn,' from the Chaddy End. The new scoreboard, already proving to be popular, flashes up 'A NEW CUP RECORD'.

The man himself is already up the tunnel. He has no idea what he has done until, while he is in the team bath, a delighted Alan Hardy bursts in spraying a bottle of champagne he has taken from the sponsors' box, like a Grand Prix winner.

The commercial manager ends up in the bath with Bunn, fully clothed.

Moments later the striker, not one for the limelight, is in front of the television cameras at the top of the tunnel. 'It's just nice to score the first one,' he says.

Later that night, following the showing of the highlights, the draw for the last-16 is made. Oldham get another home tie, which is welcome. What is more welcome is the team pulled out of the velvet bag whom they will face. 'Bring on the Champions' is the headline on the back of the following day's *Chron*. Oldham will face Arsenal, the champions of England and current leaders of the First Division.

That morning, Bunn's phone had rung. It was Hardy, and

there was excitement in his voice. 'What kind of boots were you wearing, Frankie?' he asked.

'Mitre,' said Bunn.

'Ah, that's a shame,' the commercial manager responded. 'I've just had [Italian bootmakers] Lotto on the phone. They said if you were wearing Lotto they would give you a couple of grand.'

'I was wearing Lotto, then,' said Bunn, quick as a flash.

Hardy laughed. 'You can't do that!' he said. 'There'll be photographs everywhere and it was on the telly. Let me phone Mitre and see what they say.'

Mitre were not interested but Littlewoods, the tournament sponsor, handed over a £1,000 cheque. Bunn decided to split it between two Oldham schools.

That afternoon, there was a knock at the door. Bunn answered it to a reporter from the *Daily Mirror*. The hack was armed with two pretend pistols – six shooters. As Bunn posed for a picture, his wife returned home from work from her lunch break. She took one look at her husband, aiming a pair of toy guns at an imaginary target in the front garden while a photographer snapped away, and shook her head.

CHAPTER ELEVEN

Cup Fever

THE calls, which started the morning after the Scarborough match and the Arsenal draw, jam the Boundary Park switchboard. Fans, desperate not to miss out, are desperate to know what the ticket arrangements are going to be. It is something that has never been witnessed before.

Alan Hardy, never one to miss a trick, decides to take advantage. He tells the *Oldham Chronicle* that, amid fears genuine supporters will miss out if the match sells out in home areas, they have decided to print a voucher that will be handed to fans at the turnstiles at the forthcoming Bradford City match. The voucher will entitle them to a ticket for the clash with the Gunners. Whether it works or not is unclear. Close to 8,000 turn up for a disappointing 2-2 draw, but with crowds on the rise, the figure may well have been down to the excitement growing around Joe Royle's young side.

One of the unforeseen issues Hardy faces is a reduction of capacity. Following the Lord Justice Taylor Report, into the Hillsborough tragedy earlier in the year when 95 Liverpool supporters were crushed to death on an overcrowded terrace at an FA Cup semi-final, accommodation on the steps of the Chaddy End has been cut from 7,450 to 5,530. Nobody thought that would ever be an issue, but all of a sudden, it is. To Hardy, Ian Stott and the rest of the board, the prospect of willing punters being unable to give the club their cash is unthinkable. It cannot happen.

Hardy calls the local police force and comes up with a form of a solution. Away fans who want to sit rather than stand will, as usual, be situated in the upper tier of the Lookers Stand, which means that the terrace below is set to be out of bounds to home supporters for safety reasons. Given the majority of those travelling up from North London may have difficulty knowing where Oldham is, let alone want to come and cause trouble, the green light is given for the no-go zone to be opened to home fans. All of a sudden, there are 500 precious, extra tickets to sell, and they fly out of the door.

Arsenal are providing the glamour. They are one of English football's biggest names. The champions have lifted the top-flight trophy on no less than nine occasions. In the 1930s, they landed the title four times in five seasons. They have won the FA Cup five times and, in their famous red shirts and white sleeves, are quite the attraction. But there is a genuine interest in Oldham for the football club not seen for years. The run at the back end of the previous season, coupled with the start to the current campaign, means that George Graham's aristocrats will be coming to a ground at which the home team has now not lost for 22 matches.

In the build-up, there is another Willie Donachie-inspired trip. This time, the players are taken to the nearby Tara Leisure Gym, where they don the gloves and take part in rapid-fire boxing sessions. At one point, club doctor John Kelso's wife, who is an aerobics instructor, comes in to deliver a workout. It is all part of Donachie's plan for marginal gains, which will be stretched to the limit against the league champions.

The message from Royle throughout the preparations is for the players to enjoy themselves and make sure they do not 'freeze'. He feels that some were guilty of doing just that when Spurs came to town last year for an FA Cup tie and strolled off with a 4-2 victory.

From 1-11, Arsenal are household names. The defensive pairing of David O'Leary and Tony Adams, Ireland and England internationals, is widely regarded as the best in the game. Full-backs Lee Dixon and Nigel Winterburn make up a back four that never gives an inch.

There are stars everywhere. A magical midfield features the skill and drive of Michael Thomas, whose dramatic, injury-time goal had snatched the title from Liverpool at a stunned Anfield months earlier, and David Rocastle, who is one of the most gifted players in the land.

Up front, Niall Quinn and Alan Smith, two of the tallest and most physical strikers in the country, will test the likes of Earl Barrett and Paul Warhurst like they have never been tested before. The Gunners even have a plastic pitch in their own gymnasium. They will be prepared.

Charged with keeping the visitors' midfield in check, alongside Mike Milligan in the centre of Oldham's side, is a youngster who Royle was trying to find a new club for the previous Christmas. In the midst of another injury crisis and a poor run of form, the last thing he needed was the distraction of a Wednesday trip to Middlesbrough in the Simod Cup, ahead of a league match at Ipswich on the Saturday. The competition was dreamed up in

1985, when English clubs were banned from Europe following the Heysel Stadium Disaster, when 39 Juventus fans were killed ahead of their European Cup final against Liverpool.

For Royle, the competition carried little weight. The Boro manager, Bruce Rioch, was an old friend of his Oldham counterpart and ahead of the fixture he tried to call in a favour. Years ago, they had bunked together while on trial for England's youth team, while Rioch would eventually go on to captain Scotland. Royle knew that Rioch was a very straightforward person, a man of principle. Bearing that in mind, he reached for the phone in his office. 'Bruce,' he said. 'Is there any chance we can bring the game forward to the Tuesday? We're due to go down to Ipswich on Friday. If we could shift it, it just helps me a little bit.'

The response was not what he wanted. 'Joe,' said Rioch. 'This is Middlesbrough Football Club. Middlesbrough Football Club plays its midweek games on a Wednesday.'

'I know, Bruce,' responded Royle. 'But it's me, we're mates – can you not do me a favour?'

Rioch repeated his stance several times and the conversation ended. Royle was left with a dilemma, and to consider who he will pick for what he views as a meaningless match.

One of those to be selected is a young Liverpudlian midfielder who has come through Urmson's youth system by the name of Nick Henry. Henry had been around the first team for a couple of seasons, but Royle had been trying to find him a free transfer because he did not believe that the youngster had what it took to break into the side. There was a view held privately among the staff that he had 'old man's legs' which meant he tended to run from side to side. Royle thought he was a fantastic kid, and wanted to do his best by him. He had tried to get him to both Stockport County and Chester City, but neither club would take him. The match at Ayresome Park was not so much a last chance, but a farewell.

Henry had been at Oldham since he was 15. By chance, his local Liverpool team was invited across to play against their Under 15s and they romped to a 4-0 win. He impressed, was offered a trial and it went from there. Henry, a Liverpool fan, had been training at their legendary Melwood base, but his year was stacked with England Schoolboy internationals and he felt he had little chance of making it at Anfield.

Upon leaving school he left behind his mum and moved to digs in Oldham. It had been something of a struggle. Initially, he was housed with a woman who had several cats, to which he was allergic. Often, when returning home from training, he would find one had sneaked into his bed. From there he moved to a family of devout Christians. While they were lovely people Henry, from the no airs or graces Dingle area of Liverpool, felt a little out of place when they would gather around the table at mealtime and say prayers. If he was ever injured, there would be a family prayer session where God would be asked to help aid his recovery.

The worst thing that happened to Henry was that he was selected to make his bow in the first team in the 1987-88 season and he felt like he had made it. It prompted Donachie to write in his programme notes that Henry had to know what it took to become a pro-footballer. The words had the desired effect. 'I'm going to fucking show you,' thought the youngster, and upped his game. He was ready, when his chance at Middlesbrough came.

The game started and, thankfully for Royle, the hosts went 1-0 up. But Oldham's team of misfits did not get the message. Fired-up Henry may have been playing out of position on the left, but his performance bordered on the heroic. He flew into tackles and showed an aggression that Royle did not think he possessed. He also drove forward, prompting attack after attack. Royle was amazed. The problem was, the longer this went on, the more chance there was of Oldham equalising and forcing a replay which, if possible, would have been even less welcome.

With Henry still running the show, on the bench Royle had a brainwave, and turned to Ian Liversedge. 'Get the front two off,' he instructed. 'OK boss,' his physio responded. 'Who's coming on?'

'Nobody,' said Royle, deadpan. Liversedge started laughing. 'I'm not sure you can do that,' he said.

'Of course you can,' Royle informed him. 'There's nothing in the rules that says you have to end the match with 11 men.'

Laughing, Liversedge raised the two number boards, denoting the players who had to come off. The referee jogged over and asked who would be replacing them.

'Nobody,' repeated Royle, and the non-substitution substitutions were made.

Oldham ended the game with nine men. Voluntarily. They also, more importantly, lost 1-0. There was to be no more godforsaken Simod Cup that year.

Rioch was furious, and told Royle his side had disrespected the cup. 'I tried telling you – I don't want to be in the fucking cup,' was his response.

They were out of the cup, but Henry was in the side. All of

a sudden, Milligan had a midfield partner and with Arsenal arriving, he was already a key player..

* * * * *

As it often tends to be, Oldham's preparation is straightforward, even for the visit of the champions. Each player is given a job and Royle ensures they know what is expected of them. Each has a defined role and knows what it is. On Monday morning they watch a video of the weekend's match but it is not a forensic analysis. Occasionally, Royle will press pause and point out something that he is not happy with. Often, he raises his concerns and leaves the players to sort it out.

Little time is spent on the opposition. There are no flipcharts. Little words are had with specific players, usually on Thursday, about whom they will be facing. The emphasis is on taking responsibility. 'Do your job,' is the mantra, along with 'Don't let them settle'. There is no difference in approach just because Arsenal are next, although Royle decides to play Ian Marshall up front, supporting Bunn and Ritchie. That famous visitors' backline will face three forwards.

Following the final training session, enterprising Rick Holden heads to the top of the main stand. Below him, Arsenal are going through their final paces. A walkthrough at a snail's pace gives him a good idea of what he is likely to face the following night. He cannot believe what he is seeing. The players appear to have been forbidden from playing any long balls whatsoever. All of their passes are short. Holden smiles, and heads back to his flat.

That night, Andy Barlow is one of the first at the ground, as his mind turns to his school days. He had passed his 11-plus exam and had gone to Hulme Grammar. A regular in their football team, he soon got used to taking on – and taking down – those from plusher surroundings. He sees Arsenal as football's version of Manchester Grammar, the upmarket school in the big city against whom Hulme used to battle, often with success.

Barlow is ready to reignite that spirit. This is Arsenal, whose plush Highbury ground features marble halls that are iconic throughout the world of football.

When their luxury team bus arrives outside the main entrance and the players disembark, Barlow is walking down from the car park, past a row of semi-detached houses. 'You'll find no marble halls here,' he thinks to himself.

All tickets for home areas have been sold and close to 15,000 are inside Boundary Park on what is a chilly November night. But Oldham are not cold. Not tonight. From referee Roger Gifford's whistle, they are at it. When they had triumphed 4-1 at Manchester City early in the previous season, City's caretaker manager – none other than Jimmy Frizzell – had described them as 'yard dogs'. With the inflatables craze sweeping the country, Hardy had ordered in 500 blow-up Dalmatians which had flown off the shelves – and he ended up ordering another 1,000. Tonight, the yard dogs are back, snapping at heels from the off.

For those watching, it is surreal. Arsenal, the best team in England, are finding it difficult to even get out of their own half. Milligan and Henry are relentless, like a pair of bumble bees swarming around anything in a red and white shirt.

But with half-time approaching, Latics have nothing to show for their shocking superiority. There have been chances, but there have been no goals. The Gunners' under-siege defence has been at its defiant best. O'Leary has cleared off the line, Bunn and Adams have snatched at shots which have gone narrowly wide. Marshall was pulled back when in on goal but Gifford was unmoved, much to the disgust of a packed Chaddy End. Their anger was voiced again when Bunn went down under pressure from Adams and once more there was no whistle from the Welshman in the black.

While there have been no goals, there has been pain. When Tony Adams fouled Bunn on the edge of the area Denis Irwin fired a ferocious shot at goal from the resulting free-kick. Kevin Richardson, the Arsenal midfielder, was in the way. Or to be more precise, his groin was and took the full force.

The former Everton man slowly collapsed backwards to the plastic turf as though he had been felled by a knockout punch from Mike Tyson. It had prompted loud cheers from the home support, who were enjoying what they were seeing. They were the not the only ones showing no sympathy. With Richardson prostrate, Irwin clipped over an inviting cross and Marshall, at the far post, volleyed into the crowd.

Following a lengthy stoppage, ferocious Oldham picked up where they left off. Next up Irwin caught a low drive perfectly but John Lukic, Arsenal's keeper, hurled himself to his left to keep it out.

With a gnawing feeling that you cannot create – and miss – as many chances as that against the champions without it coming back to haunt you spreading, there is time for one final effort before the break.

With another attack in danger of breaking down, Ritchie wins the ball on the edge of the area and rolls it to Henry, who quickly spreads it to Barlow, who has raced forwards down the left. Without looking up he hits a cross to the far post. O'Leary senses danger and frantically backpedals, but he is caught out by the ball's trajectory, and he cannot get there. An alert Ritchie can, but has work to do. He calmly chests the ball down. It hits the solid turf and sits up invitingly. He is around eight yards out but is to the right of the goal and the angle is tight. Lukic, like the good goalkeeper he is, has his near post covered.

Instinctively, Ritchie leaves the ground and when he connects, striking through the ball, he is in mid-air. It rockets off his boot across Lukic who can get nowhere near it. For the fraction of a second, with the ball in flight, it looks like it may hit the woodwork. It does not. It crashes into the net, just inside the far post. The delirium is instant. In the Chaddy End celebrating fans bounce over terrace steps. It is utter pandemonium.

On the pitch, Ritchie races away, one arm pointed to the sky. His old pal from Leeds, Irwin, is first to reach him and they share an embrace, but the adrenalin keeps him running. Warhurst pats him on the stomach and he is still going. Now in his own half. Barrett, as cool as ever, gives him a high five before Holden jumps on his back and, finally, Ritchie stops.

In the television booth, Tony Gubba, back again, can barely believe what he is seeing. 'The whole ground is celebrating a marvellous strike,' he says. The referee blows for half-time seconds later and the roof almost comes off for the second time in a minute.

In the dressing room, Royle's message is clear – carry on where you left off. There will be no switch to a defensive shape.

In the visitors' dressing room Graham delivers a rollicking. This is, quite simply, unacceptable. His players listen and come out firing. First, Thomas latches onto a through ball and is in on goal but Andy Rhodes, who has taken the goalkeeping spot from Jon Hallworth and who has applied what appears to be a full tub of Brylcreem to his slicked back hair for the big occasion, races off his line and blocks his shot. The keeper, under pressure from Quinn, can only punch the resulting corner to Dixon, who sidefoots a volley at goal. Rhodes dives to his right and theatrically punches it away.

It is a busy few minutes for the keeper. Moments later Rocastle and Thomas combine on the right and the latter dinks a cross over for Quinn who, almost sitting down, diverts the ball towards goal. Rhodes launches himself again, and this time tips it over the bar. After picking himself up, he calmly checks the top of his hair to ensure it has remained intact. Like Oldham's lead, it has.

The storm lasts 10 minutes and is weathered. Latics gain confidence and – with Milligan and Henry re-exerting authority in midfield – start attacking again. On 64 minutes, Milligan bursts forwards but is cynically chopped down on the edge of the area by O'Leary, who earns a booking. Holden blasts the resulting free kick into the wall and it is cleared to Henry, 30 yards out. Henry has never scored a goal in professional football. Had it not been for that night in Middlesbrough, his career may well have been over by now. As he controls the ball, he thinks about trying a shot but can hear his manager on the sideline, shouting 'Pass it!'.

Henry knows he should do as he is told. But he backs himself. As a young boy, he had played striker for his school and club teams and scored dozens of goals. As he lets fly, he thinks 'hit the target, hit the target' and he knows that if he does not, he will be in for an earful. The connection is clean. The ball hurtles low through a crowded area, miraculously evading a tangle of legs. Whether Lukic is unsighted or not is unclear – but it does not matter. It flies into the bottom corner. No keeper on the planet would have saved it.

Once again, Boundary Park erupts. Almost immediately, Milligan has his little pal in a headlock and when he lets go, Henry is laughing, arms out, as though he is trying to comprehend what has just happened. He is not the only one. They have never seen anything like this before at Oldham. In the main stand, Henry's mother, sister and brother-in-law are on their feet celebrating, along with an army of pals who have made the journey over from Liverpool. A friend's dad tosses his hat into the air, never to be seen again.

The visitors are furious. During a stoppage in play, Rocastle shouts to Smith that they need to sort this. 'We're on television,' he adds. Barlow is within earshot and can't resist. 'If you haven't noticed, lads, it's 2-0. If you get the ball it might be a start.'

Arsenal try to come back but energy is lacking. A rare attack is cut short when Winterburn is tackled by Milligan deep in the Latics' half. The midfielder immediately plays a short pass forward to Bunn, who controls on the turn and sends it right to Ritchie. The striker drops a shoulder and elegantly glides past Winterburn as though he is not there. He continues forwards before angling the ball with the outside of his foot to Irwin, who has surged up the right wing. The full-back sends over an outswinging cross and Ritchie, who has continued his run, thinks he can make it.

As he tries to get there he almost trips but somehow manages to contort his body, neck muscles straining, and connects with his forehead to send it back across Lukic, who is racing to his right. Wrong-footed, the Arsenal keeper manages to change direction and dive to his left, but he cannot get there and Oldham are leading the champions of England 3-0. Ritchie sees it hit the net and carries on running, one arm aloft again. His initial thought is 'Jesus Christ'. Holden, laughing his head off, runs after him. There are 15 minutes to play but in the away end they begin to head for the exits, to put this miserable night to bed.

'The league champions are beaten!' declares Gubba.

They are – and everyone knows it. 'We want seven!' is the chant from the Chaddy End. In injury time there is the most belated of responses when Niall Quinn hooks a volley past Rhodes but it is of little importance. There are even ironic cheers from the home fans. Seconds later, the whistle goes and it is over. This was not a giant killing in the traditional sense. There has been no luck involved. The best team in England has been outfought and outplayed. The scoreline was 3-1 but it could have been much, much worse.

In the Oldham dressing room there is almost silence as the magnitude of what has just happened sinks in. They can scarcely believe it. 'We have just taken the champions to the cleaners,' thinks Ritchie. Donachie has often told them that there are 'no limits'. They are beginning to think he may have a point.

Graham is magnanimous when he heads out to face the cameras. The pitch presents a ready-made excuse but the Scot is having none of it. He is scathing of his own team but full of praise for their hosts. 'The plastic pitch had nothing to do with it,' he says. 'The fact is that by far Oldham were the better team.'

Royle is all smiles when he comes out moments later. 'Up

until now we have had cup walks, not cup runs,' he jokes. He is not done there. 'When we have shooting practice in training everybody ducks when Nicky lets fly, but that one screamed in,' he adds.

Following the match Royle, as he often does, heads off to the nearby Old Grey Mare for a couple of pints with some of the directors. While in there, a fan walks over in a daze. 'Pinch me,' he asks the smiling manager.

The only downside of the evening is the draw for the quarter-final, which pairs Latics with Southampton. Crucially, the match will be played on the grass of The Dell, the First Division mainstays' south coast home.

Regardless, the *Chron* the next day is joyous. One of Oldham's claims to fame is that it was the first constituency of Winston Churchill. 'As a famous Oldham MP might have said, this was their finest hour (and-a-half)', Bob Young writes, referencing the former Prime Minister's famous 1940 speech to Parliament ahead of the Battle of Britain.

The *Chron* is not the only place to look for Latics fans. All of a sudden, Oldham are national back page news. 'Rags to Ritchie's' screams the *Daily Mirror*. In *The Guardian*, Stephen Bierley captures the moment. 'Oldham Athletic, who had never beaten a First Division side since they dropped to the Second Division in 1923, made up for 66 years of not altogether patient waiting with a pulsating victory over the League champions Arsenal at Boundary Park last night,' he intros. 'The Pennines fairly shook.'

CHAPTER TWELVE

Please Joe, Don't Go

PETER Swales, chairman of Manchester City, is the type of man who has a portrait of himself on his office wall. Cherubic and ruddy-faced and sporting an unconvincing comb-over, Swales, who originally made his money after setting up a business which cashed in on the 1960s boom in radio and hi-fi, is a divisive figure within the sport.

Since taking over the club in 1973 he has been desperate to see them win the often-bitter Manchester power battle with rivals United. But that desperation has seen too many managers come and go from Maine Road and has seen him pick up a reputation as a hirer and firer.

For all his idiosyncrasies, Joe Royle has always liked him. A conversation the pair had when Royle was a player at City has stuck in his mind. Swales had asked him if he could see himself managing when he hung up his boots. At the time, Royle was only 26. Clearly, Swales could see management potential.

Years later, he has seen nothing to prove that he was wrong. He is sick of Oldham taking City's fringe players for a pittance and it coming back to bite them. First it was Earl Barrett, whose £35,000 fee is looking more and more ridiculous with each game. 'Barrett's Revenge' has turned out to be a hasty description. After a shaky start Paul Warhurst – complete with his new medication – is now flying alongside Barrett at the heart of Oldham's defence and making a mockery of City's decision making.

Add to that the fact that Oldham's last visit to Maine Road ended with that 4-1 thumping and it comes as little surprise that when Swales shows manager Mel Machin the door following a poor start to the season in the First Division – despite a memorable 5-1 rout of rivals United – he knows that he only has to look a few miles up the road for his ideal replacement.

A meeting is set up at Swales's house and Royle attends. It goes well. The deal is outlined. This is a big step up. While he was born and raised in Liverpool and is an Evertonian at heart, City is a club Royle enjoyed playing for and a club that has underachieved for more than a decade.

Despite an often-disastrous transfer policy, they have a youth set-up which is the envy of Alex Ferguson, across the city at United. There are a number of talented young prospects. The support, along with the stadium, is in place and the bar is not set very high. This could be the opportunity he has been waiting for. Willie Donachie is another City old boy and Royle knows he would not take much convincing to join him. Both of them would pocket a hefty pay rise.

But something is tugging at Royle and he cannot sleep after his head hits the pillow back at his home. He thinks he is on the cusp of something special in Oldham, a town in which he and his family have settled. It now feels like home. He thinks of the hard work he has put in over the last seven years, the heartbreak of that play-off defeat to Leeds. The victory over Arsenal is fresh in the memory. He believes, after years of playing snakes and ladders, he now has a good team and their potential excites him.

While they can never compete with City on a financial footing, this feels like an opportunity to do something monumental, something historic. He feels a connection with the townsfolk. He feels he can deliver unprecedented success. To get Oldham into the First Division would represent a football miracle, something that does not happen very often. And, if he takes the job, he will become City's sixth manager in nine years. He knows that where he is, he pretty much has a job for life. In short, as Blackburn Rovers come to Boundary Park for a rare Friday night match with talks ongoing, he is wobbling.

News leaks to the press, both nationals and locals. A perplexed Ian Stott describes the timing of the approach as 'unfortunate' but adds 'we are not the type of club that behaves badly towards our employees'. Pre kick-off, the terraces are full of impending doom. Any thought that this would be the elephant in the pre-Christmas gloom is quashed by the scoreboard. Gorey has wowed fans with his graphics and his machine is the centre of attention once again. This time there are no fancy graphics, just a blunt message. 'PLEASE JOE' pops up first, followed by – flashing for emphasis 'DON'T GO'. It is a message repeated loudly by the supporters, on many occasions. Immediately, those present think that a group of fans have had a whiparound to pay for the message. The reality is that Hardy and Gorey have come up with it between themselves.

The atmosphere has got to the players. The first-half is one of the worst performances of the season. Oldham are lucky to go in level with their Lancashire neighbours. The game has become a sideshow to speculation.

Normally, Royle stands at a table in the centre of the dressing room to deliver his address. This time he decides to sit down among his players. 'What's going on out there?' he asks. 'That ain't us. Let's be open and let's be professional about this. Despite what you're hearing, I honestly don't know which way this situation is going to go. Get out there and play like you can.'

It works. Pressure released and elephant addressed, Latics get out and do as their manager says. On the hour Holden makes the breakthrough and moments later Ritchie doubles the lead.

After his players have been spoken to, Royle's style is to invite reporters into his office for a few cans of lager following the post-match press conference and a strictly off-the-record chat. He knows the importance of keeping the press onside. You never know when you may need to call in a favour. He also tends to enjoy their company. Tonight is no exception and the dissection goes long into the evening. When Royle finally departs into the December cold, he sees a fan who has been stood in the freezing night on the street opposite the main entrance, waiting for him for so long that his coat is covered in snow. He has a simple message to deliver. 'Don't go, Joe,' he pleads.

As he drives home, the fan's words stay with him. As they do throughout the evening. After another sleepless night there is a further discussion with Stott, who knows that he is onto a good thing. Should he allow Royle to depart now, what promises to be a rare shot at glory may well disappear. While the team is talented, there is a reason many of them have not succeeded elsewhere and are doing so here. That reason is the manager. Royle thinks Oldham is simmering, ready to explode. He is also friends with the chairman, the directors and the staff, and he puts a high price on friendship. The fans also play a part in this thinking. For decades they have been served up a meagre diet of relegation battles. He is in turmoil and says as much.

Stott, showing the sound business judgement that has served him well throughout his life, liaises with a like-minded board and a new contract is offered. Royle accepts it. On Saturday, he turns down Manchester City, one of the top jobs in English football, to stay at Oldham Athletic. 'It's not a City thing,' he tells friends. 'It was nothing to do with them. I just love this club. This is about Oldham. I don't want to be the one who will be remembered for running away from the best chance they will ever have.'

On the Monday he tells the *Chron* that he would have to 'have a heart of stone' not to be moved by the reaction of the fans. 'There is a unique charm about this club,' he adds. 'Totally different to any other I have been involved with.'

He reiterates his belief that they are on the verge of something special: 'Not only that but I also believe that we have a team – a unit on and off the field – that deserves First Division football and it is my ambition to get us there.' The town, now hanging on every development from Boundary Park, breathes a collective sigh of relief.

When news reaches him in his oak-panelled office Swales, who had prematurely announced Royle's capture to his board, is stunned. Days later, he calls to ask what he did wrong. Royle repeats the message. This was not about City, it was about Oldham. Swales reluctantly accepts the explanation, but has one further question. 'Joe, just one more thing,' he says. 'Is there anyone else in our Reserves who you think will make it?'

Royle laughs at what is an outrageous question. He is reminded of a recent conversation with Howard Wilkinson, at Leeds. He and Jim Cassell had identified a young, aggressive midfielder in Leeds's reserve team who was struggling to stay on the pitch because he kept committing stupid fouls. Cassell reckoned the hothead could play, and if Royle could use his man-management skills to keep him on the field he may well have had a big future in the game. Royle phoned Wilkinson and exchanged pleasantries. But before he could even get to the reason for his call Wilkinson, himself a canny operator, took control of the conversation. 'Listen, Joe,' he said. 'Before you start I know you are going to come and ask us about one of the players. Let me tell you, if I mention your name in our boardroom they all go through a different window.'

Barely containing his laughter, Royle decided to have a try anyway.

'What about David Batty, then?' he asked.

'Joe,' responded Wilkinson. 'To you, it would have to be £250,000.'

This time, Royle could not stop himself. '250?' he said, laughing. 'He's not even a regular in your reserves!'

'Well,' responded Wilkinson, no doubt smiling himself. 'I think that means that we don't really want to sell him, do we?'

The pair subsequently had a giggle and a catch-up but the message from both City and Leeds is now clear – there are no more deals to be done here.

When the nationals report Royle's decision, they all note the role that the whiparound for the message on the scoreboard had. Gorey later asks Hardy if they should correct the reporters. 'No,' he says. 'Let them think that – and never let the truth get in the way of a good story.'

CHAPTER THIRTEEN

The Tuesday Club

THIS is how it works. On Tuesday, the players are brought in for a double training session. If there is no game on Wednesday, they are given the day off. That means that, following training, they are left to their own devices. At many clubs up and down the country, groups of four or five players take the opportunity for a bit of team bonding, and head to the pub for the afternoon. At Oldham, that group numbers as many as 17.

Most of the squad take part. They meet at the Owl and Spindle pub at 2pm, close to the ground, and take it from there. Trips into Oldham town centre are few and far between. They know that the manager knows pretty much every pub landlord in the town and that their every move may well be reported back. Often they will head to Manchester.

Joe Royle knows what goes on and, as long as lines are not crossed, encourages it. He believes that the team spirit generated by The Tuesday Club is worth its weight in gold. There have been a couple of instances over the years where he has had to step in. A fracas in a Chinese restaurant and a player arrested in a nightclub, where he had ended up brawling with a chef. Royle, as he often did, knew the nightclub's owner and, following a call, no charges were forthcoming.

Nothing surprises him. One Christmas he picked up the phone and the voice on the other end of the line told him that two of his players were going to be knee-capped, which took some smoothing over. On another occasion, two of the players got into a row which ended up with them throwing bar stools at each other. When one went through the pub window, Royle was called. And on one evening, a player in the middle of a Tuesday Club session and subsequently well-oiled, decided to drive back to Boundary Park to pick up a team-mate who was appearing for the Reserves. In the process, he hit the wing mirror of nearly every car on Sheepfoot Lane.

But such instances are rare, and the positives, he feels, far outweigh the negatives. He would rather have what he lovingly describes as a team of 'raggy arses' who can perform on a Saturday, than a team of angels whose whereabouts he knows all week but who then go missing when kick-off comes around. When Willie Donachie thinks it has gone too far, he lets the manager know, but those occasions are few and far between.

If there are any issues as the result of someone not pulling their weight in training, or not grafting hard enough on the pitch, they get sorted out on a Tuesday afternoon. New arrivals are told that they must bring shoes, trousers and a shirt to their first Tuesday at the club. It is an essential part of life. Often, Ian Liversedge and Ronnie Evans join the group. Andy Ritchie is usually the first to depart, and the sessions can last until the early hours. The other players joke that Ritchie, who has a reputation for being financially frugal, is last to the bar and first to bed. In his first outing Hallworth, who joined the previous season, joked to himself that they play golf at Ipswich – a much more gentlemanly pursuit.

While he often bemoans their behaviour, Royle feels that as long as everyone is ready to train on Thursday, there are no major issues.

Unsurprisingly, Rick Holden has embraced the club, and become a key member. It is his idea to go 'over the border to Mexico', which is in effect a trip across the Pennines into Yorkshire to Ripponden where veteran defender and best friend Phil Brown, his former captain at Halifax, owns a pub.

The antics are not limited to Tuesdays. On Fridays, there is a weekly competition. Players take it in turns to bring in biscuits and cakes. There is a scoring system and things quickly become ridiculous, with giant cream cakes rolled in on trolleys as they try to outdo each other. One week, it was the turn of Donachie, who was not going to win any prizes. Donachie had a friend who was a wholesale produce supplier and he turned up with baskets of fruit.

They did not last long. Marshall started it, and within minutes, apples, bananas and pears were being launched around the dressing room. Andy Barlow, late to the party, did not realise what was going on and promptly slipped on a banana. Thankfully, he was not injured.

Nobody is spared from the abuse. Ritchie is having a sparkling season and the players have now christened it the Andy Ritchie Man of the Match Award. Rhodes has nicknamed him 'Andy Famous'. Ritchie's response is to point out that everyone knows Rhodesy is going to win the Friday cake competition because he is 'a fat bastard'. It is often blunt, and it is not subtle, but there is not one player who dishes it out that cannot take it.

On one occasion Ritchie is cornered and the players demand to know where his nickname of 'Stitch' comes from.

His explanation is that it came from fellow players when he went up for a header, clashed heads and had to have stitches in the wound.

It is safe to say that the explanation does not wash. Ritchie has developed a reputation as a man who is often last to the bar and the suspicion is that – rather than a so-called head injury – the nickname is a result of claims that the pockets of his trousers are stitched up so he cannot get to his wallet.

The cakes and biscuits are not the only poll. Each week, players vote for the worst trainer. The 'winner' is given a yellow shirt, covered with expletive messages, which they have to wear. There is fevered speculation until the results are announced, and there are often inquests, with frequent accusations of vote-rigging. You have to swim, because if you did not, you would sink. It is no place for the faint-hearted.

The practical jokes are endless. Holden has taken to bringing in the remnants of the curry he often orders at the end of a Tuesday Club outing. On more than one occasion Ritchie has found an onion bhaji in his shoe.

Unfortunately for him, Bill Urmson sometimes finds himself targeted. A bald man with a friendly face and fiery temper, he is a formidable figure to the generations of youngsters to come through the club's ranks on his watch. His propensity to explode means the players cannot resist the occasional wind-up.

Every now and then, Mike Milligan will come and watch the Reserves. A mischievous soul, he cannot help himself when someone tells him, midway through the first half of a dour game he has attended, that they have left the dressing room door open. Milligan immediately goes down the main stand steps and makes his way there. As he expected, the door is open and a cup of tea has been laid out for Urmson in the corner, where he always stands and takes sips in between bollockings. As he also expected, there is also an opened tub of Deep Heat, the warmth-triggering rub that players use on their legs in freezing temperatures. Milligan creeps across, gets a small dollop, and drops it into the steaming cup of tea, sniggering as he does it.

As a senior player, he is allowed to remain in the dressing room for the team talk and he does so. Urmson comes in and goes on his usual rant before taking a swig of his drink. Then another. Then another. Milligan waits but nothing seems to happen. He wonders if the youth coach has the constitution of an ox before he gets his answer.

'Eurrrggghhhhh,' is the noise Urmson makes when the Deep Heat finally begins to make its presence known at the back of his throat. 'Eurrrgggghhhhh!!' All of a sudden, Urmson is on the floor. Milligan can watch no more and leaves the scene before bursting into laughter in the corridor. He is not laughing for long. The next morning it emerges that Urmson's throat had inflamed so much that there could have been serious consequences. Fortunately for all concerned there were not. 'If I find out who did this there will be trouble,' he tells anyone who will listen. Milligan keeps quiet. The incident is the talk of the club and the belief among the players is that a culprit, if identified, will be sacked.

That rapscallion streak resonates throughout Boundary Park but it is usually the opposition, rather than the youth team coach, that finds itself the target. Barlow, as a local lad, often volunteers to do the school visits which take place on Friday afternoons. It means that after training he often hangs around the club for a couple of hours until it is time to do his bit. It also means that he is in the ground when the away team turns up for the training session it is permitted to stage on the plastic pitch. He has a routine. There is a fear of Oldham's artificial surface that has spread throughout the league and beyond, a distrust that means opposition players will often bring as many as five different types of footwear to road-test before deciding which one best fits the turf.

Barlow, coming across as a friendly fellow professional, often makes his way over to the group. 'Ever played on one of these before?' is his opening gambit. He then searches for the most suitable pair and picks them up. 'Don't wear these,' he tells his appreciative audience. 'If you do you'll be wrecked for three months.' Barlow, having obtained the trust of his soon-to-be opponents, then goes for the most unsuitable shoes that have been brought along, usually trainers. 'Use these, lads,' he says. 'That's what I'd do.' The results, with the recipients of his advice often sprawling about the pitch like they are playing on an ice rink, are often hilarious.

The best type of footwear, as the Oldham players have learned, are boots with moulded studs. They are experts on the surface. Before home games they train on it, before switching to Little Wembley's grass ahead of away matches. Ahead of the Boxing Day fixture with Port Vale, which ends in a 2-1 victory and a hold on fourth place, Marshall is in the tunnel, eyeing up the opponents. As he always does, he looks down at their feet to see what they are wearing. One player has decided to go with a pair of Dunlop Greenflash, the unforgiving plimsolls given to firemen to be worn in the gym. 'For fuck's sake.'

CHAPTER FOURTEEN

Back To Plastic

'YOU'LL fucking love it here.' Rick Holden, instructed by his manager, is on a charm offensive. He continues. 'It's a great craic and the manager lets us do what we want on Tuesday – and it's a fucking good team.'

Holden is on the phone to his former Watford team-mate and fellow Yorkshireman Neil Redfearn. Joe Royle has admired Redfearn, a midfielder, for a long time. He knows that he has been in and out of the side and has instructed his winger to find out if he would be interested in following his footsteps back to the north. Redfearn is, and he is intercepted as he leaves Chelsea's Stamford Bridge home following a Reserve match. At the side of the coach, Royle asks him if he fancies it, makes an offer and that is that.

Increased attendances – more than 11,000 were present for the Boxing Day victory over Port Vale – have loosened Ian Stott's vice-like grip on the club's wallet. Redfearn arrives for £150,000 and settles in immediately. Importantly, he adds an extra dimension to Oldham's midfield.

A son of Batley, in West Yorkshire, he is given the nickname Casper, after the kestrel-loving schoolboy star of the film adaptation of the Barry Hines' classic *A Kestrel For A Knave*, thanks to his broad accent.

Redfearn, however, is cup-tied and so will not be taking one of the seats on the plane for the flight to Southampton for the Littlewoods Cup quarter-final. Stott, who once drove to Swindon and back to prove it could be done on the day of a game and that there would be no need for an overnight stay, is now sanctioning plane trips.

The chairman has had his arm twisted by Alan Hardy. While a certain number of seats will have to be allocated to the squad and management team, the rest can be sold to supporters at a cost of £120 each, and demand is high. If it sells out – and it does – there is money to be made.

The task that awaits on England's south coast is a daunting one. With the brilliant Channel Islander Matt Le Tissier, who already has 14 goals this season, pulling the strings in midfield, the Saints are hopeful of a place in the top six of the First Division. They are a mix of experience and youth. The Dell has hosted top-flight football since 1978, two years after they won the FA Cup. They are a top-tier staple. In 1984, they were runners-up in the league.

For Royle, injuries are starting to bite. There will be no Frank Bunn or Denis Irwin, both injured. After opening 1990 with a point on the road at table-toppers Leeds, defeat at Swindon and a home draw against Newcastle, who headed south with a five-man defence thanks to Oldham's quickly-spreading reputation, has seen Latics fall eight points behind Sheffield United, who occupy the second promotion spot.

The match, strangely, has not been made all-ticket. Oldham have been promised three pens on the away terrace but, as home crowds begin to build up, the Hampshire Constabulary change their minds and designate one of the three to Southampton supporters. As a result, around 600 Oldham fans cannot get into the ground, after having made a trip of 235 miles. Some head to the pub, devastated, while others try and sneak into the home enclosures. The two pens they are allocated resemble sardine tins. Within them, there is concern. Those packed together do not need reminding of the Hillsborough Disaster, given it was only eight months ago.

It all adds to what is a hostile atmosphere. This is a compact, claustrophobic old ground where the fans are close to the action. Nobody outside of the tiny pocket of blue and white in the corner cares much for Oldham or their romantic cup run. The promise of a semi-final is in the air and the Saints fancy their chances.

As has been the case with the rest of the tournament, the match will not be screened live but extended highlights will be shown later on ITV. Back in Oldham, thousands gather around radios to listen to popular, Manchester-based independent station Piccadilly, which is providing commentary.

Ahead of kick-off there is an odd development when veteran referee Roger Milford enters each dressing room. He tells the managers that, instead of adding stoppage time at the end of each half, he will finish the first stanza on 45 minutes and add both sets at the end of 90 minutes.

Those listening hear their team go close to taking the lead twice, before, with just eight minutes gone, Southampton do just that. With Irwin unavailable thanks to a groin strain, Ian Marshall is playing in defence. Le Tissier, who is switching between wings and already proving to be a menace, cuts inside the makeshift right-back and hits a low drive from the edge of the area. Jon Hallworth, who has taken back the goalkeeping place, has it covered, but Earl Barrett sticks out a boot and it deflects just out of the big man's reach.

The home supporters celebrate wildly. This is in the script.

Oldham, however, respond by piling on the pressure, but cannot find a breakthrough. In the second half, Royle takes a gamble. He decides to take off Neil Adams and send on Scott McGarvey, a veteran back-up striker picked up in the summer for £25,000 who has not had the impact he had hoped.

Swapping a winger for a forward leaves the visitors vulnerable out wide and on three occasions Hallworth magnificently defies counter-attacks to keep Latics in the tie.

With 12 minutes to go, it remains 1-0. Nick Henry picks the ball up on the edge of the area and takes it past Francis Benali, the Saints full back. From the right, he sends over a cross which appears to be aimed at the middle of the area, but there is nobody there. Fortunately, the cross is lacking in height which means Ritchie, around 10 yards away, can react quickly and get his head on it. The ball hurtles towards the goal and even Tim Flowers, who has been superb for Southampton, cannot react quickly enough. It creeps inside his near post and, in a flash, Oldham are level. At the other end, there is mayhem. Any distancing is forgotten as those who have managed to get into the ground go berserk and cannon into each other. After trailing for so long, a replay will be a wonderful outcome.

But Southampton are not done. Five minutes later, with his back to goal, midfielder Glenn Cockerill hooks the ball over his head. It falls into the path of team-mate Barry Horne, who is in on goal. A desperate Andy Barlow makes a challenge and can argue that he gets the ball. Milford, however, is having none of it and points to the spot. Disaster.

Le Tissier does not miss and duly slots the penalty past Hallworth, who guesses right but cannot get there. Once again, the home supporters celebrate but this time there is an air of certainty. That must be it. 'Que sera, sera, whatever will be, will be, we're going to Wem-ber-lee,' echoes around The Dell. Many of those who surround the Oldham fans hurl abuse and make mocking hand gestures. It remains an unpleasant environment.

Back on the field, the blue shirts swarm forwards but cannot create a chance as the match goes into injury time. Jimmy Case, the firebrand Liverpudlian and Southampton skipper, is constantly in Milford's ear, demanding that he blow for full-time. The whistles from the home fans get louder and louder. This has been a tremendous run for Oldham, with Leeds, Scarborough and Arsenal seen off, but now the end is nigh.

On the Southampton bench, manager Chris Nicholl is following his captain's lead. His backroom staff, on their feet, are pointing at their watches and trying to catch the referee's attention.

Royle is angered. He knows that Milford told both sides about his plan to add on time at the end and feels the First Division side and its staff are trying to trigger a premature conclusion. The clock ticks into the 93rd minute and the whistles get louder. There is a rousing chorus of 'Oh when the Saints go marching in,' as Barrett punts the ball forwards in desperation. It is headed back, over his head and out for a goal kick to Oldham. The whistles turn to audible anger as Milford again fails to blow.

Hallworth races out of his goal to grab the ball. He puts it on the ground and quickly passes it to Barrett who gives it him back so he can now launch one out of his hands into Southampton territory. 'I think it may be too late,' says commentator Brian

Moore. 'Roger Milford is looking at his watch.' He is, but still he does not blow his whistle. The kick is a booming one, and drops out of the Hampshire night beyond halfway. McGarvey gets to it first as it descends and blindly nods it on in the hope it will find a team-mate. It does. Milligan picks it up and, moving forwards, passes it outside to his left. Holden, as he always is, is there. He has no time to control it and he sends a low cross into the box with his left foot, first time.

The speed of the attack has caught the tired hosts by surprise. Ritchie, unmarked at the near post, slides forward and at full stretch, sticks out his right boot in hope, rather than expectation. It connects with the ball and sends it goalwards. Flowers, guarding his near post, is stranded and beaten but Benali is on the goaline. The ball hits the defender but there is not enough power on the deflection to take it away from goal. Instead it crashes into the roof of the net. 'They've done it!' declares Moore in the commentary box. And they have. For the second time in 12 minutes, there is a joyous melee in the away end. There is fury on the home terraces and it is matched on the pitch, where Southampton's players are incandescent. Case tries to confront the referee and Ritchie, who played with the former Liverpool hardman at Brighton, holds him back.

There is no holding back the Oldham bench, which has erupted. Royle, still angry at their hosts' persistent time-wasting, cannot help himself. 'Back to plastic!' he shouts across at the home dugout. 'Back to plastic!'

It is too much for some of the home supporters to deal with. Celebrations have instantly turned to boiling anger. A few climb the fences, invade the pitch and the police have to get involved.

In the midst of the chaos the ever-wise Willie Donachie, who has come on as a substitute, urges the Oldham players to get back into position for the kick-off.

The full-time whistle the home fans were demanding moments earlier finally blows and triggers more fury. 'The referee's a wanker,' chant the Saints supporters. They are not celebrating any more. They are not singing about Wembley any more. Ritchie again has to hold back Case.

The anger is understandable. Southampton, who thought they were in the semi-final, will now have to go to Boundary Park and – as Royle shouted – go back to the plastic.

There is more drama on the way back when the players board the plane and some of the more nervous souls claim they can see smoke from the cockpit. They are told that it is nothing to be concerned by but when the flight leaves the ground and breaks the cloud, turbulence tosses it from side to side, prompting panic among some. Andy Rhodes, not a good flyer, throws up, much to the delight of some of his team-mates.

Earlier that evening, in the debating chamber at Oldham council, the town's councillors, including John Battye, flew through the agenda of a monthly meeting. The aim was to get out before full-time, where the politicians who supported Latics could get to the pub and listen to what was remaining of the match on the radio. Early in proceedings, deputy council leader Jack Armitage had told all who would listen that he did not want to know the score from The Dell because he would be going home to watch the match on television later that night.

Regardless, as the debate flowed, pieces of paper began to be passed around the chamber, each containing score updates. Eventually the room got one which said that Southampton were winning, 2-1. As the meeting concluded, one of the councillors – presumably wanting to save Armitage a from miserable evening watching a fruitless cause – shouted out 'Jack – Latics have lost 2-1.'

'Thanks for that!' Armitage responded sarcastically. 'I'm watching it anyway,' and stormed off.

Battye was also disappointed at the news, but was proud of the club and what sounded like another phenomenal effort against a much bigger opponent. He got up and made his way out of the chamber to the main doors. Before he could get there, he heard an almighty roar from down a corridor. He ran towards the noise and was greeted by a bunch of celebrating night shift staff. 'It's 2-2!' they shouted. It turned out that one of the porters had misheard the radio, had thought the final whistle had blown and passed a mistaken update to the politicians.

Already on his way home, Councillor Armitage was oblivious to what had happened. When he arrived, he told his wife that Latics had lost but that he was still going to watch the highlights because they had done so well. When Ritchie made it 2-2 on his television he thought that the goal must have been disallowed and that Oldham really had been unlucky. Then Southampton kicked off and the full-time score, confirming a draw, flashed up on screen. Armitage raced upstairs and awoke his slumbering wife. 'Kathleen!' he shouted. 'Kathleen! It's 2-2'. Mrs Armitage was less impressed. 'Go away you daft bugger,' she told her ecstatic husband.

The replay will take place a week later. On the Saturday, Second Division rivals Brighton and Hove Albion arrive for an FA Cup fourth round fixture, set up after a replay victory over Birmingham City in the previous round. The matches are beginning to mount up and Royle is concerned over the impact on the priority, which remains promotion. Brighton are seen off 2-1, the match only being tight thanks to the heroic performance of the visitors' goalkeeper. John Keeley nearly always plays well against Oldham, and Royle makes a mental note. Before Southampton head north, the draw for the fifth round of the FA Cup is made and Oldham get a home tie. Even better, their opponents will be none other than Everton, Royle's club.

CHAPTER FIFTEEN

It Weren't Me

'IT weren't me,' is the catchphrase of Oldham's young captain, Mike Milligan. The curly-haired Mancunian motormouth may only be 23 but his influence on and off the field is as big as his personality. Off it, he is often at the centre of any mischief and his slogan – repeated after the latest batch of shenanigans – often sends Joe Royle's eyes searching for the sky.

On it, he is rapidly gaining a reputation beyond the floodlight pylons of Boundary Park as one of the finest holding midfielders outside the top flight. He is expected to play a key role in the replay with Southampton, which comes just four years after he was working on a building site and contemplating a career outside the game.

In 1985, Milligan was at Maine Road, but he was not there to play football at the home of Manchester City. The houses close to the ground, which included the one Willie Donachie perceived as luxury when he first landed in England, were spacious and cheap to run and, as a result, many of them were rented out to the thousands of students who flocked to Manchester's universities to study.

In that long, hot summer the area was quiet, with the students back at home. But one house was a hive of activity. A group of builders, plasterers and electricians worked on refurbishing a property which was bought at auction by a developer for a song. With time at a premium, they grafted in the long hours of sunshine to get the house into a fit state in time for when the students returned, so that their employer could get his hands on large chunks of their grants and loans and they could get their hands on a bonus for finishing the job on time.

One afternoon, their progress was halted by laughter. A young lacky had been drafted in to fetch materials and to clean up, but he proved to be something of a character.

The labourer told his more experienced colleagues that he would soon be playing football in front of a cast of thousands at the big ground over the road, and that the lackying was only a temporary fix. The other men immediately took a shine to him and his optimism, but they were sceptical of his claims. They had heard it all before.

Milligan did not care. 'You'll still be putting this roof on and I'll be over there, scoring goals,' he boldly told his new workmates.

His confidence was admirable. Only recently, Milligan had been told by his boyhood club, Manchester United, that they would not be taking him on as a professional. Even worse, City had also said no.

The son of entrepreneurial, pub-owning immigrants, Milligan was bright and was privately educated, over the Princess Parkway and across Alexandra Park from where he was working on houses, at St Bede's College, the city's top Catholic school. It was an all-boys school, but as an enterprising teen, Milligan would often head up to Loreto, a sixth-form college up the road, to chat up girls.

His obsession, however, was football and the resolute belief that he would make a career in the game saw him leave without taking his 'O' Levels. 'There's no point,' he told his mortified parents, 'I'm going to be a footballer.'

By the time he came to be working on houses in Moss Side, a year had passed since that day. There had already been a list of jobs. First up was an assistant role at a computer company, but that did not last. Too boring. Then came a stint in the sports section of Debenhams on Market Street, in the heart of Manchester city centre. But periods of inactivity, standing by waiting for customers to sell tracksuits to, did not suit a jumpy Milligan. He was a flurry of activity and needed to keep his overactive mind occupied.

His parents moved from the pub game into the hotel game and would often put up residents who were in the area to work on building contracts – and that is how he found himself lackying thanks to a chat with some of the guests.

The hours were long but the money was good. Seven days a week for £300 to £400. Football took a back seat and was almost forgotten.

But one day the phone rang and it was Allan Grafton, an old contact from the city's amateur scene who wanted to see if he would play for Manchester Football Association against their rivals from Liverpool.

'Are you sure?' Milligan asked Grafton. 'I've not played for ages – I'll look a fool.'

Grafton was sure and Milligan pitched up. He was not impressed with his performance. Despite keeping in shape working on houses, his football fitness was not what it was and he was plagued by cramp.

After the final whistle, a man on the touchline headed over. It was Jim Cassell.

Milligan had caught the keen eye of the Oldham scout. In particular after he led one attack, lost the ball on the edge of the opposition penalty area and then raced to the other end of the field to win the ball back on the edge of his own penalty area. He appeared to Cassell to be a bumble bee of a midfielder. His pressing was relentless. His interception rate was off the charts.

'Do you fancy going to Oldham so they can have a look at you?' Cassell asked.

Milligan did – and was told to be at Boundary Park for a gym session to build his fitness the following evening. He had no car, and so he borrowed his father's Fiat Marea Fury Estate. The journey was not straightforward. Milligan, born and raised within a stone's throw of Manchester city centre, had rarely had occasion to travel the seven miles east to the not-so-bright lights of Oldham and struggled with directions. He also struggled with the car, which had seen better years. A combination of putting it into neutral, touching the brakes and revving kept it from stalling. It was a good job his feet were as quick as his mouth or he would never have arrived.

Milligan eventually rolled up at Boundary Park 10 minutes late. Gym bag in hand, he knocked on the door of the first-team dressing room and entered, without waiting to be asked. The first thing he noticed is that everyone inside was wearing full kit and boots. The second was that there appeared to be an angry, bald man screaming at him.

'Who the fucking hell are you?' the bald man asked. 'And what the fucking hell are you doing in here?' Milligan muttered something about Cassell and a trial and was quickly sent packing to the away dressing room by the red-faced shouter, Bill Urmson.

Eventually, someone took pity on the new boy and lent him some boots. He headed down to a sodden Little Wembley and was given the grand total of 10 minutes to show what he could do. Nobody said anything afterwards. The whole thing felt like a huge waste of time.

As he repeated his pedal balancing act in the car on the way home his fury mounted. 'What a fucking shambles,' he said out loud, to nobody in particular.

When Milligan got home he was straight on the phone to Cassell to let him know what had happened. The scout apologised, told him that there had been a mistake and to come back for training.

Against his better judgement he did that and, despite his confidence, was knackered by the end of the session and stunned with how difficult it was.

He returned home suitably chastened by the experience and contemplated a life on the building sites. At least the money was decent. Not long after the phone rang. 'Hi, it's Bill Urmson from Oldham,' the caller said. 'We have got a cup game tonight against Liverpool County at Anfield, will you play for us?'

Milligan, himself a born prankster, thought he was being conned and promptly put the phone down. It rang again. 'It's fucking me!' roared Urmson, sounding a lot more like the man who had given him a rollicking in the dressing room the previous night.

'I know it's you now because you're swearing,' Milligan responded, barely managing to conceal a fit of the giggles.

He did as requested and went to the famous home of Liverpool for his Oldham debut, where he performed well as the visitors took their hosts to the cleaners.

Then came a call from Joe Royle, who asked him to come in to the club. He was subsequently offered the princely sum of £65-a-week, courtesy of a European Council grant Oldham – following John Battye's lead – had somehow managed to secure. Unable to conceal his emotions, Milligan protested that he was earning much more than that and simply could not afford to live off such a paltry sum.

The response was blunt, along the lines of 'take it or leave it'. Milligan was many things, but he was not stupid. He backed his own ability and knew that this may be his foot in the door. A shot at the big time. He accepted the offer.

With borrowing his father's car every day out of the question, he caught two buses a day – one to Manchester and then one up Oldham Road. He impressed in his first year, a tenacious midfielder with an impressive knack of winning the ball and no little skill, and saw his salary upped to £400. He could finally afford a car, and became the proud owner of an MG Metro.

By now a fixture in the first team, Milligan, as good as his word, got tickets in the posh seats for the lads he was working with years later, with whom he has kept in touch, when Oldham played at City on an August Bank Holiday Monday in the 1988-89 season.

The groups took their seats in time to see their gobby former workmate seize on a misplaced back pass by City defender Paul Lake on the edge of the area and then dink a delightful lob over keeper Tony Coton to give Oldham the lead.

With Milligan snapping at heels in midfield, former City striker Roger Palmer – another with a point to prove – grabbed a hat-trick and the visitors gave their big brother neighbours a 4-1 pounding on their own patch in front of a furious home support. In the players' lounge under the Maine Road main stand afterwards, Milligan was reunited with his former colleagues.

'You finished that fucking roof yet?' he asked.

* * * * *

The police officer, stationed outside the Rochdale Road End turnstiles, cannot believe what he is seeing. 'This is incredible,' he tells a colleague. The Chaddy End is full, the main stand is full, the Lookers Stand is full. They have never seen anything like it. The only place with room left, half an hour before kick-off, is the away end. Knowing that, around 4,000 home fans, who cannot get in anywhere else, gather at the turnstiles.

Chief Superintendent John Halliwell has a decision to make. If he does not allow these supporters into the ground, he is concerned about how they react. If he does let them in, they will have to mix with those who have travelled up from the South Coast. In turn, he also does not know how the visiting supporters will respond. Segregation is the norm in English football. After the rise of hooliganism, metal fences were installed at grounds which are partitioned off into sections to keep rival fans from fighting with each other.

Oldham has its fair share of idiots, but for the main part it is a family club and that stretches to the terraces. Last week, the 600 locked out at The Dell could have caused trouble but they did not. The situation would not have been the same with fans of many other clubs. The Chief Superintendent knows this, and decides to take a bold gamble. He orders his officers to allow the home supporters into the away end. He will take the chance.

On the exposed terrace, there is initial shock from those who have travelled north, but it quickly becomes clear that those who are pouring in have no desire to cause trouble. They just want to see their town's football team, which is rapidly making history. By the time kick-off comes around, there are close to 19,000 people inside the ground. There have been numbers like this here in the past, but only when the likes of Manchester City and Leeds United have turned up, bringing half the gate with them. There are around 2,000 inside tonight who will be cheering on the away team. This is an Oldham crowd. The roar when, after just eight minutes, Andy Ritchie's header from an Andy Barlow cross hits the post and goes in, tells you as much. 'When will he ever stop scoring goals?' asks Moore.

The evening is a blustery one and the rest of the first-half is scrappy. Southampton bring on highly-rated young striker Alan Shearer for Rod Wallace and have the best of it but there are no real chances of note.

Five minutes after the break, that changes. Ian Marshall hammers a free-kick forward. The ball, thanks to the high wind, is moving when he strikes it but if referee George Courtney insists on it being still, the game would never end.

After an exchange of passes with Earl Barrett, Barlow dinks it forwards to Milligan, who is on the edge of the area. The midfielder, on the turn, instinctively flicks it to Ritchie. The striker gets there just as the ball is about to cross the goal line and sidefoots it back into the area. Milligan, who has turned away from his marker, has raced into the box and, with the freedom of Boundary Park, sidefoots into the net from six yards out before climbing onto the fence and celebrating with the Chaddy End, which is bouncing again.

For the first time in this epic tie, one of the sides has breathing space. There are nervous moments, Nick Henry clears a header off the line, but the life has been sapped out of Southampton.

'We're on the march with Royle's army, we're all going to Wem-ber-lee', is the chant from all corners. Even Matt Le Tissier cannot stop them. Whistles demanding full-time begin to cascade down from the packed stands. Courtney obliges and there is a pitch invasion. Oldham are in a semi-final for the first time in 77 years. With one leg to be played at home, a first Wembley appearance – unthinkable just months ago – is now a distinct possibility.

The significance is not lost on Royle. 'The town has responded magnificently,' he tells Moore after he leaves a raucous dressing room. 'For a club that struggled to get five or six thousand for a league match, we've got 18,800 here tonight. The town has got cup fever. You saw it and you heard it.'

Royle is often reluctant to single out players but now he makes an exception. 'Mike Milligan was magnificent,' he says. 'The goal apart, he was brilliant. He read danger as well as anyone I have ever seen. He's good with the ball, he was outstanding. He started it and he finished it.' The kid from the building site has done well.

The draw, held before the replay, had paired the winner with fellow Second Division promotion chasers West Ham United. The victors will face the winners of the other semi-final, which pits last season's champions Nottingham Forest against Coventry City, at Wembley. The first leg will take place on the plastic, on St Valentine's Day night.

When the players turn up to the ground for training the next morning they, like the police officer the night before, cannot believe their eyes. There are two queues, stretching from the two ticket office windows under the main stand, hundreds of yards up Sheepfoot Lane. One is for tickets for the West Ham match, the other for the Everton match. Every few minutes, Alan Hardy looks out of his office window. He smiles, and pushes back the blinds.

CHAPTER SIXTEEN

The St Valentine's Day Massacre

THIRTY pence. It does not sound much, but to a young Earl Barrett, it meant the world. Money was tight in Barrett's Rochdale household when he was a football-mad youngster and the bus fare to get to training at a nearby youth club was precious.

Barrett's parents had moved to a cold, rainy corner of north-west England from the sunnier climes of Negril, in Jamaica. Like so many others from the Caribbean, they were sold on the promise of work and a better life in the mother country. His father ended up working as a foreman in a factory, simply because one of his friends had moved over earlier and had found a job there himself. It is safe to say that every penny counted. Each time the request went in for the thirty pence, it felt like emotional warfare. It also meant that few around the local football scene were as determined as Barrett. Fewer still had the ability to match. Barrett, a centre-half, was athletically gifted. He was also incredibly driven. Every day was about 'kicking arse'.

There were other challenges. While Rochdale was loosely seen as one of the more liberal northern towns, racism was never far away. On one occasion, as a child, Barrett was playing in the street with his friends, around 100 yards from his front door.

An older man walked past and barked 'You black bastard,' at him. At first, Barrett was taken aback and struggled to process what had just happened. He then took flight and raced back to his house. In the safety of home, his young mind raced. He wondered why a stranger would say that, racked his brain for a reason but could not find one.

A similar thing – unprompted verbal racist abuse – happened three or four times. At the age of around 17, Barrett headed into an Asian café for a curry with some of his friends. A fellow diner, an older, white man at the back of the restaurant was unimpressed. It happened again. 'You fucking black cunt,' was one of a number of vitriolic shouts. Barrett went home upset but did not tell anyone about what happened. What good would it do? He saw it as a rite of passage, part of growing up for a black kid in the north of England in the 1980s.

The only thing he could do was use the racists' bile as fuel for the competitive fires. It was similar when he was spotted by scouts and signed for Manchester City. In one match he heard the monkey chants. He had heard of another black player, at a Midlands club, whose manager had thought it funny to make jokes about his race. The usual rubbish. The player had the balls to stand up for himself and reported his boss. What happened? He never played for the first team again. It was one of a number of tales well-known in football's black community. The consensus was that you kept your head down, turned a blind eye to the nonsense, and tried to get on. Things were difficult enough without making it harder for yourself.

Barrett was desperate to make a name for himself. There had been a couple of rough games in City's reserves, where older, wiser professionals had got the better of him. But he was learning and he felt like he was improving. The problem was, first-team football was hard to come by. There was intense pressure on the manager at City and a demand for instant results. It was not the easiest place to blood youngsters and allow them the opportunity to make mistakes as they develop. Their mistake could result in the manager getting the sack. He felt like he was not going anywhere so when his boss, Mel Machin, told him that he'd had Joe Royle, at Oldham, on the line, Barrett was interested. Not that he failed to carry out his due diligence.

Barrett initially sought out a team-mate, Kenny Clements, who was in his second spell at Maine Road after being signed back from Oldham. 'Earl, it's a great opportunity,' said Clements. 'You should go.'

Barrett wondered if the older man was trying to get rid of the competition. But he liked Clements and respected his opinion.

When Royle showed him around, it quickly became clear that Boundary Park was not Maine Road. But there were plus points. The money, for a start, was not too different, and Oldham neighbours Rochdale, and so he would no longer have to be up at the crack of dawn to catch two buses to work. He had been on loan at Fourth Division Chester City and enjoyed playing in meaningful matches. The Second Division would be more challenging.

Given all he had done to get to this point, he was not about to settle for a career getting splinters in his backside from sitting on the bench, or wasting his time playing meaningless matches in the reserves. He could have waited for his chance at City but time was ticking and he had been doing that for months.

It immediately became clear that there was a down-to-earth mentality at Oldham. There were no prima donnas. 'This is real,' thought Barrett as he looked around at the empty, windswept terraces. 'Real football.' He knew that if you do not win in real football, there are consequences. He thrived on competition. Despite the lack of money, his parents had delivered a fine, happy upbringing. They had grafted to give their sons, Earl and his brother Floyd, opportunities.

While it may have appeared to be a step backwards, Barrett felt like this was an opportunity he couldn't miss. What was the point of saying you play for Manchester City, if you didn't actually play for Manchester City? Royle initially wanted to take Barrett on loan, but City refused. It was a permanent deal or nothing. Peter Swales was adamant. A fee of £35,000 was agreed and Barrett became an Oldham player.

His first game was an unremarkable goalless draw with Plymouth. Barrett made it memorable when he fearlessly did the unthinkable and attempted a sliding tackle on the unforgiving astroturf. It promptly earned him the nickname Psycho among his team-mates, which stuck, as did the sheets to his bloodied leg when he woke up in pain the following morning.

By the time of the West Ham game, Barrett is well-established in the heart of Oldham's defence. The £35,000 fee looks like a ridiculous figure. He has grown up in the two years under Royle. He has also bulked up thanks to a relentless work ethic which he carries from the field to the gym. Barrett is one of few who sits out the Tuesday Club. Few mind. He is part of the band of brothers every Saturday afternoon and that is what counts.

The work has been done. Joe Royle and Willie Donachie, aided with Jim Cassell's Opposition Report, have finalised their plan. The players are in the tunnel, about to walk out in front of another 19,000 faces. But something has been nagging at Royle since the West Ham United team sheet dropped an hour ago. He thinks the visitors will be playing three in central defence, instead of two. Oldham have gone with a 4-4-2 formation, with Roger Palmer and Andy Ritchie up front. Much to his own dismay, Ian Marshall is in the centre of the defence.

Royle does not want the Hammers defence to have the cushion of an extra man. It is a risky move, but he decides to make it. He hurriedly makes his way to his team, who are yet to walk down the concrete steps onto the plastic pitch. 'Marshy,' he says. The player turns around. 'Play up front.'

Just like that, Oldham's 4-4-2 becomes what is effectively a 3-2-5, with Rick Holden and Neil Adams supporting what is now a three-man attack. Royle will not die wondering.

West Ham are managed by Lou Macari, whose Swindon sides have done well on the plastic in the past. They have trained on a plastic pitch in London, and came up to Oldham the day before the game for another session. The Hammers manager has travelled north in the midst of a storm after being found guilty of betting on his Swindon side to lose an FA Cup match at Newcastle United in 1988. He is also dealing with an injury crisis and many of his players – new signings – are cup tied. It is hardly the ideal preparation.

Royle's gamble takes 11 minutes to pay off. West Ham are camped in their own half from the off. When Adams picks up the ball about 30 yards out, he has time. Adams hits it to Ritchie, who has his back to goal on the edge of the area. One nimble touch brings it under control, the other lays it off to his right. It is the perfect one-two. Adams, now within range, strikes the ball with his left foot off the post and into the bottom corner to trigger more bedlam in the Chaddy End. With the celebrations ongoing, there is an immediate let-off. From the kick-off, the white-shirted Hammers race to the other end. Hallworth comes off his line to clear a through ball but can only succeed in getting it as far as Stuart Slater, the gifted West Ham playmaker, on the edge of the box.

With the Oldham keeper grounded, Slater has an unguarded goal to aim at if he can get the ball over the heads of the Latics defenders. An away goal may well be crucial. Slater chips the ball towards the net and there is a sickening wait as it sails through the air. It bounces and there is relief, as it flashes by the post.

The visitors continue to press, but when an attack breaks down, they are exposed. Andy Ritchie picks up the loose ball after Nick Henry has blocked midfielder Liam Brady's pass, and is around 60 yards from goal. He turns and sets off. This is a player who has scored in every round of the competition, and his reputation has clearly spread to the East End. Nervous Hammers defenders back off as he glides along the astroturf. Ritchie approaches shooting range and still there is no challenge. Finally, Tony Gale decides to stand his ground, and the Oldham striker shoots. His effort deflects off Gale and continues towards goal. Phil Parkes, the veteran in the West Ham goal, dives to his left. He gets nowhere near it. Just 18 minutes have passed and Oldham lead the semi-final 2-0. It is a dream start.

It gets better. On 33 minutes, Holden sends in what has now become one of his trademark booming crosses. Barrett, of all people, is in the area, such is Latics' thirst for blood. The ball drops and he takes one touch to control it before diving forwards, sticking out his right boot and poking it past Parkes. The decision he made to leave City has never looked as good.

As it was against Arsenal, 'We want seven,' is the chant from the crowd, only this time they are not joking.

After a breathless 45 minutes and an unthinkable three-goal cushion, Royle makes the decision in the dressing room to pull Marshall back to defence. In his wildest dreams he could not have thought it would have gone this well and his last-second switch has worked.

The message is to ignore the hysteria that is unfolding all around them. Concentrate on their jobs. Make sure the basics are done. Do not get carried away. The tie is not over and an away goal, or even worse two, could still swing it in West Ham's favour ahead of the second leg.

Royle's words are ringing in his players' ears as they head back out down the steps for the second half. Twenty-two seconds after the restart it is 4-0.

In a television interview earlier in the week, Holden – in typically forthright fashion – had compared the attempts of visitors trying to master the plastic as 'dogs sliding around on lino'. He is a prophet.

This time, Irwin breaks free down the right and sends over an inviting cross that Ritchie just fails to connect with. It falls to Holden, at the far post, who chests it down. With the West Ham dogs sliding on the lino, he has so much space that he can allow the ball to bounce, knowing it will sit up nicely for him. It does just that, and his left foot crashes the ball across Parkes and into the bottom corner, like a heat-seeking missile. Even at 3-0 there have been nerves on the terraces, but they are there no more. It is party time. Wembley is in sight.

West Ham's players and supporters did not expect this. The frustration is summed up when Brady, a gentleman of the game, fells Milligan with a crude tackle. But it is of little importance. Moments later, it is 5-0 when Holden swings in a corner and Roger Palmer, from all of two yards out, sweeps it in. On the Rochdale Road terrace, those who have travelled up from London and who have not already written the evening off and returned to their cars, do not know whether to laugh or cry. Some, soaked to the skin, jokingly decide to celebrate the goal. There is little else to do. In the Lookers Stand seats, one strips naked and police officers are called in. The following chase up and down the aisles is the highlight of the evening for those who have made the long midweek journey north.

But their misery is not over. Oldham are not done yet. With 12 minutes to play Holden, for the umpteenth time, sends in another cross. Ritchie rises above the defence and heads it into the bottom corner. Now, the St Valentine's Day massacre is complete. 6-0.

It is carnage in the home dressing room. Almost as noisy as it is in the streets outside Boundary Park. Royle tries to keep a lid on it but he knows that there is little he can do. Already, the players are talking about Wembley. Organising a kitty, discussing what type of suits they will wear for the big day.

Back out on the pitch, a devastated Macari, not having the best of weeks, is at least honest. 'It was so one-sided it was unreal,' he says. 'We were never in it and were second best all night.'

'I'll admit that we're favourites,' says Royle, barely stifling a smile. 'There's still a job to be done.'

It should not have been like this. At £700,000, West Ham full-back Stewart Robson has cost more than the whole of Oldham's team combined.

There are vast swathes of empty space on the away terraces

long before the final whistle, but some of those who have travelled up from London are overnighting.

At The Abbey Inn, at the other end of Rochdale Road in the town centre, one such group is drowning their sorrows. They are magnanimous in defeat and generously buy a round for a group of celebrating Oldham supporters when they arrive.

Back at the ground, Jon Hallworth seeks out his old friend Parkes before he leaves. Parkes runs coaching schools in Denmark and Hallworth has gone out there and done some work for him previously. Before the match, Parkes had told him that he was not looking forward to what was to come. He was not a fan of the plastic and 90 minutes of agony has done little to change his mind. 'How on earth do you play on that every week?' asks the Hammers keeper.

Up in the press box they are frantically tapping away. The nationals have once again descended on what Royle had previously christened Ice Station Zebra, a name that sticks. In the following day's *Daily Telegraph* Ian Ross describes it as 'a near-impeccable display of football'.

In the *Chron*, Bob Young – mindful of the recent betting scandal – muses that he would not put Macari's money on West Ham overturning the deficit, let alone his own.

For the first time in their 95-year history, Oldham are halfway up Wembley Way.

CHAPTER SEVENTEEN

Ooh, Roger Palmer

EVERY day, at the same time, Willie Donachie stops his car on Washway Road, in the Sale area of Manchester. Every day, Roger Palmer gets in for a lift to training. By now, Willie has been picking up the striker for six years. He has no idea where he lives. On more than one occasion, when it has been pouring down on the way home, the coach tells Palmer he will take him to his front door. On each occasion, the answer is the same. 'I'm alright here.'

Early in Joe Royle's reign, Palmer failed to show for training. While everyone knows that he likes a drink and a bet, this was not like him. Royle called the number for Palmer's house and a woman answered.

'Hi, it's Joe Royle here from Oldham Athletic,' said Royle. 'Is Roger there?'

'He's got acute appendicitis,' the woman said.

'Oh right,' says Royle, 'is that what the doctor's said?'

'No,' says the woman. 'It's what I'm saying.'

'Send him in,' said Royle.

When Palmer arrived the following day they already had a plan for him. It was a day off but a couple of the super fit senior pros were in because they liked to come in for a run. Urmson was told to send Palmer out with them and to run him into the ground. Around an hour later, the two professionals could barely move. Palmer looked like he had just strolled in from an afternoon at the beach.

Sale, in general, is a nice area. It is a desirable suburb for those who work in Manchester to call home. It does, however, feature the Racecourse Estate, which is notorious.

The Racecourse is where Palmer was raised and where he remains. As a child, he was a Manchester United supporter and a ballboy at Maine Road. But upon leaving school it was City who snapped up his services. Club legend Tony Book, a player who became manager, gave him his debut in 1977, at the age of just 18. That season he scored twice in a draw at St James' Park against Newcastle and got off the mark at home in a 2-1 defeat of Ipswich,

The following season, he struck twice in a home win against Leeds and was part of the City team that – despite miserable league form – pulled off a 2-2 draw with the mighty AC Milan at the San Siro in the UEFA Cup.

There would be no persistent run in the team. The following season, Malcolm Allison returned for a second spell and the chequebook came out. Palmer had to wait until a late September derby against United at Old Trafford for his bow and promptly struck an equaliser in the last minute against his boyhood club.

Allison failed to have the desired effect and when he was sacked and replaced by John Bond, the writing was on the wall for Palmer. Bond was not a fan. The new manager was all about graft and hard work. Ironically, the view that Palmer was too laidback was lazy in itself. Regardless, after five years, in 1980 he was transferred to Oldham.

City's loss was Oldham's gain. For the next decade, the club counts on his goals, initially from midfield.

Denis Irwin had never seen a winger like him. 'Jesus, he likes to leave his foot in,' was the Irishman's initial thought after playing behind Palmer for the first time. 'He's a right dirty bastard.'

Oldham did have a small Caribbean community, but black faces were few and far between. Palmer was almost instantly a cult hero, a novelty. The chant of 'Ooh Roger Palmer,' would be heard week in, week out, for years.

When Donachie arrived, he made the instant diagnosis that Palmer could not hit the ball in a straight line. But when it came to finishing he had never seen anyone as lethal, as precise.

'He's a brave boy,' he told Royle. 'To get in the box, to score goals you have to be brave. Roger's brave.'

The car journeys with Donachie were the stuff of legend for others in the vehicle. Following his arrival from Wigan early in 1989, Andy Holden often drove to the coach's house from his North Wales home and was taken the rest of the way to Oldham. Holden loves Palmer. The two – a big ginger Welsh centre-half and a slight black Mancunian – are an unlikely couple but they hit it off. Palmer, who is notoriously private, even invited Holden to a night out at Belle Vue, the grubby dog track in Manchester's east. It turned out to be one of the best nights of Holden's life.

Palmer, who loved a punt, took the lead. He guided Holden to the parade area where he passed on his expertise on what to look for in the dogs who would soon be careering around the track. From there he would say 'Come on, Taff' and seek out the bookie offering the best prices and from there it would be up to the bar where he knew they would have to wait the shortest amount of time to get served. The pair become roommates on away trips and enjoy each other's company.

When Palmer gets in Donachie's motor, Holden listens for the tell-tale squeak of the back window being wound down. Palmer always sits in the back. He also always has the window down, regardless of the weather. It is part of an attempt to ensure health conscious Donachie is unable to smell the trace of alcohol on his breath.

Holden is not the only one who loves his team-mate. Milligan is also often in the car and, knowing that Palmer will want to keep his mouth shut, often tries to get Donachie started on the big football topics of the moment. He knows Donachie loves talking about the game and that Palmer will not have to get involved in the conversation. 'Keep keeping him talking, Taff,' Palmer would often say later.

The appetite for a drink, however, fails to hamper him. Holden makes a point of marking Palmer if he is on the opposite side in a practice match. The reason is that Palmer's movement is like that of nobody else and that Holden knows he will get a serious workout trying to shadow him. 'Do us a favour Taff,' Palmer often says when the session is finished, 'piss off'.

It is all part of his eternal search for elusiveness which extends to his whereabouts in the dressing room. Often he will be in the middle of a conversation with Milligan and Ritchie, whom he sits between, and disappear before it has finished. It is a knack of vanishing that earns him the nickname 'The Ghost'.

Opposition defenders spend a lot of time looking for The Ghost and his strike-rate is incredible. So much so that in April 1989 he had broken the club's goalscoring record. A Tuesday night visit of Ipswich Town saw Ice Station Zebra covered in snow for the occasion. Conditions were so poor that the clubs had agreed to use an orange ball, so it could be seen in the snow that refused to melt even on the sanded, plastic surface.

Royle often goes out to the top of the steps of the tunnel to survey all before him. On that particular night he noticed that, along with the snow, there was a strong, biting wind. It may have been a mirage, but to his eyes it looked like the four corner flags were blowing in different directions. That was April, in Oldham.

Palmer and his team-mates had taken it in their stride, but Ipswich were not prepared. Royle saw 11 men in white shirts who may as well have been waving white flags. The omens looked good for Palmer, who sat level on the club's all-time scoring charts and needed one more to go ahead of Eric Gemmell, with the pair on 109.

Ipswich had dispensed with tradition and had travelled from the other end of the country on the day of the game instead of coming up the night before and staying over. It appeared as though they were trying to spend as little time there as possible.

As kick-off approached, a blizzard rolled in, engulfing the frozen few who had made the long journey north to support their team and who were exposed to the elements on the open Rochdale Road terrace. The humane decision to move them under the cover of the Lookers Stand was taken and while the view from there was better – and the environment drier – it was a miserable night for Ipswich's supporters.

The match was barely a contest. Oldham won 4-0, with Palmer grabbing a trademark two and the record. At one point, one of the Ipswich players was substituted. On Oldham's bench, Royle thought he had never seen a footballer get off a pitch so quickly before in his life after his number was held up. But the main memory of the evening was Palmer, who cemented his place as a club legend.

In 1989-90 he remains a regular fixture in the side and is still going strong. Indeed, for the visit of Everton for the next big cup tie in a season full of them, the 31-year-old will take his place in Oldham's starting XI.

CHAPTER EIGHTEEN

Everton

ONCE again, the big guns from the world of journalism descend on a packed Boundary Park. The scenes, unprecedented mere weeks ago, are being repeated regularly now. Patrick Barclay sums it up for *The Independent*. 'Boundary Park, a few miles to the north east of Maine Road, is the sort of place we call homely, the main stand possessing the character of the red-brick terraced houses on one side – even if the bleak Pennine landscape to the other side carries with it a wind no double-glazing could defy,' he writes.

'In the last few years, despite Second Division respectability (and a narrow failure to be promoted in 1987) the townsfolk have tended to stay in their own homes and watch the Latics from a distance, displaying no more faith in a rugby league club that has the consistency of a yo-yo.

'Now, however, as you drive up from Manchester, giving your regards to Chadderton's Broadway as the Lowry-esque mills loom in the distance, it is towards a healthy congestion. Nearly 20,000 will see the Latics on Saturday, the second full house in four days.'

The journalists are not the only new, previously unseen visitors who are becoming a fixture. The main stand is now often populated with men in long coats and notepads of a different variety. Scouts from Liverpool, both Manchester clubs and both Glasgow sides are now regular punters. Word has spread to the players, who sneak into the main office to have a look at the list of visitors universally known as 'Brussels'. The world of football is taking notice of what is unfolding, as are the TV executives. The Everton match will be top billing on *Match of the Day*. A nation wants to know if Oldham can do it again, as does another packed Boundary Park.

The atmosphere pre-kick-off is celebratory. 'Tell me mam, me mam, to put the champagne on ice – we're going to Wembley twice,' sing the Chaddy End, a Lancastrian revamp of the old *Que Sera Sera* terrace classic.

There is – ludicrously – almost an expectation that the Merseysiders will go the way of the rest. But the confidence is misguided and, before long, the feeling of invincibility is shattered. Everton come out flying and it is almost instantly clear that Oldham's midweek heroics have had an impact. They are sluggish and they are not snappy. Visitors' manager Colin Harvey has clearly seen other top-flight sides approach matches on the plastic with caution. He will not repeat the mistake.

Harvey's men exert pressure and soon get their reward. A cross from the right seems harmless but Barrett's attempted clearance, in the howling wind and driving rain, scuffs off his boot and travels sideways, across two Oldham players who would have otherwise dealt with it. The ball falls to Graeme Sharp, the lethal Everton striker and Scotland international, in space on the edge of the area.

Sharp is one of the finest centre-forwards of his generation and he has no hesitation in turning and hammering the ball at goal, first time in one movement. Hallworth dives low to his left, and gets a hand to what is a fierce shot, but he can only deflect it into the net. There is a melee behind the goal as the 4,000 drenched Evertonians on the Rochdale Road terrace celebrate.

Almost immediately a thunderous chant of 'Come on Oldham' goes up from the other three sides of the ground, who are disbelieving of what they are seeing, such has been the shift in expectation. But the goal has shocked the hosts and Everton are not only canny but brutal opponents. With any notion of winning the First Division gone, the FA Cup is their only chance of silverware and it is a realistic one. In midfield, wily Northern Ireland international Norman Whiteside has targeted Mike Milligan and, as half-time approaches, has twice elbowed him in the face without any action from referee Tony Ward.

Seconds after the second incident, the visitors strike again thanks to another Oldham error. Everton's Neil McDonald launches the ball forwards and forward Tony Cottee nods it to Sharp who, for reasons unknown, is wide open again. The Scot sets off towards goal but is hacked down from behind by a desperate Ian Marshall. It is a nailed-on penalty, but the ball has rolled under an advancing Hallworth, leaving Cottee a tap-in, which he converts. There is no need for a spot kick. As the Everton players rush to join the scorer in front of their own supporters, full back Ian Snodin deliberately barges into an unawares Milligan from behind and sends him sprawling. Just like that, Oldham are 2-0 down.

On the bench, Joe Royle has seen enough. Harvey, who was at the West Ham massacre, appears to have found the answer. Oldham are not causing his side enough problems and are allowing them to attack. That has to change. His players are of the same view. Rick Holden, having seen Snodin's off-the-ball assault, takes the lead, and dumps his opponent to the floor in the next 50-50 challenge. On the bench, Royle tells sub Paul Warhurst to warm up. Moments later, he is sent on for winger Neil Adams. The defender will go into the back four and Marshall, who has been in defence, is sent up front to give them something to think about.

The move is almost an instant disaster. With the wind at his back, Everton goalkeeper Neville Southall launches a long goal kick down the field. Sharp gets there first to flick it on and Cottee steals a march on Warhurst and is in on goal again. The former West Ham man chests it down and smashes it with his right foot across Hallworth. Nobody comes back from 3-0, not even this Oldham team. But somehow the keeper, already beaten twice, manages to hurl himself to his right and gets a glove on it. This time it is enough to deflect it to the ground in front of him and he gratefully dives on top of the ball. 'How crucial might that be?' asks Tony Gubba, who may as well now bring a sleeping bag to the commentary box, he is there that often.

There is still time, before the whistle, for Marshall to latch onto a long ball from Irwin and fire past Southall but he is flagged offside. This has not been a great 45 minutes and Oldham's players, furious at the visitors' shenanigans, protest loudly when they return to the dressing room. Royle is a calming influence. He tells his men not to be drawn into confrontation and adds that if they can concentrate on their football, all is not lost.

Marshall, who grew up supporting Liverpool, knows he needs to make a nuisance of himself and sets about doing that when play restarts. From a Barrett long ball he manages to muscle off defenders and win a free kick on the edge of the area. With the wind now at Oldham's backs, Denis Irwin fancies having a crack and puts both his hands in the air with palms facing forwards, telling the referee to ensure that Everton's wall of yellow away shirts is taken back 10 yards. His shot is deflected out to Warhurst, who sends it back into the area. Andy Ritchie gets there first to flick it on but Southall manages to grab it. His intervention means little to Palmer, who carries on his run and cleans out the Everton keeper. The message is clear – Oldham will not be bullied again.

Marshall continues where he left off. This time he gets to a Hallworth goal-kick first to nod it on to Ritchie, who in turn nods it on for Palmer. The striker stretches to control and cuts inside but the wind and the bounce takes it away from him. Nick Henry is there to take over as Southall races off his line. Henry takes it past the Everton keeper but is heading out wide and struggles to get a cross in. It does not matter. Southall's momentum has involuntarily taken the legs from Palmer and Ward blows his whistle for a penalty. There is a split-second when nobody realises what has gone on. All eyes are on the ball, not on Palmer and Southall. But there is Mr Ward, pointing at the spot.

Everton's players cannot believe what they are seeing. They surround the official. 'He's took the ball!' shouts Southall, pointing at Henry. He has a point, but Ward is having none of it. It is never a penalty, only it is.

The coolest man in Boundary Park is always Ritchie. He picks the ball up and places it on the spot. With the ranks of Everton fans behind the net waving their arms and creating a din to put him off, he keeps his head down and almost casually dinks his spot-kick towards the bottom corner. Southall, arguably the best keeper on the planet, guesses the right way but even at full stretch cannot lay a finger on it as it picks up speed off the turf. The packed landscape behind him freezes as the ball hits the net for Ritchie's 25th of the season, apart from a grey tracksuited ball boy who leaps up and down in perfect contrast. Southall grabs the ball out of the back of the net and boots it high into the Lookers Stand in fury.

Game on.

Now, finally, the pressure begins to build. Ritchie turns, a thing of beauty, and deceives three Evertonians. Palmer crosses and it looks like Marshall will finish it from close range but the magnificent Southall, brave as a lion, makes a point-blank block and takes a boot in the eyebrow, which has to be stitched up at the side of the pitch. There is a delay in the game for the procedure to take place and, following a thumbs-up from the brilliant keeper, the only stopper to wear shorts in the history of the Boundary Park plastic, we are back at it.

The noise cranks up a volume. This is now a blood and thunder cup tie and this is far more like it from Royle's men. They hassle and mither and do not give the visitors a second on the ball. 'I think Everton are just happy to keep possession,' says Gubba, as the ball for the umpteenth time goes back to Southall. There is nowhere for them to go. No space to find, no relieving ball to play. All angles are covered. The blue energy machine that Royle has created is finally in full flow.

Another blind pass forwards from the visitors is intercepted by Henry and it falls to Rick Holden in space on the left. Holden is a sharp operator and, in training, has noticed that the open terrace at the Rochdale Road often means the ball is held up in the air if there is a wind blowing down from the hills. There

Royle arrives at Boundary Park in 1982, the only manager in football to arrive on the back – or, to be more accurate, the front – of a lorry

Joe Royle's frequent raids on Leeds brought Denis Irwin (top picture) and Andy Ritchie (above) to Oldham. The club's new manager Howard Wilkinson would later joke that his directors 'went through a different window' when they heard Royle was on the phone

Earl Barrett shows why he was nicknamed 'Psycho', risking a crash landing on the plastic to score in the St Valentine's Day Massacre of West Ham (top picture), while Andy Ritchie celebrates knocking league champions Arsenal out of the League Cup (above left). Meanwhile, Frank Bunn gets deadly after his record-breaking six goals saw off Scarborough in the same competition (above right)

Top flight Everton presented a formidable physical test across three FA Cup matches, with Ian Marshall (above) and Nick Henry (left) in the thick of the action against the Toffees

Ian Marshall is mobbed by fans after Oldham overcome Everton 2-1 in the second replay to claim another big scalp

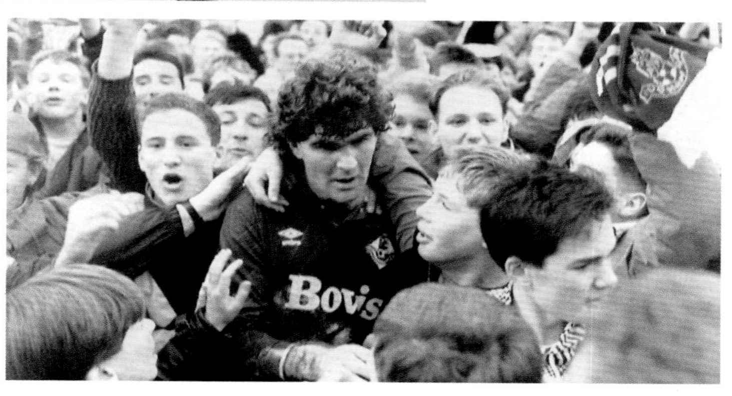

Palmer Sunday as Roger strikes in extra-time against Manchester United in a thrilling 3-3 encounter at Maine Road (above) – not that the elusive man of the moment hung around for long afterwards...

The Latics faithful urge on the boys in blue against United (above), while Ian Marshall does battle against Gary Pallister on a magical FA Cup afternoon (right)

Joy unconfined in the FA Cup replay against United, with Pallister and Steve Bruce powerless to prevent Andy Ritchie scoring against his former club in the closing stages of another pulsating fixture

Roger Palmer is thwarted by Jim Leighton at Maine Road, while Latics would eventually be eliminated in late and controversial fashion

Ready to chop down the Forest. Mike Milligan and Andy Ritchie pose for a staged press shot before the 1990 League Cup final and (right) Joe Royle and Brian Clough lead the teams out at Wembley

Neil Adams goes close at Wembley as Oldham chase an unprecedented League Cup triumph

An emotional lap of honour gives the travelling hordes a chance to thank the players for their efforts after a heartbreaking 1-0 defeat, while (above right) Brian Clough and Joe Royle plot a well-earned drink after the final whistle. The following day, Royle remains positive as supporters throng the streets of Oldham to welcome the squad home (below)

Joe Royle's men win Division Two in scarcely believable fashion thanks to a very late Neil Redfearn penalty against Sheffield Wednesday, sparking jubilant scenes as the fans toast glory with Ian Marshall (above) and converge on the Boundary Park pitch (above right, as seen in grainy YouTube footage, and right)

is today. He surges down the flank and hits what is by now a familiar, trademark early centre, deep towards the far post. Palmer, the man who makes a living out of evasion, the man christened The Ghost, has done it again. This time it is not Willie Donachie's watchful eye that he has averted but that of his marker. A little nudge in the back has done for McDonald – along with Holden's wind-assist – and the ball drops out of a murky afternoon and he has room. The header, down and into the turf, is the stuff of a coach's dreams. It bounces off the plastic, skids past Southall and Oldham have done it again.

Marshall, whose own run has taken him in front of goal, cannot help himself. While at Everton, he had once given an interview to the *Liverpool Echo* in which he unwisely outed himself and his dad as Liverpool supporters. The next day, his dad had a brick thrown through his car window. That, added to the feeling that his talents were never really appreciated at Goodison Park, added to the fact he loves a debate, prompt his next action. He races towards the disbelieving away fans, raises both hands and gives them a double two-fingered salute. 'Fuck off!' he shouts, 'have that you little twats!'

Twenty minutes remain. Milligan finds Palmer on the left. One touch to Irwin. Irwin gives it back. Palmer, on the turn, plays it inside to Ritchie. Ritchie takes a touch and taps it to Irwin who has driven forward. Irwin pulls it back to Henry who is one of three Oldham players who can finish and he does just that. It is a mesmeric goal, something from the court of the Harlem Globetrotters, not a windswept artificial football pitch in northern England. It is peak Oldham Athletic. At the far post Holden celebrates wildly, and rightly so. But it will not stand. Irwin was a fraction offside. The linesman has raised his flag and the cup tie remains level. Undeterred, Oldham go again. Ritchie sends a cross over, Marshall wins his header and at the far post it is another race between Southall and Palmer. This time the goalkeeper gets there first to send the striker tumbling. Their battle continues.

Another cross, this time from Barlow. Palmer, back to goal, chests it down. Ritchie, coming in from his side, drills it towards the bottom corner. Southall flings himself to his right and manages to palm it away. The Welshman is earning his money today.

As full-time of a breathless afternoon approaches, Milligan tries to win it but his drive sails wide. The seconds tick down and the TV cameras focus in on Everton's bench. Harvey is now visibly distressed, hand in mouth, biting his nails. He is pale and he does not look like a well man. It then turns to Oldham's bench. Royle is laughing, and is jokingly massaging the shoulders of Donachie, looking like he is having the time of his life. And he is. 'Don't take anything away from Oldham because of their playing surface,' Gubba tells his audience. 'They've got a team of really good young players.'

Hallworth sends another kick down the middle and Ward blows his whistle. That unwanted replay is a reality.

As they head towards the tunnel steps Ward is surrounded by angry Evertonians. Snodin gives him a Yorkshire mouthful, while captain Kevin Ratcliffe spits Welsh-accented abuse but, as Gubba says, the draw was the least that the Second Division side deserved.

On *Match of the Day*, veteran pundit Jimmy Hill does not agree. 'That was not a penalty,' he says. Hill does, however, tell host Des Lynam that he does not understand all the fuss over the plastic pitch. 'If you've got touch, if you can control the ball, you should be happy on that kind of pitch – I don't understand the fuss that's made about it.'

Royle, when interviewed, is almost as mischievous as his players. Asked about the penalty, he tells Gubba that you cannot see much from the dugout and so he did not get a view of it. 'I saw one in the first half when Andy Ritchie went flying off the ball but the referee didn't,' he contradictorily adds for good measure.

When he goes to face the written press he is in a more jovial mood. The replay will be another cash generator. 'What are we going to do with all this money?' he asks the reporters.

* * * * *

That replay comes four days later, on Wednesday evening. While any visit to Goodison is a grand occasion, Royle wants more than a day out. This should be the norm, not a one-off, he tells his players as they make their way across the M62 on a Mostonian coach. In front of a sell-out 35,000, with Ritchie sidelined thanks to a thigh strain, one of many of the walking wounded, the task is made more difficult.

Cries of 'Come on Oldham' from the 4,000 who have travelled to fill the Park End ring out as Everton – in their familiar blue – kick off. But this time it is Oldham who start the quickest. Following a surging run and cross-field pass from Barlow, Irwin whips over an inviting cross but first a sliding Palmer and then Marshall, on his knees, are inches away from connecting.

They are almost made to pay seconds later when McDonald sends over a looping ball from the right which catches Warhurst out of position. Kevin Sheedy, owner of arguably the best left foot on the British Isles, chests the ball down. It hits the grass and bounces up invitingly. The Irishman is around eight yards out and there is nobody between himself and the Oldham goal other than Hallworth. Sheedy pulls the trigger and the connection is clean. It hurtles past the Latics goalkeeper who has zero chance of getting in the way. There are hearts in mouths for a fraction of a second, but it narrowly flashes over the bar and into a relieved away support. Gubba, commentating again, can barely believe what he has just witnessed. Sheedy does not miss those and he is furious with himself.

The frustration arrives early and it arrives raw. Moments later Whiteside, whose behaviour in the first game came into question, goes over the ball and mercilessly stamps on Henry. Mr Ward, back in charge, goes for his yellow card. It could easily have been red. This is going to be another bruising encounter. Whiteside now has eight yellow cards for the season. He has already been banned once and another caution will trigger a second suspension.

Oldham maintain the pressure. Barlow, given licence to press forwards, hammers a volley from 30 yards. It takes a high bounce in front of Southall, which ends up helping the Everton goalkeeper who gets a fingertip to it to deflect it wide.

The Oldham defender then sends over a booming free-kick towards goal. Southall rises to claim, as does Marshall. The striker leads with his elbow and takes Southall's arms away. The ball drops into the goal but Mr Ward has seen the foul and we remain goalless.

With the Milligan and Henry axis running midfield there are more attacks. Holden sends over a cross and Southall punches clear, Marshall and Ratcliffe collide and when the pair hit the ground, Marshall mischievously grabs the Everton skipper's leg. Ratcliffe does not take it well, and punches – punches! – the Oldham man around the side of his head. In fairness to Mr Ward, it is an off-the-ball incident and his eyes are elsewhere. We play on.

It is the final action of the first-half of another tempestuous, pulsating affair. Little changes following the break. Henry goes in for a 50-50 with veteran Everton defender Dave Watson. Watson responds by stamping on the young midfielder, right under the official's nose. Again, it goes unpunished. The Liverpudlian collapses to the grass of his home city in agony.

Next it is the turn of his midfielder partner. Milligan nips in front of Whiteside and the Everton man kicks him, above the waist. Perhaps he could argue that he was going for the ball. Regardless, it is reckless. The assault takes place in front of the Oldham bench, which erupts. Milligan is down and Ian Liversedge races the short distance to him. Ward calls Whiteside over and there are five Everton players in his face, hurling abuse. He goes for his top pocket and pulls out red. Whiteside is off. The First Division side will see this one out with 10 men.

Milligan makes his way to his feet and is confronted by Sharp, screaming anger in his face. It is an ugly sight. The Mancunian, never short of a word, remembers what his manager told him, keeps his head down and says nothing. Out comes another yellow, for the striker. Cottee is also booked. Everton are losing the plot.

They regain composure and, despite the numerical disadvantage, begin to attack. A free-kick on the edge of the area gives Sheedy a chance to atone for his earlier miss. He rifles in a shot around the wall which Hallworth manages to get behind. It is an ugly save, bouncing off his chest, but it will do. This is not a night for aesthetics.

They come again. This time Cottee bursts clear and is brought down by Barrett in an almost identical position. Sheedy again lines it up. There is one minute to play. The hosts are attacking a Gwladys Street End which is willing the ball into the back of this pesky Second Division side's net. This time Sheedy curls it around the wall again but aims for the bottom corner. Hallworth can get nowhere near it. Is this it? Are Everton, with 10 men, finally going to break Oldham's run? No. They are not. The ball cannons off the post and Royle's men breathe again.

All of Goodison is now on its feet, urging its men forwards. There is still time for one more attack. Oldham are out on their feet. The cross from the left finds Sheedy and he is in. He stabs it at goal from close range. This has to be it. It is not. Hallworth's reflexes are up to the task. He instinctively flings out an arm and the hosts are denied yet again.

Ward blows for extra-time and the Oldham goalkeeper juggles the ball on his head and his shoulders as though he is playing on the beach.

Following a quick chat on the pitch, the additional 15 minutes start. Still, Everton attack. McDonald volleys one narrowly wide, with Hallworth stranded.

At last, thanks to Milligan, Oldham get the ball. Irwin, wide on the right, sends over a cross but it evades all and looks to be heading out for a goal-kick. It does not cross the line. Holden, who has cut in from the left, manages to get there first. He swings his left boot and connects 'like a sand iron', says Gubba.

His cross is delicate. It is also accurate. Marshall has been waiting all night for this. He leaps high, between two Everton defenders and, from six yards out, heads it towards the bottom corner, firm and true. Southall is a wise man. He does not move. He knows it would be futile. The ball hits the net and the Park End terrace erupts. There is dew on the surface and Marshall races towards the celebrating supporters. He knee slides and is almost inadvertently clothes-lined by Adams as the two former Evertonians embrace. Joy. Sheer joy. Everton 0, Oldham 1.

On the other side of the field Barrett and Warhurst race over to Holden. His delivery made it almost impossible to miss. The dream is alive.

But Everton are not done. A long punt downfield sails over the head of Barrett and Sharp is through. He chests it down and it is only him and Hallworth. Perhaps it is the intensity of the occasion, but his calmness deserts him and he wallops a volley instead of placing it in the corner. The ball sails over the Oldham stopper and dips, dips, but not enough. It clips the top of the bar and goes over. In the Gwladys Street, 10,000 heads descend into 20,000 hands.

Into the second-half and the aerial bombardment continues. Oldham are withstanding everything but are dropping deeper and deeper. Another long ball catches Warhust out and Sharp is in again. He dinks it over an advancing Hallworth but Warhurst has recovered and manages to scramble the ball away just as it is about to bounce into the goal. The Park End erupts again at an astonishing, acrobatic stop.

But they are not celebrating long. Mr Ward is pointing at the spot. In an eerie replay of what happened at Boundary Park, Hallworth – like Southall – has inadvertently taken away the legs of the striker. While the ball had gone, again it makes no difference, Everton have a penalty. Warhurst is visibly stunned. 'What was that for?' he asks the official. Irwin steps in to argue the toss but there will be no reversal. Sheedy steps up and will not be denied again. He absolutely hammers the spot-kick down the middle. Hallworth has dived to his left, the net bulges and once again, we are level.

Not long afterwards, the final whistle blows. After 210 minutes the two cannot be separated. There will be another replay. But where will it be held? What those still inside the ground do not know is that a coin-toss was held before kick-off in the Everton boardroom. Oldham vice-chairman David Brierley, given the hospital pass of representing his club, had been told by the rest of his board to call 'tails'. But as the coin was flipped into the air he had changed his mind and went for 'heads'.

The news is relayed to those still in the ground to loud cheers from the away end. The trilogy, unless it provides another draw, will conclude at Boundary Park. The coin had fallen with the Queen's face looking upwards at the crowd of gathered faces and Brierley had won.

In the press room, Royle is grilled about Everton's behaviour. He tells the reporters that it is for them to write what they have seen, but adds that his players kept their self-control admirably and emerged with their dignity intact.

In the *Chron*, Bob Young rises to the manager's challenge. 'Everton's verbal abuse of the referee and attempted intimidation of Athletic's players was one of the most disgraceful exhibitions I have seen,' he writes.

The following morning, Liversedge's physio room looks more like the Accident and Emergency department at the Royal

Oldham Hospital, a short walk up Sheepfoot Lane. Outside, there is a queue of battered and bruised footballers. It turns out that a punch in the face, which went unpunished, has broken Marshall's nose. Holden's leg needs treatment, as do Irwin's leg and ankle. Henry, who was on the thick end of it all evening, has shin, chest and thigh injuries. Adams's hip and thigh require treatment.

Meanwhile, Ian Stott is back in his Jag. The chairman heads across Lancashire to the Football League headquarters at Lytham St Anne's. Top of the agenda is how to address what is becoming a ludicrously congested fixture schedule.

CHAPTER NINETEEN

Put That F***ing Champagne Down

ALAN Hardy has a decision to make. He has been in talks with a number of merchandise suppliers ahead of what will be a money-spinning trip to Wembley. But a realisation has quickly dawned on him.

If he wants the best prices on Wembley flags, hats and t-shirts, the deals which provide the best margins, he needs to pay the suppliers and put the orders in before the second leg of the semi-final kicks off at Upton Park because the manufacturers have a longer turnaround time. It is a tough one. Oldham are six goals to the good. Never in the history of English football has any side overturned such a margin in the second-leg of a cup tie. It would take an unforeseen collapse of historic proportions to keep them from the famous twin towers. Common sense tells him to put the orders in and spend the £30,000, and he does so.

But as Oldham's coach approaches Upton Park, he has a sickly feeling in the pit of his stomach. Even though this has been a record-breaking season financially, £30,000 is still a lot of money to set fire to, should West Ham do the unthinkable.

Unlike his commercial manager, Royle is taking no chances. He has taken the unprecedented move of naming a goalkeeper on the bench. Andy Rhodes has been out of the side since the New Year and has not been flavour of the month. Royle felt his goalkeeper was overweight and had told him so. For a memorable week he had even sent him to live with Willie Donachie, where he had existed on a diet of salads and had come back a broken man. 'I need to eat,' he told anyone who would listen, usually to laughter.

Things had come to a head when, on a final warning, Rhodes got into trouble with the police for drink-driving. While that was not a great look, another issue was that he had been approached by officers of the law because he had parked his car outside a Chinese takeaway on the main road in the early hours when he was meant to be looking after himself.

Rhodes is on the transfer list, but he has made the trip to London's East End.

The hosts are a radically different proposition than the meek lambs who were slaughtered on the plastic weeks ago. For a start, Macari has been sacked. His replacement, Hammers' legend Billy Bonds, has quickly set about fixing things. The Londoner played more than 600 games for the club and this, his first job in management, is one at which he intends to succeed. It is as much a passion as it is employment.

The environment is also different. The Boleyn Ground is a hostile venue at the best of times but tonight it is a wounded beast. The locals are out for revenge. While they accept that a seven-goal swing is unlikely, they want their side to right a few wrongs. This is a proud football club and the events at Boundary Park were hard to stomach. There is aggression in the chilly air and it promises to be a challenging night for both Oldham's players and supporters.

Bizarrely, there is little segregation between the Oldham fans who have paid for seats and the home supporters elsewhere in the stand. Before kick-off there have already been a few altercations. Many of those who have travelled are told, in direct Cockney, that they are not welcome here. Many keep quiet. Some even practise their London accents, as squads of thugs approach on the concourse under the stand and demand to know where they are from. Any trace of a northern accent is met with a swipe to the face. There is almost zero police presence and the abhorrent behaviour goes unpunished.

Royle and Donachie have been doing their best to keep minds focussed but it has not been easy. Since the first leg thrashing, there has been plenty of talk of Wembley. A kitty has been set up, and even Phil Black has been involved in the planning, although Andy Ritchie has convinced the squad he can get them a better deal on their Wembley suits.

West Ham's players are as fired up as their supporters and they come out to attack. There is no other option. Julian Dicks, the left back, gets in a cross which striker Leroy Rosenior rises, unchallenged, to head. It looks destined for the top corner but Hallworth acrobatically leaps to his right and claws it out. It is a warning that is not heeded. The resulting corner is outswinging and the goalkeeper comes to collect but cannot get there. Tony Gale flicks it on and Alvin Martin forces in the opener.

Oldham regroup and see out the first half. Hardy thinks he can soon relax. But not long after the break Rosenior flicks on a huge goal-kick by Ludek Miklosko, the Hammers' new, impressive goalkeeper, and Kevin Keen bears down on goal. Hallworth races from his line and is always going to get there first but for reasons unknown he leads with his feet and clumsily takes out the West Ham striker. The resulting penalty is blasted in by

Dicks and there is a sniff. Not long after, it becomes a strong scent. Another huge kick from Miklosko causes problems and this time it is a panicked Earl Barrett who makes the mistake, heading it into the path of David Kelly, who drills it across Hallworth for 3-0. West Ham are halfway there and there are still 24 minutes to play.

In the main stand, Hardy's face has turned pale. He looks like he has seen a ghost. On 80 minutes, Dicks crashes a trademark shot at goal. Hallworth is beaten. At 4-0 with 10 to play it is anyone's game. The ball thunders against the bar and there is relief. But the onslaught continues. There are only 15,000 inside Upton Park – it would have been twice as many had it not been for the first-leg massacre – and they are creating an East End din. Royle decides to bring Marshall back into what is now a five-man defence but the chances keep coming. Martin is sent up front and Keen and Rosenior both go close but, mercifully, another goal does not arrive.

Finally, as time ticks down, the end is in sight. In the corner of the North Bank, behind the West Ham goal, realisation dawns and the pocket of 2,000 begin to celebrate. The scarves come out, along with some knock-off Wembley flags that have already been decent sellers on the stalls of Oldham Market. On the bench, Rhodes pesters Royle to send him on. He is desperate to play up front but his manager is having none of it.

It has been a nervous night but the finishing line is in view. Wolverhampton's Terry Holbrook puts his whistle to his mouth and it is over. For the first time in history, a team from Oldham will play at Wembley.

At first, the players do not really know what to do with themselves. But with the stadium emptying, the racket from the away section gets louder. There is a belief that they have let themselves down, and it takes a while for the irrelevance of the scoreline to dawn on them. But as they walk towards a sea of smiling faces, the penny drops. They have made history. Oldham Athletic – little Oldham Athletic – are at Wembley and before long they are enveloped in euphoria.

The feeling does not last. In the dressing room, a furious Willie Donachie awaits. He tells the players in no uncertain terms that what he has just seen was unacceptable, that the benchmark has been set much higher than that and that they have just lost to a team they had recently beaten 6-0 by three clear goals. In cutting, intimidating Glaswegian, he tells the group that some of them think they have made it when the reality is that they have won nothing. It is almost surreal. 'Anyway,' he ends, 'you've got to Wembley – enjoy your night.'

When Royle gets in, the message is similar. He knows he has to try and keep his team's feet on the ground. The second Everton replay is on Saturday. Promotion is still the priority, there is still much to be done. Halfway through what is a rare bollocking, director Rod Adams ill-advisedly sticks his head around the door, carrying a bottle of champagne. He is given both barrels by a seething manager.

But after the point is made, Royle congratulates his players. It is some achievement, he tells them, and one to be proud of.

Next through the door is a magnanimous Bonds, carrying bottles of Budweiser. He congratulates Royle and his players before handing the booze over. 'You've done brilliantly,' he tells them. 'Have a great day out and have a few drinks on us.' It is a fine gesture from a fine man. Another flight home has been arranged and it is a joyous one. There is more champagne and, after landing, the party is taken to a pub called The Black Ladd, in the hills above the town. They get in at around 12.30am and quickly get down to it. At 8am, dawn has broken and the drinks are still flowing. A TV reporter that the players like is celebrating with the group but he keeps repeating that he has to be in work in central Manchester at 9am.

He makes various attempts to leave but is continuously foiled. Eventually, Denis Irwin locks him in a toilet. The reporter's cries for help are ignored. 'You're not fucking going,' the Irishman shouts through the door. When 9am passes, he is finally let out. Irwin, Henry and Milligan continue what is now a momentous session throughout the day. The players have been given the Thursday off and they are making the most of it.

Oldham Athletic are at Wembley and the fact will be celebrated.

In his office, Hardy checks in on the progress of his orders and makes many more.

The second leg had happened to clash with another council meeting for John Battye and co. This time, they managed to make it out in time to listen to the second half. A group headed to a pub named the Three Crowns, and huddled around a transistor radio at the bar. When the third goal went in, it all got too much. 'Turn the fucking thing off,' someone demanded, and was obliged. For the next 30 minutes, everyone in the pub stood around barely making eye contact and nervously sipped their pints. Eventually, when they knew full-time had passed, the radio was switched on and the news that disaster had been averted was relayed. Champagne was ordered.

CHAPTER TWENTY

The Killing Field

ROYLE turns to kit man Ronnie Evans on the bench. 'I think this lot are still pissed,' he says. Twenty minutes have gone and Oldham trail Everton in the third fixture between the two sides by a goal to nil. Royle is not impressed. He knew that his players would let their hair down following the defeat at West Ham which saw them secure a trip to Wembley but his spies have told him that some of them took it a little too far.

If he is looking for evidence, he needs gaze no further than the plastic turf in front of him. Once again, close to 20,000 have packed into Boundary Park for a fixture that has had to be rearranged after gales damaged a partition wall, and, once again, the team in the yellow shirts has taken an early lead.

This time, the scorer is Tony Cottee. The Everton striker turned on a simple ball from Neil McDonald before dinking over an advancing Jon Hallworth and giving a stunned Chaddy End a mouthful. With Paul Warhurst out of favour after the reverse at Upton Park, Earl Barrett is the only centre-half in the team. Royle has gone for a bold 3-5-2 formation and it has not taken long for it to be exposed.

Injuries are taking their toll. Again, there is no Andy Ritchie. It is a season that would break squads that run deeper than

Royle's but there is something about the group that he has assembled. The average age is 24 and that youthful exuberance means that they do not know when they are beaten. They have already scored nine equalisers in cup competitions this season. At every training session, Donachie tells them that there are no limits and they believe it. Gradually, summoning reserves of energy from who knows where, and with Milligan and Henry seemingly over their hangovers, they get a grip.

That there is no Norman Whiteside helps. Everton can again try to bully their lower league opponents but they miss the banned Northern Irishman's mastery of the dark arts.

There is also no Tony Ward for the game. This time, the Football Association have gone for veteran Roger Milford, no doubt thinking that his knowledge will come in handy in officiating a match between two teams which, by now, do not like each other.

But Milford plays a key role in Oldham's equaliser. It comes when McDonald plays a ludicrous backpass which Neville Southall is never going to get to first with Roger Palmer hanging around. The Oldham striker pounces but misses the ball with his outstretched leg. Southall is caught by surprise and is, perhaps, slower than he may have been to collect the ball. When he does get down to it, he fumbles and a sliding Palmer, who has committed to the challenge, upends the goalkeeper. He also gets a boot on the ball, which rolls into the net. To many, it is a clear foul. Not to Mr Milford. He keeps his whistle away from his mouth, stretches an arm out in the direction of the halfway line and Oldham Athletic and Everton are level again.

Royle tells his players at half-time that they have got away with it, and to go out there and finish their illustrious visitors off.

Chances arrive. Rick Holden is almost on his knees at the far post to head in a Palmer cross but a desperate, sliding Ian Snodin blocks his effort and risks the wrath of the turf. Neil Redfearn, following a corner Southall cannot take, hammers a volley into the Chaddy End before Irwin rifles a long-range effort that swerves in the wind which the Everton keeper can only deflect over his own bar.

Milford blows for full-time and Royle makes his way onto the pitch to address his men. He is smiling and he is laughing. He puts his arms around some of his weary charges and whispers words of encouragement. Holden gets a jovial bollocking for his Wednesday night and Thursday morning exploits and is told that if he can win this epic war in the next half an hour, all will be forgiven. Meanwhile, Harvey is barking instructions and pointing fingers. The contrast will not be lost on Jimmy Hill later on that night's *Match of the Day*, for which Oldham are top billing once again.

The first-half of extra time kicks off and McDonald quickly makes himself the toast of Oldham for the second time. There is virtually no danger when Palmer plays a pass for Marshall to chase. The striker will get there first, but he is barely inside the area and is heading towards the corner flag.

For reasons only known to himself the Everton man clatters his opponent from behind. It is reckless. It is also a penalty. Tony Gubba, who now knows these two sides inside out, can scarcely describe it. 'What a foolish tackle,' he declares. 'That was stupid, absolutely pointless.'

The issue Oldham have now is who will take it. There is no Ritchie, who would have the task in normal circumstances. In the dressing-room before kick-off, Marshall declared that he would take a penalty if they got one. At first he forgets, and is looking for Ritchie to pick the ball up.

'Oh fuck,' he thinks as the delight of winning the spot-kick wears off and he recalls his earlier promise. 'It's me.'

Marshall knows Southall from his time at Goodison Park. He thinks that he cannot try to outsmart him. He also knows that if he tries to be clever and misses, he will never forgive himself. This is a man who will not die wondering. He will be hammering this one as hard as he can.

Marshall rolls up his sleeves and makes his way towards the penalty spot. Milford has barely even blown his whistle before he runs up and absolutely belts it. Southall dives the wrong way and it whistles into the back of the net, down the centre of the goal. The penalty has taken place in front of the Everton supporters, some of whom have clambered to the top of the fence to try and put him off, but this time there will be no flicking of the Vs. No abuse. The overriding emotion is relief.

Marshall is shattered but raises both arms aloft as he wearily runs back to halfway. This is what it is all about, he thinks. This is why he prefers being a striker to a defender. This feeling, when you score a goal and bring all these people to be on their feet with their arms in the air because of something you did, this is what it is all about. It is better than anything. Better than sex. Anyone can have sex. Not everyone can score a penalty against Neville Southall that will be broadcast to the nation later that night. Royle has already told him that he will play for England if he stays as a central defender. But last-ditch clearances do not generate the reaction that this does. The noise is incredible. This is football. This is life. England can wait.

The niggle remains. Barlow crosses to the far post and Everton clear. With the ball gone, Southall pushes Redfearn to the floor. The goalkeeper gathers the resulting corner but is then clouted in the small of his back by Palmer while he is on the floor. Oldham are wise to it now. No act goes without retribution.

McDonald comes off but it is not a mercy substitution. Another forward, Mike Newell, replaces him.

The second-half starts and something is different. This has been a war of attrition but Everton, at last, appear to be broken. All the attacking is coming from the home side. A Redfearn cross sails over the bar and a Chaddy End ballboy, perhaps intentionally, volleys it away from Southall and gets a mouthful of abuse from the Wales international in response. Everton are getting desperate and are throwing bodies forwards, which is making them vulnerable to the counter attack. It is one-way traffic and it is not heading in Oldham's direction.

Marshall, a man possessed, wins the ball on halfway and then jinks past a tired challenge from Kevin Ratcliffe. He is chased into the area by Martin Keown but feigns to shoot and the defender is done for. The hard work has been done – the goal is at his mercy. But the shot, on his weaker left foot, is a poor one and Southall can deflect it away with his knees. It falls to Holden, who crosses and Marshall is there again. He heads into the turf but it bounces agonisingly over the bar to howls of angst from the home hordes.

By this time Marshall can barely move, but he needs to because from the goal kick Oldham are attacking again. Irwin has released Milligan down the right hand side and the captain is approaching the area. He crosses and Marshall is in again, six yards out. All he has to do is sidefoot it into the goal. But he is shattered and he mistimes his shot. The ball almost comically hits his leg and the chance is gone. Marshall collapses to the turf and the game continues around him. Irwin gives the ball away and the spell of pressure is over, but the Oldham crowd roars its encouragement.

Another attack. This time Holden pulls it back for Redfearn, who is six yards out. The midfielder, who is enjoying a rare start, keeps his calm and directs it across the goalkeeper. But Southall is brilliant. He dives to his right and not only saves but catches the ball and within two seconds he has belted it down the field.

It does not matter. With the ball in the air, Milford blows his whistle for full-time. It has taken 350 minutes of gruelling, physical football, but Oldham have done it. Everton have been in four of the last six FA Cup finals. They will not be in the next one. The pitch is flooded with delirious supporters. Wembley twice is on. Another big name has bitten the dust.

This is not a plastic pitch, it is a killing field. Oldham are redefining the act of giant killing. Previously in this nation's long history of football, instances of David and Goliath have been mainly limited to one-offs. Flukes. There are no flukes to be found here. The best teams that this country has to offer are coming to Boundary Park and they are being blasted away. The electronic scoreboard shows a final score of 2-1 but the droves of Everton fans now making their way towards the exit underneath it know that their team could have been humiliated. In extra-time there was only one team in it, and it was the one assembled at a fraction of the cost of the other.

The former Manchester United manager Tommy Docherty

is sat in the main stand and is overheard telling those around him that Joe Royle must succeed Bobby Robson, the England manager, following the forthcoming World Cup in Italy.

Oldham's players are so tired that they cannot get off the pitch before the invasion makes it impossible. They wearily trudge their way through supporters who are delirious for the second time in a week. This just does not happen. Teams like Oldham do not do this. Only they are doing. Wembley twice is something those at the top of the table dream of, not those who fend for scraps. But Aston Villa, more top-flight aristocracy, will arrive on Wednesday for an FA Cup quarter-final. As Arsenal were when they arrived for the Littlewoods Cup tie, they are the current First Division leaders. The country's current best. And if they are defeated, Royle's men will be one match away from two visits to the home of football in the same year.

The manager is grinning as he heads up the steps to the tunnel to dozens of slaps on the back. His decision not to go to Manchester City makes more and more sense with every passing 90 – or 120 – minutes.

In the tiny boardroom, with its wall-mounted optics and sparse trophy cabinet, Oldham's directors are commiserating with their Everton counterparts, who they have come to know well over the past few weeks.

As the defeated party from Merseyside rises to leave, Oldham's president, Dick Schofield, stands to bid them farewell. 'Well, lads,' he tells them. 'At least tha' made a few bob.'

A story that gets harder to believe with every passing act of gianticide is not lost on the national press. In *The Sunday Times*, Peter Ball writes: 'This match was decided purely on footballing merit, and the First Division team were outclassed to an almost embarrassing extent. There is much more to Oldham than plastic pitches.' For good measure, he adds: 'Tactically, the Second Division team was in a different league, Royle staging one of the game's most brilliant and bravest coups with his decision to line-up with only one central defender, the excellent Earl Barrett, and use two full-backs to pull in to supply support when necessary. A familiar formation to the over-forties, it was a hair-raisingly brave decision in today's game'.

In *The Guardian*, Stephen Bierley muses colourfully: 'Boundary Park has flowed with milk and honey this season. One half expects the plastic turf to blossom roses after every extraordinary win: Wembley reached once and now, on Wednesday night, an FA Cup sixth-round tie against Aston Villa. At any moment the Pennines will skip like rams and the little hills like lambs.'

CHAPTER TWENTY-ONE

Tricky Ricky

AT Webb's chicken factory in Keighley, West Yorkshire, they called the job 'live hanging-on'. What it entailed was taking terrified chickens out of boxes, turning them upside down and clipping their wrinkled feet into shackles on a conveyor belt. Once attached, the animals would then be propelled to the hanging room, where they were dipped in electrically-charged water and stunned, just before they approached the three-way switch-blade that would decapitate them and bring their short lives to a close.

Perhaps it was because they knew what was coming, or perhaps it was the shock of being turned upside down, but for whatever reason the chickens would lash out and use their only defence against the worker tasked with the 'live hanging-on' role, using their claws and beaks. They would also empty their bowels. The result was that the staff member often ended up with dozens of little slashes on their hands which would sometimes become infected, thanks to the stinking environment in which the grim scene was repeated 100,000 times each week.

For three summers in the 1980s, one of the live hangers-on was Richard William Holden. A graduate of Leeds Carnegie, who had designs of being a professional footballer, he was on non-contract terms with Fourth Division Halifax Town, which meant that when the season finished, so did the money. The rent – along with the student loans – would not repay themselves.

Holden started life at the factory by folding back the wings on recently sliced-in-half chickens, before putting them on the conveyor belt bound for the freezer. From there it was the freezer itself, where he would place the packaged poultry onto pallets, ready for shipping to the nation's supermarkets. The temperature – minus 30C – meant that he had to wear a special suit and take a break every half an hour to 'defrost'.

And then it was on to 'live hanging-on'. Perhaps unsurprisingly, Holden developed an appetite for dark humour, and promptly christened himself 'chief executioner'.

It was not his only side job. Each Christmas, he would join the postal service and head out into the freezing, dark mornings at around 5am to deliver cards and presents to the residents of North Yorkshire.

Holden is a principled soul. He had turned down an offer to train full-time at Burnley as he was in the middle of his degree and it would have meant dropping his studies. It could have been the end of any hopes of a career, but a phone call out of the blue saw him invited to train with Halifax Town. At The Shay, he quickly began to gain a reputation among the dozens of scouts – including Jim Cassell – who would head to the ramshackle ground on Friday nights to watch Mick Jones's impressive young team.

From nearby Skipton, Holden – also a talented cricketer – was in his element. Finally, he gained a full-time contract and graduated into one of the highest earners at the club. He was also popular with his team-mates. In one programme interview he was asked for his favourite food and responded 'fish and chips'. One of Halifax's main sponsors was a chip shop and they promised to feed the team whenever Holden won the man-of-the-match award. It happened often.

While not blessed with explosive pace, a degree in sports science and three years studying body movement gave him an edge on most Fourth Division full-backs. Holden had the knack of frequently being able to find the room needed to deliver a cross – and he could centre the ball like few others.

His ability meant he was often targeted with a crude challenge. But once you have worked as the live hanger-on, you are pretty much ready for anything that can be thrown at you.

An inevitable big move – to First Division Watford – saw him head south. But when it became known that things were not going to plan at Vicarage Road – and when Tommy Wright left Oldham for Leicester ahead of the 1989-90 season creating a need for a new winger, Joe Royle made his move.

When he sat down with his new manager to discuss personal terms, Royle had asked him what he thought he would bring to the club. Holden had told him that both crosses and eccentric goal celebrations would arrive in abundance. He was as good as his word.

At an early training session, Willie Donachie told him that he would take the side to the next level, and he has certainly had a huge impact.

The Oldham fans almost immediately took to this eccentric character. Wingers are often popular, especially if they can beat a man and get a cross in. Now, whenever he gets the ball, there is a buzz of excitement and anticipation. His interviews and knack of delivering forthright, frank opinions, has struck a chord in a no-nonsense northern town. He even has his own chant: 'Tricky, Tricky Ricky, Ricky Holden on the wing.' However, the public's admiration did not stretch to a sharing of his fashion sense. An eccentric character, Holden had taken to wearing Trilby hats and was often spotted strolling around Springhead, where he had rented a flat above a glass and mirror shop, wearing it. Holden is also entrepreneurial. A conversation with Alan Hardy resulted in a number of the hats being ordered in for sale at Latique. They have not been great sellers.

The players, like the fans, have quickly taken to him. Holden is not your average footballer. He is an intellectual dressed in tramp's clothes. Each day before training, he brings the *Daily Telegraph* into the players' lounge and sits down to pore through global events, at least until one of his team-mates attempts to set fire to it.

On Saturday home matches he sometimes drives a campervan and parks it next to the Clayton Arms, the supporters' bar behind the Chaddy End. On Saturday nights he will socialise and then sleep in there, saving on a taxi fare.

Royle is delighted with him. He knows that a happy team is usually a winning team and Holden – and his antics – ensure that the club often has a smile on its face.

He is a valuable member of the dressing room and the first team. In this incredible season he has provided the bullets for the likes of Frank Bunn, Andy Ritchie and Ian Marshall to fire home, and has developed a knack for scoring beautiful goals.

The draw for the semi-finals has been made before Holden and Oldham face Aston Villa. The winner will face Manchester United for a place in the FA Cup final. Villa are a huge club who are dreaming of former glories. In 1982 they lifted the

European Cup, before the rest of the decade saw leaner times. But under the astute guidance of Graham Taylor, who is being tipped as the next England manager, they are again on the rise. They will become the second side to visit Boundary Park this season while occupying first place in the First Division.

The talk in Birmingham is of a Double for a side which was in the Second Division two seasons previously. They are being driven by David Platt, a brilliant young midfielder who was ironically born a stone's throw away from Boundary Park. Such was Platt's reputation, built playing non-league football for Chadderton, just a mile away from Oldham's home, Manchester United came in. But after failing to make the breakthrough at Old Trafford he headed to Crewe and within three years was on his way to Villa for a bumper £200,000. Platt, all energy, aggression and touch, is having a magnificent campaign. He is timing his runs to perfection, scoring goals for fun and a place in the England squad at the forthcoming World Cup in Italy is a no-brainer. The Villa defence is marshalled expertly by another former United man, Paul McGrath. The classy Irish centre-half is also a cert for Italy, with Jack Charlton's Ireland side.

It is, in short, another challenge for Royle's youngsters, who will again be without Andy Ritchie. The talk in the press is of burnout. Villa arrive just four days after the Everton epic. Oldham simply have to run out of gas at some point. The consensus is that Taylor's men may prove to be too much of a challenge. Holden will be up against right-back Chris Price. Price is a solid professional. At 29, with more than 400 appearances, he has seen plenty.

It is another near 20,000 sell-out. On the BBC's *Sportsnight*, Barry Davies refers to 'the increasingly famous steps' as both teams make their way towards the pitch. It is another blustery night and it is another febrile atmosphere. Early on, Price tries the old trick of barging into Holden, off the ball. The winger takes it in his stride. Moments later he tries to go past the defender close to the goalline, knowing full well that his opponent will get to the ball first and attempt to shield it out for a goal kick. Price does just that and Holden promptly smashes him into the advertisement hoardings. It is his blunt way of letting his opponent know that he will not be bullied.

For what feels like the umpteenth time, the blue shirts swarm and it is one-way traffic. Surrealism descends upon Boundary Park once again. It is now an old friend. Villa may be top of the First Division but they cannot get to grips with Oldham or their plastic pitch. As they have done against everyone else, Mike Milligan and Nick Henry are dominating midfield. Oldham, without Ritchie, have missed chances as half-time approaches, and do not hold what would have been a thoroughly deserved lead.

A throw-in on the left, midway inside the Villa half. Andy Barlow runs across to take a quick one and hurls it to Roger Palmer, back to goal, on the edge of the box. Palmer chests it down, holds off his marker and lays it back to Holden. With one touch of his left foot, he takes it outside a wrongfooted Price and there is a precious sight of goal. What happens next is a work of body mechanics that his lecturers would have been proud of.

Holden plants his right foot on the Astro, next to the ball. His cross for Ian Marshall to equalise at Goodison was described as a 'sand wedge' by Tony Gubba. This time he brings out the five iron. Head down, backside sticking out, Holden hits through the centre of the ball. It sets off like a rocket. Nigel Spink, who has been unbeatable in the Villa goal, dives high to his left but cannot get there. The ball, flying through the floodlit night, looks destined to crash into the crossbar. But as it gets beyond Spink something strange happens. Its trajectory changes and it dips, ever so slightly. The result is that it clips the underside of the bar and bounces down into the net for Holden's eighth goal of the season.

Once again, three sides of Boundary Park explode. While this is getting to be a familiar feeling, there is still ecstatic disbelief at what is being witnessed. It is the 36th consecutive home match in which Oldham have scored. They are unbeaten in all of those games. Villa have one of the country's best managers and some of the country's best players but they cannot find the answers relentlessly being asked of them.

Half-time comes and goes and the second-half brings more of the same. Oldham's stunning energy reserves show no signs of depletion. The visitors are being harried and hassled on every square inch of artificial turf.

A long ball from Paul Warhurst, aimed at Ian Marshall, is too deep. It will be covered by Price, who is having a miserable evening trying to keep Holden in check. Marshall, mullet flying in the gale, charges after it, like a wounded wildebeest, knowing he will not get there. Price does. He takes the safe option and sidefoots the ball back to Spink. But his brain is frazzled.

He has had so much to think about, so much to contend with, that his basic senses have deserted him. He has not realised that his goalkeeper has come out to meet the ball. He has not heard the shout of 'leave it', if there was one, in the ferocious din that has enveloped this quarter-final from kick-off. His back pass goes to where he thinks Spink should be, not where he is. The ball rolls past an aghast goalkeeper towards the Chaddy End goal. Before it hits the back of the net, Marshall turns away with arms in the air. In the main stand, where they get the best view, 4,000 Oldham fans have followed Marshall's lead and are also celebrating. Price has scored an own goal. The Second Division side lead 2-0. 'Eee aww,' is the unforgiving chant.

Price's evening of misery is not finished there. On 68 minutes he wearily tracks Holden out wide on the left. The winger, in his element, teases him. He drags it to the left, drags it to the right and then, in one movement, nudges the ball between his legs and he is gone. Holden, free of his man, veers into the area and hammers a low shot at goal with his right. Spink manages to get down and block it, but the rebound falls to Neil Redfearn, who sidefoots it into the empty net and it is another pasting.

On the terraces and up in the seats, thoughts quickly turn to the semi-final. 'We've got a bye in the semi,' is the chant from the Chaddy End, interspersed with 'Are you watching, Manchester?' United hold no fears and why should they? Arsenal, Southampton, Everton and now Villa have all been seen off and each sits comfortably above Alex Ferguson's side in the First Division.

'Ha, ha,' chuckles Davies as time ticks on. 'And the crowd are shouting "we want seven" in memory of the six against West Ham'. The cameras pan to the front of the Lookers Stand and on an army of young boys wearing brightly coloured ski jackets, which are of the current trend. There are beaming faces everywhere. Clenched fists, youthful hands to the night sky. Many hold their blue, red and white scarves aloft. A generation has been converted in the space of a couple of months.

In his usual spot behind the goal in the middle of the Chaddy End, Graham Lambert feels vindicated. Earlier that day he had been in London with the rest of the Inspiral Carpets, practising for their big day. The band's new single, *This Is How It Feels*, has been a huge success and crashed into the UK Top 40 at number 22. It means that tomorrow, they will record their first appearance on *Top of the Pops*, a Thursday night-ritual on the televisions of many. Lambert figured out that if he caught an afternoon train he could make the game, then he could get the 6am service from Manchester Piccadilly the following morning and be back with the rest of the band by 9am. In the midst of a scene of pure joy, it feels like the right decision.

The final 20 minutes of the latest cakewalk play out without major incident. With two minutes to go Palmer should make it 4-0, which would probably be a scoreline which accurately reflects the vast gulf between the two teams, but he shoots straight at Spink from around eight yards out. It is of little importance. Not long later, the whistle goes and triggers another pitch invasion. 'Oldham Athletic will play Manchester United on April 7,' says Davies. 'This remarkable story continues.'

Over at Old Trafford, where United are in midweek, First Division action, the score from Boundary Park is flashed up on the scoreboard. There are audible gasps.

'The two little lads in midfield never gave them breathing space,' Royle tells an enthralled nation.

'People keep expecting you to run out of puff,' Davies observes.

'They're young lads,' Royle responds. 'They're very fit lads and we're not doing a lot of training at the moment…we seem to be drinking more champagne than training!'

Later, it is Taylor's turn to come out and face the cameras. He is a wise man, a good man, a football man, and his interview echoes that of George Graham, following Arsenal's defeat.

'Every player knows his job,' he says of the victors. 'They know what they are doing and they will give any team in the land problems. They are confident in their own ability but I think the biggest thing today was that they get the ball into areas that hurt you, irrespective of the surface. The surface does not come into it for me. It's the way they play. It's nothing to do with the surface at all.'

Not everyone shares Taylor's view. In a petulant whinge disguised as a match report in the following day's edition of *The Times*, Stuart Jones moans that Villa 'were knocked out of the FA Cup in circumstances which should be regarded as unacceptably unfair'. He is not done there. 'It remains inexcusably unjust that they (Villa) should have to perform in such conditions in a tie of this stature', he adds before claiming that Tony Daley was 'rendered inaffective by the artificial surface'. Jones does, however, point out that 'Oldham were as persistent as an angry sea rumbling into shore'.

Across the packed press box, Stephen Bierley, clearly enjoying his trips to Boundary Park, begged to differ from his fellow reporter. 'Many will continue to mutter about the unfairness of the plastic pitch,' he writes in *The Guardian*, 'Oldham will only laugh. They are already at Wembley for April's Littlewoods Cup final. And now, with their first FA Cup semi-final for 77 years, who would bet against them doubling up?'

CHAPTER TWENTY-TWO

The Boys In Blue

BOBBY Ball is used to tough crowds, but the players of Oldham Athletic are something else. The comedian, one half of duo Cannon and Ball, is with the squad at a recording studio, on the outskirts of the town. They are all there to cut Oldham's Wembley record.

The obvious choice had been the Inspiral Carpets, and Alan Hardy had held meetings with guitarist Graham Lambert, an avid Latics fan who had stood in the Chaddy End for years and who had grown up on the terraced streets almost within the shadows of Boundary Park's towering floodlights.

The reaction from the group was lukewarm. Football songs tend to be wholesome family affairs, widely mocked by the critics. For an image-conscious, cool indie band attempting to break through, a cheesy single with a local club did not feel like the right step. Indeed, it could have been fatal. And while Lambert and Clint Boon are Oldhamers, the rest of the band is made up of United and City fans who were less than keen.

Jilted, Hardy approached Ball, who, as one of the borough's most famous sons, was more suited to accompany Royle's squad. It is a Thursday afternoon and the players are lively. Ball's fame cuts no mustard with them. Along with his partner, Tommy Cannon, he became a household name in the 1980s thanks to what was, in principle, a cabaret act. But the Oldham dressing room is an unforgiving place. If you cannot give it out as well as take it, you are in trouble.

Ball is having to take it. An early gag was made about his size or, to be more precise, his lack of it. It has not gone down well and things have gone downhill from there.

Cannon and Ball starred in a spoof police film in the early 80s called *The Boys in Blue*. Someone has made the link and decided that Oldham's cup final record should be called *The Boys in Blue*. The lyrics are simple, the tune catchy. It starts with Ball: 'Get up early every day, soccer is the game we play, we are the Boys in Blue, we're going to beat'cha, beat'cha.' Then the players join in for the chorus: 'We're the Boys in Blue, a woo, woo, woo, woo, and we'll win for you, a woo, woo, woo, woo, 'cos the Latics will do anything for Oldham.'

The players, however, are not as interested in their musical debut as they are taking the piss out of the vertically-challenged comedian. Eventually, he can take no more. 'You're a lousy set of bastards,' he says, before storming off.

Record done, the group decides to head to the nearby Three Crowns for a spot of lunch. The pub's landlord, Ray Hicks, is a former professional rugby league player who represented Oldham. What the group does not know is that he is also a friend of Joe Royle's. Upon seeing the players enter his bar, Hicks pulls out a visitor's book and asks each to sign it. They happily oblige. By Oldham standards, the afternoon is a sedate affair. Not many have more than a couple of pints with their food and nobody thinks anything of it when they turn up for training the following morning. That is, until they see Royle, who appears to have the visitor's book under his arm. He is not happy.

'Right,' he tells them. 'This is how we are going to do this. By lunchtime, I want a list of everyone who was at The Three Crowns yesterday.'

Rick Holden cannot resist. He heads into the office and asks one of the staff if they can get the last match's team sheet up on the computer. They can. Holden changes the name of the opponent from 'Aston Villa' to 'The Three Crowns (away)'. He prints out the spoof document and puts it on the desk in Royle's office.

The manager cannot help but see the funny side. 'Right,' he says, regardless. 'If you don't win tomorrow, you're fined a week's wages.'

The record is part of a relentless commercial drive. Something strange has happened. The town of Oldham has turned royal blue. At Latique, there are fans awaiting deliveries. Stood in the shop for as many as two hours. When the packages arrive there is no time to put their contents on the shelves. Punters are literally taking Oldham Athletic t-shirts, jerseys, towels out of the boxes.

Hardy often holds brainstorming sessions with his staff at which ideas of new products that could be good sellers are invited. His assistant, Gordon Lawton, had the idea of an 'Andy Ritchie Appreciation Society' t-shirt. It is simple. A picture of the striker with the slogan beneath it. They have flown out of the door. Demand is through the roof. So much so, a second outlet has been sourced in the Town Square Shopping Centre, in the middle of the town centre. It is also rammed. A short walk from the second shop, through Boots the chemists, takes you to Littlewoods. The League Cup sponsor, which also has a huge distribution plant in Oldham, has dedicated its shop front to the final. For a time, the trophy itself is put on display with fans able to have their pictures taken with it for £9.99 (including frame). As Jim White notes, having been sent to see what all the fuss is about for *The Independent*, on the main shopping drag, blue and white bunting hangs from the lampposts.

In the bakeries, they are selling gingerbread men wearing iced blue Oldham jerseys. Street cleaners are wearing blue rosettes and taking more pride in their jobs than ever before. At Top Man and Burton's, the mannequins are dressed in blue suits, as are the dummies in the bridal shops. At McDonald's a poster reads: 'Littlewoods' Cup Final 1990: Come on Oldham.'

White heads up to the Civic Centre to interview Battye, whom he writes 'is the kind of Labour council leader who would give Margaret Thatcher heart failure'.

'It's given everybody something to talk about other than the bloody Poll Tax,' he tells the reporter. 'It's like having another Christmas. I suppose the most tangible effect on the council will be that the rent arrears go up as people find the money for Wembley tickets.'

White notes that academic achievement in the town is as low as anywhere in the country, despite its motto of 'Sapere Aude' – 'dare to be wise' – and that the owl on Oldham's shirts is not a nod to wisdom, but to the accents which pronounce it as 'Owldham', instead of 'Oldham'.

No doubt briefed by Battye, White also points out the drive to demolish the mills and bring new, hi-tech industry to the town. He adds that 33,000 of the residents rely on one form of housing benefit or another and that unemployment stands at a gut-wrenching nine per cent.

Back at the ground, Latique has started doing late night openings. Hardy and Lawton often help out the staff. They have upselling competitions. One night it is mugs, the next it is crystal glasses. When customers take their gear to the counter they are told that a mug would look great in their office, or in the staff kitchen. A large chunk of Oldham's population works in nearby Manchester. Up until now, there has been little to brag about. Now everyone wants the world to know who they support. The pair have no issues shifting more stock.

Sales in the shop are approaching £500,000. It is incredible. Savvy Hardy has had a percentage included in his contract and is doing very nicely from it. The bank is contacted. The loan they handed over – the one that was to be paid back over four years – can be paid off in full in less than one. Plans are submitted for a second-storey.

Requests to sponsor matches have also gone through the roof. In the 1960s a young, ambitious chairman by the name of Ken Bates built a series of what you could loosely describe as 'boxes' in the main stand, effectively lean-to sheds which are attached to the wall which separates the seats above from the terrace below. One of the tiny boxes is given to Hardy to sell to the match sponsors. There is room inside for 12 and a small bar, along with a buffet. At half-time, the occupants can stand at the door and peer out to the tunnel, catching a strong scent of wintergreen and hearing the noisy clattering of studs. It is an amazing experience.

Up until this season, there have been matches that have been unable to attract a sponsor. JW Lees Brewery help out where they can, with their wine merchant Willoughby's committing to sponsor a couple of games a season. There have been no such issues this time around. Then there are the ticket sales. Oldham have been given 33,000 tickets for Wembley and they will all be sold. They have had to open turnstiles to sell them as the ticket office – two tiny windows on to the street – cannot possibly cope with demand. Coupled with gate receipts from the cup runs, they are looking at a profit that may not be far short of £2m. There have been six capacity gates and more than 350,000 have clicked into Boundary Park over the course of the season.

This incredible year has also seen others cash in. At the *Oldham Chronicle*, they are experiencing staggering rises in sales on Mondays after Latics have won at the weekend. John Battye is hearing from retailers in the town who are reporting increased sales. It appears the football club's unlikely success is creating a feelgood factor which is prompting the Oldham's residents to open their purses and wallets.

Factory owners have also been in touch with Battye. On the mornings after Royle's men have worked their magic, productivity levels have risen. It is not a coincidence.

All of this is not lost on the players who are now getting recognised wherever they go. Ian Marshall is stopped by one supporter doing his shopping in Sainsbury's and promptly cops for a stern lecture because his fellow shopper has spotted a six-pack of beer in his trolley.

Most of Royle's squad live in the town. In the Shaw area, there is Marshall, Andy Rhodes and Andy Ritchie. In Saddleworth, it's Bunn and Holden. Andy Barlow, the only member of the side who originally hails from the town, calls Moorside his home.

Barlow is a complex character and often feels the need to detach himself from what is going on. To do so, he takes his dog out for long walks to Strinesdale Reservoir, high above the town, which affords views across the sprawling borough.

He often looks down at the town. All the people who live in those houses, who work in those factories, who drive on those roads he surveys from on high are relying on him and his team-mates. He takes deep breaths, surveying the scene, regains his focus and heads home. As a local lad, he volunteers for much of the community work. When he first started going into Oldham's schools all he would see were shirts of both Manchester clubs and Liverpool. Gradually, it all turned into the blue of Oldham. Barlow prefers to shop at Hillards rather than Sainsbury's, and, like Marshall, he is often stopped.

But this is a friendly town and to these people they are now heroes. Most of the time they just want to pass on thanks and wish him luck. There are no issues, other than the fact it is often taking him twice as long to do his weekly shop.

The connection is a strong one. Not only do the players mix with the supporters, the borough's children are no strangers to playing on the plastic themselves. Almost every night a number of different schools are in action under the floodlights. Often, Royle makes sure one of his players is there to referee the games.

And, bizarrely, it is not just the football team who are putting smiles on faces. Up at Watersheddings, the rugby team is enjoying a wow of a season. They are in the Second Division, but under the astute guidance of coach Tony Barrow and a board who believe they must speculate to accumulate, they are set for promotion and are on a cup run of their own. Already in this campaign, they have been to a Lancashire Cup Final, which was narrowly lost to First Division Warrington. The same opponents await them in the semi-final of the Silk Cut

Challenge Cup, the sport's pinnacle fixture, which will be held at Wembley the day before the Littlewoods' Cup Final. For fans of both clubs, there is the ridiculous prospect of three trips to the twin towers in the space of a few weeks, should the rugby team overcome Warrington and Latics see off United.

Even the Oldham Celtics, the town's basketball side, which features Floyd Barrett, brother of Earl, among its players, has got in on the act. They have won the second tier National League title and National Trophy double and have also attracted a visit from the national press, with chairman Pat O'Donnell telling *The Times* 'Maybe it's the water we drink,' before adding: 'This town cares passionately about its sport – there's not a lot of other things to get excited about in Oldham.'

It is not lost on the music world, either. The Carpets appearance on *Top of the Pops* airs in the middle of an unlikely storm which is not lost on presenter Simon Mayo. 'Oldham's the place to be,' he declares. 'What with the Oldham Celtics basketball team, the rugby league side and, of course, the football club. Now they have a group in the Top 20 and here they are – The Inspiral Carpets.'

Lambert cannot believe it. As the group waits to be called onto the stage he reflects on where they have come from, of writing songs in his mum and dad's back bedroom. Now he is wearing clothes picked for him, after the band struck a deal with fashion designer Sonetti. Brands want him and his bandmates to wear their clothes. They have mixed with the likes of legendary former Smiths' frontman Morrissey, they have a tour to America lined up. It may only be 400-capacity clubs but each one is sold out. The band is growing increasingly popular.

This Is How It Feels is essentially a song about loneliness and depression. It provides a snapshot of working-class life in a northern town and is a million miles away from the happy pop dominating the charts. It starts with the story of a row between a husband and a wife which impacts on the couple's children before the chorus declares: 'This is how it feels to be lonely, this is how it feels to be small, this is how it feels when your word means nothing at all.'

The second verse has been changed for radio. The original album version told: 'There's a funeral in the town, some guy from the top estate, seems they found him under a train, and yet he had it all on a plate.'

The new version: 'Black car drives through the town, some guy from the top estate, left a note for a local girl, and yet he had it all on a plate,' is a little less graphic, but the message is the same.

The video is suitably bleak. Shot in January on moorland at the highest part of the Snake Pass, which crosses the Peak District and connects Manchester with Sheffield, it captures the band blasted by wind and rain in almost darkness.

Dominated by Clint Boon's organ and featuring haunting harmonies, *This Is How It Feels* has, like Oldham's football team, struck a chord across the country.

A student has been arrested in Oxford for wearing one of the Carpets' 'Cool as fuck' t-shirts. That slogan, with the 'fuck' changed to 'milk' has been etched into milk bottles delivered across the town promoting their forthcoming July concert at G-Mex, Manchester's former Central railway station that has been converted to a giant exhibition centre, with room for 10,500, and there is a confidence that all tickets will be sold. At the bohemian Afflecks Palace indoor marketplace, on Oldham

Street in the city, there is a t-shirt with the slogan 'Manchester, north of London'. You can now also buy an equivalent with the message: 'Oldham, north of Manchester', even if technically it is east of the city.

Back in Oldham, White, who is putting some graft in for *The Independent*, heads over from the town centre to the ground for a chat with Alan Hardy, who lays out the financial ramifications. Last year, the club shop turned over £1,200. It is currently bringing in £35,000 a week. Four extra staff have been drafted into the commercial department. Burton's have been on the phone – they have seen the success of the concession over the road at Littlewoods and want to know if they can have one in their shop.

'Listen, if you want to know how this club's success has helped this town,' says Hardy, 'I'll tell you about one of our game's sponsors, Thorn Securities, who have a factory in the town. They paid £5,000 for the West Ham semi-final. For that they got 18 free tickets, a free bar, food and some advertising around the ground. They brought some clients, who had been talking about signing contracts for over three months. The day after they had brought them here – and we had beaten West Ham 6-0 – they signed the contracts.'

Warming to the theme, he adds: 'It was worth a lot of money. It secured a lot of long-term jobs in the town. I think they would have had to work a lot harder for that contract had we been scrabbling around playing Hull City in a relegation game.'

CHAPTER TWENTY-THREE

Fatigue

BY the time Sheffield United, the team most likely to grab the second automatic promotion spot behind league leaders Leeds, arrive at Boundary Park on March 28, their hosts have already played 50 matches. In the league, they still have 12 to play. There will be at least one more than that in both the Littlewoods and FA Cups. While the bruising Blades, all long ball and brute strength under manager Dave Bassett, lost to Manchester United in the FA Cup quarter-final, they were out of the Littlewoods Cup before August had elapsed.

Joe Royle is not blessed with a big squad. Often, reporters repeat Barry Davies's question after the Everton epic. When are they going to run out of steam? Royle, Willie Donachie and Ian Liversedge do what they can. Training sessions are limited and players are given as much rest as they can possibly get. But injuries bite everywhere. Some of the cup money – a record £225,000 – has been spent on a striker called Paul Moulden, a former Manchester City man who has been prolific at Bournemouth. Moulden is a welcome arrival, but more like him are needed and there is no time to get deals done, and nobody wants to sell their players at this stage of the season. Ritchie remains out for the Roses battle, which will see Oldham attempt to protect a 38-game unbeaten home record.

Bassett's men do not care much for statistics or for fatigue. In their fluorescent yellow shirts, they weather an early storm and deservedly take the lead on 29 minutes when big striker Brian Deane heads in a corner. Oldham should equalise on 51 minutes but Ian Marshall misses a penalty and Deane lobs in to kill the game with 12 minutes to play. As Ian Ross writes in *The Times* the following day: 'The unthinkable happened in Greater Manchester last night when Oldham Athletic were defeated on their own ground for the first time in 14 months.'

It may have been unthinkable to many, but to Royle and Donachie it was almost inevitable. They can see that their men are running on dangerously close to empty. The South Yorkshire side were the worst possible opponents. Well-organised, tough to break down and supremely fit, they held three ingredients of a formula that the likes of Arsenal, Everton and Aston Villa were unable to find.

Worse is to follow. A 1-0 defeat at Middlesbrough comes on a traumatic day for the town.

At Central Park, home of Wigan, Oldham's rugby league club has put in a tremendous performance against First Division Warrington. With time running out, they narrowly trail a gruelling battle 10-6 but are on the attack. Mike Ford, the gifted hometown scrum-half, spots a gap behind his opponents defence and dinks a perfect kick towards the try line. Paul Lord, on the left wing, knows what is coming and races for the ball. He is going to make it. He does make it.

Half of the 15,000 present go berserk. If Oldham's reliable goalkicker Duncan Platt can kick the two-point conversion, they have done it. They have broken their own hoodoo. They will join Latics in London for Oldham's Wembley weekend.

Oldham, as the BBC's rugby commentators have already said, will be a burglar's paradise. On the steep Wigan terraces there is delirium. While the football club's consistent failure to get to the twin towers has been understandable, the rugby club's non-appearance has an almost eerie edge to it. Rugby league is more of a level playing field. Oldham, a founder member, are one of its traditional names. There are no other clubs of a similar size and with a similar tradition, who have never made it to the showpiece fixture since it was played at Wembley. In 1964, they were leading Hull Kingston Rovers in a semi-final and were on the verge of breaking what was, even then, being referred to as a jinx, 12 minutes into extra-time when – bizarrely – fog descended on the ground and the match was abandoned. To the surprise of no-one, Rovers won the replay.

The guttural roar that greets Lord's try is reflective of all those years of hurt. The one which will greet Platt's winning kick in a minute or so will be even louder. In the split second that Lord touches down generations clad in red and white hoops embrace.

But there will be no winning kick. Referee John Holdsworth has blown his whistle. He has given Warrington a penalty. He has ruled that Lord was in front of Ford when he kicked the ball, even though replays subsequently show he was well behind him, and has adjudged him to be offside. The try is disallowed. It is a traumatic, unjustified end. A horrendous decision has robbed the town's rugby club. Seconds later the whistle is blown. Grown men and women and children are in shock. There are hands on heads and there are tears. The jinx continues.

Days later, the town's football club cannot provide a small pick-me-up. A 3-0 thumping at Leicester severely dents hopes of promotion, which was always Royle's first priority. Three defeats in a row. Following the mauling at Filbert Street, the manager is so angry that he leaves without speaking to the waiting press. His team are creating chances but they do not seem to be able to convert them, outside of Boundary Park. In 18 league games on the road they have scored only 15 goals. They are often going behind and having to get men forward to chase the game and their defence is being left vulnerable. Above everything else, however, they are shattered.

Suddenly, there are doubters. Oldham have won only three times away from home in the league all season and it gives the plastic pitch naysayers more ammunition. It is not ideal preparation for their FA Cup showdown with Manchester United, whose form has picked up. There has been some good news – Andy Ritchie is back in the fold and long-term injury victim Andy Holden played 90 minutes at the heart of the defence – but there is a grave concern that promotion may well be slipping through their fingers.

In the physio room, Liversedge and his assistant Ronnie Evans do their best. The pair are part of the fabric of the club. Liversedge is a former footballer who failed to make the grade after starting out at Everton and the players can relate to him.

He enjoyed a career at semi-pro level, mainly in Wales, where he picked up the nickname 'The Soss' after one fan, having presumably read a programme, started referring to him as 'liver sausage', much to the bemusement of all present. Such is his desire to enjoy life that he came to Oldham from the mighty Newcastle United because the club's then manager, Arthur Cox, refused to let him play amateur football in his spare time. After spotting an advert in the *Daily Mail* not long after Royle's arrival, he turned up for an interview at Boundary Park where the manager – who remembered him as a youngster at Everton – spotted him. Never one to miss a trick, Royle had asked him if he was still playing in his spare time. When Liversedge said he was but that Cox was stopping him, the job was as good as his. At the time, Royle needed a physio but also needed numbers for the Reserves. At a previous fixture one of the office staff had to turn out. Liversedge would fit the bill nicely.

Evans, who also looks after the kit, arrived a short time later. Another former player, he had come through the ranks at City and joined Bury, where a broken ankle finished him before he had started.

Evans had been forced to take a job at Manchester Airport, where he delivered pre-packed meals to the waiting airplanes. It was a miserable way to make a living and when he went to his local for a pint he said as much to Tony Henry, his pal and former City team-mate who was playing at Oldham. Henry told him that the lads were off to Magaluf for a week for their end of season trip, and asked him if he wanted to come. Evans did, not knowing that it would be a week away which would change his life.

On one afternoon, the players had been in the same bar for a number of hours, knocking back pints and eating lunch. Someone asked the waitress for a bill. When she brought it over, Evans asked her if she had any tomato ketchup. She said that she did and returned with a sachet. Evans promptly emptied the contents of the sachet over the bill and ate it.

At a separate table a watching Royle, who knew Evans from his City days, called Liversedge over. He is a good man, liked Evans and felt like he was in a position to help. 'Soss,' he said.

'We're going to have to get Ronnie a job, aren't we?'

'Yes boss,' was the reply.

Not long after, Evans was on the staff and was quickly given a rapid introduction into how it worked.

'All those meals you were meant to deliver to the planes,' said Liversedge. 'I reckon you ate half of them, you fat bastard.'

The pair set about their daily tasks with relish. And with United days away and the season run-in just behind, they know that now, more than ever, Royle is depending on them.

There is much to do. Frank Bunn is back from injury, as is Andy Holden. The pair have been out for three months and seven months respectively. Andy Ritchie also played the full 90 minutes at Leicester. But the niggles and knocks, and the scars of what is already a punishing campaign continue to arrive with alarming regularity. Rick Holden has an ankle injury which keeps reappearing and was substituted early at Ayresome Park – a match which saw Paul Warhurst shifted up front as an emergency striker. A thin squad is being stretched to its maximum.

CHAPTER TWENTY-FOUR

Palmer Sunday

'IF Oldham had a coach the last time they reached the FA Cup semi-finals, it was horse drawn,' David Lacey, of *The Guardian*, writes. He is not wrong. Seventy seven long years have passed since their last outing at this stage, a defeat to Aston Villa. 'Football matches were played on Saturdays then,' Lacey adds, 'and on Sundays, far from allowing football matches, they locked up the swings in the local park.'

Lacey notes that the United fixture, to be played on the grass of Manchester City's Maine Road, will provide Oldham with a chance to show the country that their success is not simply down to their plastic pitch. It is a subject which has caught the imagination of other members of Fleet Street. In the *Daily Telegraph*, John Ley carries out a statistical study into the effect of artificial surfaces on the results of the clubs who have installed them, QPR, Luton, Preston and Oldham. He finds a marked improvement in cup competitions, and a slight rise in league performance.

For the first time, both semi-finals will be played on the same day and both will be televised live on the BBC. Three-and-a-half hours before Oldham face their big neighbours in Manchester, Crystal Palace and Liverpool will kick-off at noon at Villa Park.

Palace, promoted from Division Two last season, were

thrashed 9-0 at Anfield earlier in the campaign. Few give them a prayer in Birmingham. It would appear that, despite their repeated antics, some hold the same view of the prospects of Royle's men.

One scribe writes the two matches make up 'what looks like the most one-sided pair of semi-finals in living memory'.

United have had a dreadful season in the league but the cup has been their – and under-pressure manager Alex Ferguson's – shot at salvation. It has been widely reported that the Scot, who has spent much but delivered little since his arrival from Aberdeen in 1986, would have been sacked had they gone out at Nottingham Forest in the third round. Ferguson was saved at the City Ground by a goal from a young striker from Chadderton by the name of Mark Robins, who lives a couple of doors down from Neil Adams.

United remain arguably the biggest club in the world. But since Matt Busby's Babes lifted the European Cup in 1968, a wonderful young side emerging from the Munich wreckage to capture the trophy and millions of followers beyond Manchester, there have been more than two decades of serious underachievement. A series of managers have come and gone without being able to return a beast of a club to its perceived rightful place at the summit of English football. Each has been backed heavily in the transfer market and each has failed.

So far, Ferguson has been no different. On the opening day of the season, a 4-1 victory over champions Arsenal in front of more than 47,000 at a rocking Old Trafford delivered genuine hope of a challenge for a league which bitter rivals Liverpool have dominated, with a squad full of expensive new arrivals playing the Gunners off the park.

But injuries and a loss of form hit hard. Around Christmas, the clamour for Ferguson to be sacked grew louder and louder. After a home defeat to Palace a banner calling for his head was unfurled in the stands.

But following the victory at Forest, form improved and the Scot is likely to be able to pick England's midfield two, Neil Webb and Bryan Robson, in his XI. The team that Oldham will face is likely to have been assembled for around £13m. Royle's XI cost no more than £600,000. It should not be a contest.

In the build-up, camera crews descend on Oldham and on Boundary Park again. But this time the atmosphere is slightly different. Reporters are surprised to see that Royle does not appear to be his usual self. He is not. The three league defeats in a row have hurt. 'I've said for a long time that promotion is the priority,' he tells one journalist. 'I'd swap both cup runs for that.' There is a glimpse of his humour, however, when he is asked by the BBC if the underdog could have its day on Sunday. With a trace of a smile, he responds: 'Who's the underdog?'

Despite the three defeats, the town is almost neurotic. The High Street is awash with blue Bovis shirts. The United match is hotly debated in the bars and clubs on its Saturday night eve. There is a local rivalry but it exists almost entirely on Oldham's side. Few in Manchester support Oldham, but the same cannot be said of the opposite. Up until very recently, there were almost as many match-going United fans in Oldham as there were supporters of Royle's side. The view from those who choose to follow the team from the big city has, for years, been patronising.

The hope among Latics fans is genuine. In *The Observer*, Hugh McIlvaney makes the point that Oldham are not your traditional giant-killing act. 'Being overawed is not a habit with the squad

Joe Royle has so admirably developed on a meagre budget,' he writes, before lauding the talents of Rick Holden, whom he says 'crosses the ball as well as anyone in the First Division'. 'The news that the ankle Holden twisted is responding to treatment will certainly reassure Royle,' he adds.

* * * * *

The big day arrives. Palace and Liverpool go first and produce a classic. Over a see-sawing 120 minutes of mayhem in sun-drenched Birmingham, the lead changes hands four times. The unfancied South Londoners fare better than the 9-0 debacle but look to be heading out when a John Barnes penalty puts Kenny Dalglish's men 3-2 up. With three minutes to play and the strains of *You'll Never Walk Alone* echoing around the old ground, Andy Gray finishes a scramble to send the match into extra-time, where Alan Pardew snatches a dramatic victory by heading in the seventh goal of the game.

The nation watches, enthralled. In the TV booth Des Lynam, presenting the double-header, asks, 'How can we follow that?'

Around him, Maine Road is bursting at the seams. It is also more red than blue. The FA has decided to give United 27,000 tickets compared to 18,000 for Oldham following last year's Hillsborough Disaster. In the aftermath of the tragedy the FA were criticised, with many claiming that they had not taken strength of the support of the two competing clubs into consideration and, as a result, they could not satisfy demand on Merseyside, having not allocated enough tickets. A knock-on effect is that United enjoy a numerical advantage on the terraces and in the sky blue seats at the home of their cross-city rivals.

Under bright, warm skies, both teams emerge from the tunnel to a wall of noise. They may be outnumbered, but the 18,000 followers of the underdog are contributing to what is a racket. 'Come on Oldham' booms out from the wooden benches in the Platt Lane End, half of the seats in the main stand and a tiny slither of the cowshed-like Kippax Street terrace, which the smaller of the clubs has been allocated. 'United, United!' booms out from everywhere else.

The players cannot make themselves heard. For Jon Hallworth, it is a novel experience. He has played in the First Division, but he has never known anything like this.

Royle has picked Andy Holden to play at centre-half instead of Paul Warhurst. He knows that Mark Hughes, the robust United forward, carries an immense physical threat and believes Holden will be a better match-up. The pair, both Welshmen, know each other well, having been in the Wales squad together. When Oldham played United in a practice match ahead of the season at The Cliff, United's training ground, it was a war.

They are soon at it again, when Hughes' first action is to elbow Holden in the Adam's apple. The defender is furious and fired up. So are his team-mates, even more so when Robson cleans out Andy Ritchie. It is a frantic start but if anything it is United who are the more nervous. A harmless looking ball from Andy Ritchie should be easily picked up by United goalkeeper Jim Leighton, but he gets involved in a mix-up with full-back Mick Phelan, who has Rick Holden breathing down his neck.

The defender knocks it past his advancing keeper and Holden just cannot get there as the ball rolls out for an Oldham corner. The winger sends it to the near post, where it is cleared back out to him. With one touch, Holden brings it under control and with another he clips in a low cross. Again, it should be Leighton's. Again, there is a cock-up. The Scottish goalkeeper somehow manages to dive over the top of the ball, with Andy Ritchie perhaps blocking his view. Time appears to slow as the gravity of the keeper's error hits home. The ball bounces and Earl Barrett, of all people, is left with an open net, which he taps the ball into. There is a suspicion, perhaps, of offside, but there is no flag. The goal stands.

Immediately, Barrett is mobbed. Andy Holden plants a kiss on his cheek. The roar from the Oldham fans is almost hysterical. Yet again, their team has landed a punch on football's aristocracy. David, in his blue shirts, shorts and socks, has smacked Goliath in the chops.

'What a mess for Manchester United, what a delight for Oldham Athletic,' proclaims Barry Davies, as the camera pans to those inside the ground who are celebrating. 'All Barrett had to do was wave his foot.'

The match continues at a frantic pace. Andy Holden gets his own back with a crunching tackle as Hughes looks set to pull the trigger, while an audacious, long-range lob from Ritchie drops narrowly wide with Leighton, embarrassed once, frantically backtracking.

There is no doubt that Oldham are the better side as the half hour mark approaches but the pace remains ferocious and there are concerns over how much they have in the tank. United have shown few signs of life but all of a sudden, out of nowhere, they are level. There appears to be little danger when United's tough defender Steve Bruce slides to win a 50-50 ball with Ian Marshall just inside the Oldham half, but it rolls forward to Webb who, with a deft two touches, plays it behind Latics defence to Robson, who has timed his run to perfection.

The England captain is through on goal. Hallworth races from his line to meet him and manages to get a hand on Robson's low shot but it continues beyond him. Hallworth, on the turf, turns his head. For a moment it looks like the ball is going to bounce wide and his first reaction is one of relief, but then something happens. The ball hits a piece of uneven turf from a pitch that is showing signs of wear and tear following a long season. The dislodged grass changes its trajectory and it creeps inside the post. United's support erupts. Their numbers include small pockets who have managed to secure tickets in Oldham areas and whose presence is not entirely welcome. There are minor scuffles, which add to the drama of the day.

Suddenly, United are on top. Barrett, who has started well, nips the ball away from the striker Brian McClair just as he is about to fire one at goal. The swathes of United supporters are now making all the noise but Oldham regroup and win a corner as Rick Holden manages to cause Phelan problems.

Perhaps wary of the first goal, United are nervy. As the winger gets ready to put it into the area Leighton, for reasons known only to himself, shoves Ritchie in the back with both hands. It is a penalty, a blatant penalty. Referee Joe Worrall, from Warrington and reportedly a Manchester United supporter, marches over to the goalkeeper. But he is wagging his finger, rather than pointing at the spot. He is giving Leighton a warning. On the Oldham bench, they cannot believe what they are seeing. Rightly or wrongly, they had their concerns over Worrall and they are incandescent.

Regardless, Royle's men continue to press. Irwin races beyond the United defence and sits up a cross to the far post, where Marshall awaits. The big man powers a header at goal. Leighton, wrongfooted, has no chance, but Gary Pallister, another expensive recruit, manages to block it. The ball rolls to Rick Holden but the sturdy defender repeats the trick and it goes out for another corner.

As the ball comes across, Leighton is at it again. This time he flaps and it drops to Nick Henry who, along with Milligan, has entered into a fierce battle with Robson and Paul Ince in the centre of the field. Henry connects cleanly and drills it towards the corner. Again, Leighton is beaten but again, there is a red shirt in the way. This time it is Ince who blocks the shot on the line and United breathe again.

Within seconds they are almost in front. Down at the other end, Irwin manages to partially clear a McClair cross but the loose ball is rolling to Robson who must score his second of the day. Exploding off their marks like Olympic sprinters, Irwin and Barrett charge fearlessly towards the United man and throw themselves in front of him, blocking the ball in the process. There is a pile up of players on the turf. This is relentless.

Finally, almost mercifully, Worrall blows his whistle and the players traipse off to an ovation from all. Inside the Oldham dressing room, Royle is walking around his group as he does, delivering short bursts of inspiration. While there are 45 minutes still to play, his side have already proved that the big question is a nonsense. They can play on grass, make no mistake.

The second-half starts like the first, with Oldham on top. Worrall, who seems to have decided that he will not be booking anyone today, delivers another telling off. This time it is to Bruce, who has, once again, gone in hard on Ritchie. Royle's men are enjoying themselves. They are showcasing their talent to millions of enthralled viewers. Milligan pulls off a high speed Cruyff turn and leaves Ince floundering. Ince fouls and there is no card. On the hour mark Hughes, clearly frustrated, boots Barrett in the air. Again, there is no card.

A minute later Irwin, who has been excellent in both attack and defence, sends a long ball forward for Marshall, whose control is a work of art. He charges towards Leighton and hammers a drive at goal. Is this it? No. The Scot manages to block the shot and is almost knocked over by its power. It is a fine save and the score remains at 1-1.

Still, Oldham push forwards. A loose ball sees Marshall connect with Leighton's shorts rather than the ball and there is a stoppage in play as the goalkeeper, with his backside now on display thanks to the subsequent tear of material, calls for a new pair. It is comical and it is almost symbolic. While the scores are level, Oldham look like they are in the process of pulling their big neighbours' pants down.

The chances continue to come and go. United have a strong appeal for a penalty turned down when Andy Barlow appears to push Webb in the area. Then Redfearn has the ball in the net but the goal is disallowed for a push by Ritchie in the build-up. Replays suggest the decision was harsh.

Ferguson replaces Robson, who has given him more than an hour, with Danny Wallace, a pacy winger. Royle is yet to make a move.

On 73 minutes, there is a rare United attack and Wallace manages to evade Barlow on the right. He heavily slices his cross which ends up being headed towards the six-yard box by a backpedalling Phelan. Hallworth, in the Oldham goal, is left with a choice. Andy Holden is in the area and should be able to clear given that Webb is the only United player nearby. If he comes for the ball now, however, he should claim it. Initially, he decides to let Holden deal with it, but adrenaline takes over and rationale flies out of the window. The goalkeeper, a fraction of a second too late, rushes off his line. His move makes Holden hesitate. The pair collide and both miss it. Webb facing away from goal and hardly having jumped, deflects it gently. Had Hallworth stayed where he was, he would have caught it. But he did not choose to do so. The net is unguarded and the ball hits the back of it. United lead for the first time.

Holden is furious. He knows that Hallworth should have come and punched it clear but he also knows that he should not have been beaten in the air by Webb.

Regardless, the United man – sidelined for months with an Achilles injury – fist pumps towards a bouncing North Stand. There are only 17 minutes to play and this long, miserable season for United may just have some light at the end of it.

It is a gut punch for Oldham who, by the time they kick off, have 15 minutes to respond. The first assault comes on the right. Irwin throws to Redfearn who gives it back to the Irishman and heads towards the edge of United's area. Irwin plays the ball back to the midfielder whose sharp first touch with his left foot, towards the touchline, is too good for Ince, and he leaves his marker trailing behind him. Redfearn, blonde highlights twinkling in the Manchester sun, dinks over a cross towards the six-yard box. Phelan, who has been superb, manages to get his head there first ahead of an incoming Ritchie and Holden, but his touch does not change the ball's flight and it continues across the face of goal to the far post.

Marshall, who has had a frustrating afternoon, is ready. With a ferocious swing of his right boot he absolutely belts it, on the volley, back towards goal. The ball takes one bounce and flies into the bottom corner. As it hits the net, it springs the 5,000 behind the goal to their feet. 'Marshall!' exclaims Davies, before pausing and letting the noise do his talking for him. 'What an unbelievable day this is!'

The striker races away and performs the knee slide he made famous at Everton. Milligan and Barlow embrace him. Young, angry United fans at the foot of the Kippax, celebrating Wembley seconds ago, hurl abuse. 2-2.

But there is still time for a winner. United, stung into action, have their chance when Webb races away from Holden and hits a fine shot which Hallworth beats away. It bounces to Hughes who hits the target but Barrett, back at the ground where he failed to make the grade, blocks it on the six-yard-line. His performance has been magnificent. Flawless.

Royle, with an eye on extra-time, replaces Henry in midfield with Warhurst. Almost immediately, his side are back on the attack. Rick Holden, who has been quiet by his own standards but who is now causing problems, finds Marshall in the United half. Buoyed by his equaliser, he shimmies away from Pallister and races into the area from the left. In the centre, Ritchie is waiting to apply the killer touch. On the Oldham bench Jim Cassell, along for the occasion, is willing Marshall to play his team-mate in. But Marshall backs himself and who can blame him? It is the wrong decision. His weary leg slices the ball wide. Ritchie may well have tapped it into an open goal.

It continues. Now, United are defending desperately. The cameras, as they have often done during this remarkable run, cut to the Oldham bench. Royle, again, is smiling. Ferguson, yards away, is almost ashen-faced.

Worrall blows for full-time and there is a chance to catch breath. Royle is getting used to these situations. He walks around his men, placing arms on shoulders, clips around ears. Donachie is delivering instructions. They are the good cop and bad cop.

* * * * *

Thirty more minutes await. Thirty minutes to find a winner. A cup finalist. For the third time on this momentous afternoon, Oldham start the quickest. Rick Holden, now in his element, finds space and crosses to the far post. Redfearn nods it down and Marshall blasts towards goal but these United defenders are resilient. Bruce, a warrior of the north-east, performs the umpteenth block of the day and the chance is gone.

Seconds later, United respond. McClair nicks the ball from Ritchie and goes past Warhurst before sending a ball through the middle. Andy Holden and Barrett have been dragged out of position by the runs of Webb and Hughes, which has created a huge gap which the rapid Wallace is now charging through. Barlow is outpaced by the substitute. Hallworth races off his line but sells himself too quickly and dives to his right.

'Test of his pace, now test of his finish,' says Davies, who is providing the perfect narration to what is pure theatre. Wallace scuffs his shot but it goes beyond Hallworth's outstretched leg. The ball rolls into the net. 'And he's equal to both,' the commentator adds. 3-2 to United.

Royle makes his second change. Ritchie, still short of fitness, is replaced by Roger Palmer, another back on his old stomping ground. Finally, the pace slows. It is looking like this is it. Oldham Athletic are finally going to lose a cup match at the 16th attempt in this incredible season. Royle, who is celebrating his 41st birthday, is simply not having it. As he has done so many times over the years, since he arrived at Boundary Park off the back of the lorry, he decides to get creative.

He tells Redfearn to move into a number 10 role, behind the front two. Barrett switches from the centre of defence to right-back. Irwin is pushed forwards into midfield. Against the mighty Manchester United, in an FA Cup semi-final, Oldham are now playing with one centre-back.

The break comes and goes and the noise from the United fans gets louder. Pallister heads away a free-kick to loud cheers. Milligan intercepts a subsequent pass from substitute Robins, just inside his opponents' half as their defence pushes out, with his chest. He quickly and intelligently plays in Marshall, on the left, who has sneaked in behind. Hang on. Hang. On.

'Yes, there's space here for Marshall,' says Davies, a hint of excitement in his voice. The defender-turned-striker has a sight of goal but instead of shooting again, he slides the most precise pass he will ever play across the area with the outside of his left foot. Leighton is in two minds. Palmer is lurking at the far post. The United keeper comes off his line to gather but the pass is too good. He cannot get there and he has, again, exposed himself. 'And Palmer's far side!' the commentator relays, almost hysterical. Palmer, the elusive, has done it again. He is in front of an unguarded goal. His connection is not the cleanest but it does not matter. There is nobody there to stop the ball as it rolls in for the sixth goal of the game.

The striker runs away with both arms outstretched in celebration. Palm Sunday has now become Palmer Sunday. On this day of religious feast, he looks like he should be standing atop a mountain above a Rio de Janeiro beach rather than on a bone-dry field in Moss Side. Roger the Redeemer. In the North Stand there is disbelief. Some erupt out of their seats, furiously pointing fingers at the players they are meant to be supporting. There is no overconfidence now. No sneering at little Oldham. No songs about trips to Wembley.

'This is the stuff of schoolboy comics!' exclaims Davies, capturing the moment perfectly. The cheers have barely died down before an explosive chant of 'Ooh Roger Palmer' envelops the arena.

Eight minutes remain. Redfearn whistles one over the bar and Oldham get carried away. Their thirst for a winner has left them open. McClair has space in the area and all the time in the world to deliver the killer blow. The only lives he threatens are the ones of the pigeons flying overhead as the ball sails over the bar and into the relieved Oldham fans at the back of the Platt Lane. Another let-off, this time when Webb, who has been superb, crosses for Robins, who gets ahead of a shattered Irwin but whose header is, slightly nervously, blocked by Hallworth.

Royle's men come roaring back. The pace turns up again. Two minutes to go. Holden, now playing like a man possessed, surges past Phelan, who has had enough. He crosses for Marshall, one of his trademark up-and-unders, but the header goes narrowly wide. The 120 minutes are up. Ferguson has seen enough. He comes off his bench and raises his arms towards Worrall to make his point. He wants a replay and he wants it now.

But Worrall does not whistle. Two minutes into added time

and the attacks continue. Pallister heads one clear and Rick Holden controls, 30 yards out. The winger from the chicken factory hints at taking it down the line and then swerves inside.

He looks up. The goal is in range but he is going to have to hit it with his right foot. His connection, as it was against Villa, is firm and true. The ball sets off towards goal, rising and rising. Leighton, caught unawares, dives to his left but cannot get near it. The curl takes it beyond him. 'Good try!' shouts Davies. The net shifts but the ball has whistled past the outside of the post and cannoned into the side-netting. Centimetres from glory. Leighton, arms outstretched, remains on the turf, half time-wasting, half in need of a rest. This has been a busy afternoon. The cameras again pan to the Oldham bench. This time it is Donachie, chin resting on his hand, who delivers the wry smile. 'Goodness me,' says Davies. 'How beautifully struck by Holden. And for a moment there I think that Joe Royle thought that that might be the decider.'

'Keep them in their den,' roars Donachie, always alert to danger. With Milligan set to launch another attack, Worrall decides enough is enough and blows his whistle. The two will have to come back on Wednesday night. A still-smiling Royle puts his arm around Ferguson, who looks like he has just been hit by a truck.

Across the country, families sit back on their sofas. Those who are not United fans have fallen in love.

Both sets of supporters rise to their feet to applaud. Oldham's players head to the dressing room where their manager tells them how proud of them he is. They have shattered the plastic myth and they have almost shattered United. They will have another crack on Wednesday. A replay is the last thing he needs but for now, that does not matter.

After showering, the players head to the lounge for a well-earned drink. An over-officious character on the door fails to recognise them – even now – and blocks their path because they do not have the required passes to enter. Steve Bruce, weary and in need of a pint himself, sees what is going on and promptly barges the security guard out of the way, telling him in no uncertain terms who these people are.

Back out on the pitch, after interviewing Royle, Davies asks him if he will make any changes for Wednesday night. 'Would you?' says the manager, with a smile.

Royle then heads for the coach where the atmosphere, despite the draw, is buzzing. Director Norman Holden in particular, is beside himself. Oldham have given Manchester United the fright of their lives. They have gone toe-to-toe with their illustrious rivals, they have not lost and – if anything – they should have won.

One person who is not on the coach is the scorer of the final goal. Palmer sees no point in heading back to Oldham, given his Sale home is not far from Maine Road. He has no lift from Donachie but he is not concerned. The few fans still milling around outside do not recognise the black man with a bag over his shoulder as he makes his way among them.

Palmer walks through the streets of terraced houses to nearby Princess Parkway, the dual carriageway that connects Manchester with many of its southern suburbs. It is a route he knows well. Having just scored the goal that millions watched, he approaches the bus stop, gear in his bag, and silently waits for the next service as the cars pass.

The praise in the media the following day is aplenty. Under a headline: 'Tenacious Oldham refuse to die' Stephen Bierley, for *The Guardian*, writes, 'Oldham looked by far the most balanced side,' before adding 'the middle name of Joe Royle's team is resilience – plastic pitch or no plastic pitch.' The reporter concludes his match report with 'Sunday, bloody marvellous Sunday'.

CHAPTER TWENTY-FIVE

A Russian Linesman

ANDY Holden entered the door of his local, the Red Lion in Northop, Mold, and the man he was coming to see was already sat at a table in the corner, with two pints in front of him. It was January 1989 and Holden, of Fourth Division Wigan Athletic, was close to joining Crystal Palace. A fee and wages had been agreed but, before he could head to London to sign the paperwork, his phone had rang and the man he was now heading towards was on the other end of the line. Joe Royle. 'Andy, I want to come and see you,' he had said. 'Where's your local pub?'

Holden liked that. He had nothing to lose in seeing Royle and decided to meet him. To make life easier he offered to meet him in Chester, closer to where Royle would be coming from. 'No,' the manager had said. 'You're from Flint. That's not your local. Where do you drink?' Holden had told him, and here, as promised at 7pm, he was.

Within 20 minutes he has agreed to join Oldham, then battling relegation, instead of Palace, who were then heading for what would become promotion to the top flight. He walked into the bar 6ft 1. When he left after the chat, he felt 6ft 9.

Royle told the defender, who has never lived outside his hometown, that he has done his homework. The mileage from

Mold to Oldham is not an issue. He can sign for him and not have to move house. He has also told him that he will get him back into the Wales squad. Oldham have suffered from injuries but they are on the cusp of great things, Royle added.

The deal, for less money than he would have earned at Palace, was done. Holden's first game on a plastic pitch was against Manchester City. There was a crowd of 19,536 – far more than he was used to playing in front of – but more than half of those were supporting the visitors. It was raining. His first touch in the blue shirt of his new club was shanked into touch. The second actually went behind his head for a corner. Oldham lost 1-0. They had not won for a long time.

In the dressing room, Royle ordered his players to report to Clayton Playing Fields, behind the Chaddy End, first thing Monday morning. Holden did as he was told. Willie Donachie split the players into groups of three. Holden is with Earl Barrett and Roger Palmer. Within 20 metres the pair left him for dead. As he traipsed after his new team-mates he had to keep his eyes on the floor to ensure that he did not tread in dog muck on what were public playing fields. 'What the fuck am I doing here?' he thought. 'Joe's sold me a dream and here I am doing drills and jumping over dog shit'.

It got better. Oldham started to win matches and the laps of Clayton were few and far between. Holden fitted right in. Unimaginatively christened 'Taff' he provided substance at the back which was desperately needed. He marshalled the defence and if Mike Milligan and Nick Henry ever dropped too deep from midfield he would tell them to get out of his fucking way and the message would be received loud and clear.

The training sessions were quickly a highlight. The intensity under Donachie's watch was something which he thrived under. Everybody kicked lumps out of each other because they all wanted to play on Saturday. He loved Donachie's insistence that every day saw an improvement. Every day, everyone had to strive to be better. The journeys flew by, especially after he started dropping his car at Donachie's house.

He also enjoyed playing for Royle and the sense of humour which prevailed at the club. Every week, Royle would take the teamsheet and walk around the dressing room, whispering words of encouragement. 'Andy,' he would say to Ritchie. 'You're too good for this centre-half that's marking you. Get your backside into him and get your shots off.'

'Rick,' he would say to Holden's namesake. 'The full-back cannot deal with you. Take him on and get your crosses over.' Then he would turn to Milligan and Henry. 'Boys – you have far too much energy and quality for this midfield. You will overrun them.' The compliments would flow until he reached Holden. 'Taff,' came the message, and his voice would drop to almost a whisper. 'Discourage the number nine.'

One day Holden had pulled his manager up. 'You always tell everyone else to do great things,' he said. 'But all you ever say to me is discourage the number nine. Why don't you tell me to get the ball down and hit a 60-yarder into the channels?'

The answer was short and sharp. 'Discourage the number nine,' growled Royle. 'And if he scores, it's your fault.'

Holden was also a paid up member of The Tuesday Club. A wiser, older player, he could see the method in the madness. 'You could show your arse in Woolies window and there'd be no comeback on Saturday as long as you were at it,' he thought. And he was right.

Holden was loving life. The son of an English farmer and Welsh mother, he had played Sunday League as a youngster. He did not turn professional until he was 20 after the father of legendary Liverpool striker Ian Rush had recommended him to Chester City, where his own son had made his name. At the time, he was also working in a toilet roll factory.

While at Wigan, he had been forced to have major knee surgery. Perhaps he should have known that Oldham's unforgiving surface may have exacerbated the issue. But Holden's bravery meant that he took on any challenge he faced. The injuries arrived frequently. Training sessions often saw him running up the Chaddy End steps with weights on his back, two at a time.

In one comeback match, Oldham's Reserves were winning 5-0 with minutes to go when a ball bounced in between Holden and in front of the man he was marking. The striker lined up a volley. Most players, with one eye on their health, would have taken into account that this was a Reserve match, that their team was winning 5-0 and that there was literally no point in making a challenge. Not Holden. He launched himself at the ball and blocked the shot, keeping the clean sheet intact. Unfortunately, the same could not be said of his face. Having headed the ball away, his opponent's boot instead cannoned into his head, just above the eye, splitting it open and sending blood pouring from a considerable gash that needed many stitches.

The following season has seen him out for long periods but he is now enjoying being back in the side. He loved his tussle with Hughes at Maine Road and he thinks he will be better for the replay with more mileage in his legs. And he is sure that there will be no repeat of the disaster that allowed Webb to somehow score the second United goal.

Before the replay, Ian Stott has work to do. An already ridiculous situation is now farcical. Oldham face 11 games in 25 days. For the second time, the chairman heads to the Lytham St Anne's headquarters of the Football League to argue for an extension. This time he is met with a pathetic admission. The league is willing to allow them to play one match beyond the final Saturday of the season. One match.

Tuesday night's planned fixture with Bradford City has been postponed and will be the game shifted. It means Oldham will play United on Wednesday and then Leeds United, who are set to win the league, in a vital clash at Boundary Park on Good Friday. United Sunday, United Wednesday, Leeds Friday. To make matters worse, the Leeds match has to kick-off at noon, on police advice. If Oldham beat United, they will be due to play in the FA Cup final a day before the scheduled first leg of the play-off semi-final competition, which they are desperately trying to be part of.

* * * * *

Royle walks around the dressing room. He pauses by Henry. 'You're going to score tonight,' he tells him. The two sides head out of the Maine Road tunnel for the second time in four days. United's numerical advantage in the crowd is even greater for the replay. The harsh reality of life for many in Oldham is that, with a Wembley trip to pay for and following cup match after cup match, they simply cannot afford the price of another ticket and, as a result, their numbers are a couple of thousand down on those who were present on Sunday.

In the makeshift studio perched between the North Stand

and Kippax there is excitement. Des Lynam and Jimmy Hill cannot wait for what is in store. Asked for a prediction, Hill says he believes that Oldham are the more balanced of the two sides. The BBC are getting their money's worth from Royle who, earlier in the week, followed in the footsteps of the likes of Racquel Welch, Rock Hudson and Joan Collins when he was a guest on BBC1's prime-time *Wogan* show.

If anything, despite fewer numbers, the noise – this time from a crowd under floodlights – is louder. This time United come out on the attack, but it is Oldham who have the first opportunity when Marshall gets a boot to Pallister's attempted backpass. The striker manages to get to the ball just before it goes out of play and dinks it over Leighton but it drops just behind the goal.

On five minutes, a corner. In the commentary booth, Trevor Brooking remembers that the first goal came from a corner at a similar time. Rick Holden whips it in. It hits the post with Leighton nowhere near it. Two minutes later, another corner. Redfearn plays it short to Rick Holden, who crosses. McClair heads clear but only as far as Henry, on the edge of the box.

With his boss's pre-match words ringing in his ears, he chests it down and hits it with his right on the volley. Leighton dives to his left and gets a touch but cannot stop it. The ball hits the bar and drops down a yard behind the line. The Oldham fans erupt. Behind the goal, in the North Stand, a United fan puts his hands against his face in despair. But something strange happens. Leighton catches the ball when it bounces back into play and belts it up the field. United play on as if nothing has happened. Crucially, Joe Worrall – who is perfectly positioned to see where the ball has dropped – also plays on. And, just like that, the goal is not given. Henry screams at the referee. So does

Redfearn. But they have to get on with it because United are on the attack and within seconds Hallworth is diving to his right to deny Webb. 'Every promise of Sunday afternoon continued,' says Davies, back in the chair.

The basketball game continues. Holden and Phelan tussle on the touchline. The ball goes out for a throw. Phelan refuses to let go of Holden's leg. When he does, the winger throws the ball at his back, takes the rebound and sends over a cross which Leighton just manages to hold under pressure. Absolute genius. 'Full of enterprise, this Oldham side,' says a laughing Davies, who is by now a convert to the Church of Royle.

Hughes stings Hallworth's palms, Ritchie fires across Leighton but narrowly wide. And so it goes and goes on a glistening pitch following a day of rain. Leighton gets down well to deny Marshall from long range after Ritchie tees him up with a glorious touch as the ball dropped from the sky. 'The pace is unrelenting,' purrs Davies. Marshall, however, has picked up a thigh strain stretching for the shot and does not come out for the second half. Paul Warhurst comes on and heads up top to partner Ritchie.

In the first clash, United's second and third goals featured large slices of luck. Someone is smiling down on them. It happens again. Wallace, whose mishit cross was part of the build up to Webb putting his side 2-1 up, hits another aimless centre, which strikes Henry. The ball ricochets dangerously across goal. Hallworth dives forward but cannot get there. McClair taps in. Out of nothing, and thanks to yet another twist of good fortune, United have scored. Again, they have the lead. Again, Royle gets creative. His response is to bring off Barlow and send on Roger Palmer.

Time ticks by. Rick Holden continues to torment Phelan, who has to hack him down when he is beaten yet again. The yellow card comes out. It exists! Irwin belts the free-kick low and true. It strikes his fellow Irishman Milligan in the chest, wrongfoots Leighton and looks to be rolling into the goal, but it hits the post and bounces clear. For the third time tonight, Oldham have struck the woodwork. They keep up the pressure. Leighton brilliantly tips a Milligan volley wide of the post. 'This is a fine comeback by Oldham Athletic,' says Davies.

Amid the onslaught Ferguson drops Robson back alongside Bruce and Pallister. The blue waves continue to roll but there are only 10 minutes to play. Royle tells Andy Holden to go up front. Oldham will not die wondering what may have been.

A free-kick wide on the right, in United's half. Ferguson makes as though he is going to bring on a sub. There is a delay. Royle, for the first time, snaps and asks him if he is going to do it or not. He is not. It is a time-wasting technique.

Amid the boos of the Oldham fans, Holden slips it to Irwin, whose low cross is nodded away by a diving Ince. Irwin picks up the loose ball and passes forwards to Milligan, in the area, with his back to goal. The midfielder slides it wide to Holden who hits over another low cross which is deflected back to him by Robson, the makeshift defender. He feigns right but goes left and Robson is done for. There is room for another cross.

Over it comes, towards Palmer and Barrett, who is now attacking. Webb, arguably United's best player, launches himself forwards through the air and gets a touch. It takes it beyond everyone in the centre of the box towards the far post where Ritchie stands. He has waited a long time for this. The United fans, presumably oblivious to what has happened this season, have often chanted 'United reject', when their former striker has touched the ball throughout the two ties. But this is about more than shutting up a few morons. Ritchie loved United. He is a Manchester boy, a United fan. The decision to leave was his, but it should not have been like that. It felt unjust.

The ball flies across him at speed. There is no time to use his right. In a fraction of a second he opens his body. In the same, measured movement, he sidefoots it with his left. It explodes off his boot, above a despairing Leighton, and crashes – crashes – into the roof of the net. The Platt Lane erupts again and it is carnage in the corner of the Kippax. The tie is level again.

'Andy Ritchie,' says an almost gleeful Davies, 'the man who began his career as a teenager at Old Trafford, has beaten Jim Leighton and again, in this quite remarkable FA Cup semi-final, it is all square.'

As his team-mates celebrate, Andy Holden turns to his bench and asks Royle if he should go back into defence.

The manager thinks about it. Even in the madness unfolding around him, he retains his belief that promotion is the priority. His side simply cannot afford another replay if they are to make it to the promised land, where they can take on the likes of United twice a season. He tells the Welshman to stay up front. It is a risk and he knows it. Ferguson keeps Robson in defence..

* * * * *

All the noise is now coming from the Oldham supporters. Phelan sends a cross out for a goal kick and there are loud boos from the United fans.

Worrall blows. Another 30 minutes. Extra-time.

United, clearly under new instructions, come out on the attack. A Phelan cross is cleared as far as Ince, 30 yards out, who thrashes it at goal with his left foot. Hallworth can barely move before it is past him, but it hammers against the post. The tempo slows. Oldham are still playing five up front. Ferguson brings on Robins. The first period ends with little drama. The second begins. Rick Holden takes the ball on the left. Phelan invites him inside. He accepts the invitation and hits a deep cross with his right toward the far post. Redfearn is underneath it with Colin Gibson, the United defender. Redfearn gets his head on it. It bounces down into the turf. Leighton is scrambling. It hits the side-netting.

Still Oldham attack. Redfearn cuts inside Ince but the United man, sliding, executes the perfect tackle and wins it back. Danger. Gibson plays it forwards to Hughes who gives it him back. He dinks it over the heads of Oldham's back three for Phelan, who has surged down the right. Barrett comes across from the centre to deal with it. Phelan touches it inside him.

There is nobody there for Oldham. Andy Holden, having heeded his manager's instructions, watches from the other half of the field. This was the gamble. Robins, the substitute with the fresh legs and killer instinct, the Oldham boy, picks it up and heads through the giant gap towards goal. Hallworth, exposed, races forwards. Robins takes one touch, two touches, and coolly stabs it across the goalkeeper. Time stands still. To those on the bench it looks like it is heading wide. It is not. It creeps inside the far post. United lead. United lead.

A few miles away, a cab leaves Manchester Piccadilly station with the Inspiral Carpets in the back. They have returned from London, where they have signed their first big deal. Keyboardist

Clint Boon has already spent some of his royalties on a battery-operated portable television. For the whole of the journey back from the capital he has tried – and failed – to tune it in to BBC One. All he has managed to do is get the sound, which has kept them updated. Now, within sight of home and as if by magic, a picture appears. The grainy images show Robins wheeling away in celebration. Graham Lambert, next to Boon, sinks back into his seat.

Five minutes to go. Four, three, two. 'We're by far the greatest team, the world has ever seen,' sing the same United supporters who were, less than half an hour ago, berating that team.

Into the last minute. An Oldham throw, midway inside the United half. Rick Holden hurls it to Milligan, who volleys it to Palmer who heads it to Ritchie, out wide on the left. He looks up. He sees Leighton off his line. He hits it with his right foot. Leighton backpedals, frantically, dives half sideways, half backwards, stretches out a white-gloved palm and just touches it behind for a corner. Redfearn sprints across to take it. The cross eludes all but Rick Holden, who controls, but Phelan, who just will not give up, manages to boot it into touch.

The whistles are deafening. One last chance. Hallworth volleys it down the field and it drops for Ritchie, who exchanges passes with Rick Holden and heads down the left. He beats Danny Wallace and there is room for a cross. He pulls it back to the edge of the six-yard box. Palmer is there and he is in space. Surely, surely not? Palmer turns and angles his body for the shot but there is no time for that. The ball cannons off his leg and goes high, high, over the bar. A glorious opportunity is lost. On the United bench Ferguson turns to his nearest member of staff and embraces them. He then checks his watch and wonders how many beats per minute his heart is doing. Leighton's clearance goes the full length of the field. Hallworth catches and immediately belts it back.

'Oldham fear it may all be over,' says Davies, whose timing is a work of art. Worrall blows his whistle. 'And all over it is now.' And it is. Those in blue sink to their knees as Robins is hoisted aloft on the shoulders of delirious pitch invaders. Finally, in this momentous, ludicrous season, Oldham have lost a cup match. It is a cruel, cruel exit and the realisation dawns immediately.

The reality is that the semi-final could easily have gone the other way. With a better referee it may well have done. Royle's men could have been at Wembley twice in the same season. But they are not. Instead, those racing onto the field from the stands are wearing the red, white and black scarves of United. All that is left for Oldham's supporters is to applaud their team from the field and to make their way quietly into the Moss Side evening.

In the BBC studios they go to Lynam and Hill. Someone from production has clearly had a word and suggested it might be a good idea to talk about the Henry goal that was not given. The replay is shown and finally the question of whether the ball was over the line is belatedly asked. Then it is down to Ferguson who points out that this could be a turning point for his club, before declaring that Oldham are the best team they have played against this season.

In the Oldham dressing room, it is deathly quiet. They have been beaten in a cup match at the 17th time of asking. There is a burning sense of injustice and anger which grows when Henry's goal is shown on the monitor. 'It's over the fucking line,' one of the group shouts. The silence that follows is broken by a knock on the door. The globally recognisable bald head of Bobby Charlton, Manchester United legend and England World Cup winner, appears. Charlton, dressed in his black United blazer and club tie, almost apologetically shuffles in. He quietly congratulates the players, tells them that they should be proud of themselves and adds that they were desperately unlucky to lose, before shaking hands and leaving them to their misery. It is a magnificent gesture from one of the sport's greatest names.

Royle leaves his weary men and heads out to see the press. The corridor is still noisy with celebrating United players and staff. Almost immediately he is asked about Henry's goal. Remarkably, he gives a dignified response that even contains a little humour. 'The referee can't see that from his angle unless he's got a Russian linesman,' he says, with a nod to England's third goal in the 1966 World Cup final. The reality is that inside he is seething but he is an intelligent man who knows that there is little point in criticising the official after the act.

He is full of praise for his side. 'I am so proud of them,' he says. 'We have been true to ourselves, we have tried to play football, we have not come near a booking. But semi-finals are cruel.'

Ferguson repeats to the written press the message he gave to the BBC. 'They are the best team we have met this season and they are out of place in the Second Division,' he says. 'I just hope now they win the Littlewoods Cup. No disrespect to Brian Clough, but they certainly deserve something from the way they played this season.' He is asked to qualify. Does he mean that? That he thinks that Oldham are a better side than champions-in-waiting Liverpool?

'They are a tremendous side,' he adds. 'They are so quick, they never let you settle for a moment and they play. You are fully extended all the time, and what other side would play with just one centre-half against us? Would Liverpool?'

The stress was clearly visible on his face throughout and he is in no mood to deny it. 'I've never felt such pressure, so much strain in a game,' says a man who won the European Cup Winners' Cup with previous club Aberdeen.

Robins also faces the media. 'I don't know what sort of reception I'll get when I get home,' he jokes, all smiles.

The following day's papers heap on more praise. Stephen Bierley, back at Maine Road for *The Guardian*, writes: 'It would be a hard man or woman who did not feel a little sympathy for Oldham Athletic.' But Royle cannot allow his players to feel sorry for themselves. They are three points outside the play-off places and, less than 36 hours after Worrall called time on their FA Cup dream, they will face league leaders and old enemies Leeds United at Boundary Park.

As things transpire, Good Friday is not a bridge too far. Leeds, incredibly, are despatched 3-1 in front of an appreciative crowd of more than 16,000 on a sunny afternoon that almost feels like a homecoming. The scoreline flatters Howard Wilkinson's side, who must be sick of the sight of Oldham. Rick Holden scores two, Frank Bunn gets the other. The gap on the play-off places narrows to two points, but the games keep coming and the injuries arrive with them.

Easter Monday sees a trip to Port Vale which ends in the down-to-earth thump of a 2-0 defeat. Wednesday night and it is Plymouth Argyle, at the other end of the country. Seven days have passed since the United replay and Oldham have played three times. Another 2-0 defeat arrives and, just like that, all seems lost. They are now seven points off the play-offs. At one point at relegation-threatened Plymouth, Oldham are playing with a 3-3-4 formation. If it looks desperate, it is because it is.

A relatively huge gap of three days follows before West Ham are blown away 3-1 on the plastic, with Bunn and Ritchie's partnership picking up where it left off before Bunn picked up a knee injury that kept him out for three months. There is one more long trip to navigate before Wembley, a Tuesday night encounter at Portsmouth. The 60th game of the season ends in a sixth successive away defeat. Nick Henry twists his knee, Andy Holden suffers a season-ending hamstring injury, Earl Barrett picks up a concussion and Ian Marshall again misses out, having not played since the replay. Oldham are now five points outside the play-offs with four matches to play. The price of cup success is a heavy one and it is hardly ideal preparation for a first ever Wembley appearance.

As he reflects on his side's faltering form Royle begins to think that he would have been better off bringing Andy Holden back into defence at Maine Road and taking a replay, had it been needed. Hindsight is a wonderful thing.

CHAPTER TWENTY-SIX

Wem-ber-lee

ANDY Ritchie is in a pickle. After the two-legged victory over West Ham the players, looking for ways to supplement their income, held a meeting about Wembley and the potential for making a few quid on the side via endorsements. Thrifty Mike Milligan told them that he could sort a deal with Japanese sportswear firm Mizuno for boots for those who did not already have boot deals, which amounted to most of the squad. When it came to the suits, it was widely thought that Phil Black would look after them, but Ritchie said he knew a man and told the group he could get them a better deal. Some were dubious, given Ritchie is not known as the most sartorially elegant member of the group, but he was given the green light.

With just days to go, the contact has let him down and he is now beyond desperate. Cup final suits are a big deal, part of the tradition of English football. The players do their walkaround of the stadium wearing them, and like to be at their best for the television cameras. Ritchie swallows his pride, calls Black to relay the news and asks him if he can pull him out of the shit.

Black, laughing, agrees to help. He now has the task of finding somewhere that can fit and make 26 suits in the space of a few days. He makes a few calls to trader pals but there is no success.

Finally, he makes a breakthrough. A connection says he can help and he will come over to his swanky Manchester store to show him what he has. The man turns up at the shop with a sample suit under his arm. It is all Black can do to stop himself from laughing again. The suit, to be frank, is dreadful.

For a start, it is made of linen and is a pale shade of grey. Add to that, it has shoulder pads that would not look out of place under an American football jersey and giant lapels that a 1950s Teddy Boy would be proud of. Black thinks it is funny, but before saying yes, thinks he had better check with Royle. He puts the suit in his car and drives to Oldham to see the manager. Royle takes one look and immediately has a glint in his eye. 'Fantastic, Blacky,' he says. 'They'll do.'

When the players step out onto the famous turf in their last-minute attire, they will see 33,000 of their own supporters in the stadium. Tickets have sold out. It has been a gargantuan effort from the club's staff to ensure demand has been satisfied. Les Olive, who retired as Manchester United secretary two years ago after a lifetime's service, has been drafted in to help. Olive, who played for the club and who was made a United director after retirement, is a veteran of organising trips to Wembley and his help has been invaluable.

It has not all gone without a hitch, however. As part of the project, tickets were sold at the turnstiles to ease congestion at the ticket office. In the Rochdale Road End, they ran out of the cheapest tickets, priced at £15, and another box was sent for. When the new box arrived, it was quickly opened and the tickets sold. It was only later on when the realisation came that the new box contained £25 tickets. When it came to balance the money against the value of the tickets, they were £15,000 short.

There were many tasks to be completed. The Football Association needed a copy of the club's badge for the flag which will fly high above Wembley, along with that of Nottingham Forest. Secretary Terry Cale picked up a sponsorship brochure, which was green-coloured but which had the badge in the middle of it, and sent it to London.

On a midweek TV show, Rhodes and Rick Holden performed a sketch of the Smith and Jones TV comedy, where they sit opposite each other, foreheads almost touching, and discussed the Oldham squad and manager.

'How is Brian Clough different from our manager?' asked Rhodes. 'Well,' said Holden. 'He wins trophies.'

Back in the studio, Royle laughed. 'That's two late team changes,' he told presenter Elton Welsby. The pair were in their element. 'Have you been to Wembley before?' asked Holden. 'Yeah, I went down to Live Aid,' responds Rhodes, referring to the historic 1985 benefit concert. 'Who won?' said Holden.

'Well,' Rhodes responded, 'nobody as such – it was like mankind winning over famine.'

'What was the score?'

'Well, it was like all the money raised. It was like mankind millions, famine nil.'

Holden then delivered the punchline. 'You weren't the famine goalkeeper, were you?' he asks.

There has also been a photoshoot with the Inspiral Carpets for *Shoot!*, the children's football magazine. The band descended on Boundary Park, all baggy jeans and bright-coloured cagoules, posing for a variety of staged snaps with Andy Ritchie, Nick Henry and Frank Bunn. The article, complete with puns linking the band with the plastic carpet pitch and an 'Oldham Rave On' sign, appears in the mag the week of the final.

It has been decided that the players will travel to London on Saturday, for the Sunday fixture. Royle had wanted to head down earlier, but his squad wanted to keep things as normal as possible and, on this occasion, he is happy to listen to them.

It is a good job for Milligan that he had. Friday comes and there is still no sign of the Mizuno boots he has promised his team-mates. There is widespread panic throughout the squad. Eventually, they arrive that afternoon and his relief is palpable. Some are not impressed. 'They're fucking heavy, these,' observes Nick Henry. If they are wearing new boots they could have done with a couple of training sessions to break them in.

Two coaches have been arranged for the trip. One for the players and staff and one for their families. They travel down to the Marriott, in Slough, and on a restless Saturday night, many cannot sleep. When Sunday arrives, it is absolutely baking. The temperature that afternoon, in the 80s, will ensure that Wembley will be like a furnace.

The group already knows the team because Royle had pinned it on a wall before they had set off. He has made a huge call. Andy Rhodes will come in from the cold and take his place in goal instead of Jon Hallworth. Royle has agonised over the decision all week. He knows his regular first choice will be distraught, but he thinks that he had a 'nervous' semi-final and is concerned that, in front of 75,000, there will be a repeat. He does not discuss the decision with Hallworth. No words will improve the situation.

What also fails to improve the situation for the dropped goalkeeper is his suit. Hallworth is rooming with Neil Adams.

He pulls his suit out of the bag. His jacket fits but his trousers barely go below his knees. 'For fuck's sake,' he exclaims. Adams takes one look at his team-mate and starts laughing. He knows he should not, that he is not having a great day, but he cannot help himself. Hallworth mutters another expletive and puts a tracksuit on. In another room, Nick Henry puts his suit on. The sleeves of his jacket cover his arms. On their big day, the players of Oldham Athletic are not going to look like catwalk models.

Like Hallworth, Ian Marshall has not made the cut. His thigh has not responded to treatment. He has failed a fitness test and he is inconsolable. Oldham are the walking wounded. Royle is hoping that the adrenalin triggered by the occasion will see them through. Henry will have cortisone injections into his knee. Frank Bunn will start but his knee continues to give him discomfort. Denis Irwin needs a minor operation but is playing through the pain, as is Milligan.

The two coaches make their way towards Wembley and when they get within view of the famous old stadium, those onboard can barely believe what they are seeing. The area is a sea of blue and white. It looks like the whole of Oldham has turned out. As the team bus makes its way through the crowds, thousands of well-wishers, with flags and banners, roar their support. None of Oldham's supporters have gone inside the stadium until they have sent their team on the way.

Some of the players, including Ritchie, are close to tears. This is what it means. Never before in the history of Oldham Athletic has there been a day like this.

For one member of the party it is not the first time that he has represented Oldham at the iconic venue. Andy Barlow played for Oldham schoolboys rugby league team in a curtain raiser to the 1977 Challenge Cup Final. Oldham took on Hull and in the tunnel their opponents from East Yorkshire, with a number of bigger boys in their ranks, were throwing their weight around, telling Barlow and his pals that they were going to get smashed. Oldham won. He thinks back to that day and is confident the underdog will prevail once more.

The staff and families' coach follows behind. As their vehicle pulls within view, Hardy's commercial assistant, Gordon Lawton, looks up at the twin towers. 'What the fucking hell is that?' he asks, pointing towards the sky. The flag of Oldham Athletic, who play in blue, is flying proudly above the national stadium. It is bright green. Cale had presumed that whoever picked up the green brochure at the FA would know what Oldham's actual colours were. He was wrong.

On the other side of Wembley Way a minibus carrying the Inspiral Carpets crawls along. The band have been spotted and groups of kids are holding up *Shoot!* magazines for them to sign. Their new album, *Life*, has rocketed to number two in the charts, second only to *The Best of the Carpenters. This Is How It Feels* went as high as number 14. They are currently on tour and have headed down the M1 from Sheffield's Octagon, where they played a sold-out gig the previous night.

Once they are inside, the players give their television interviews in their shiny suits. It is sweltering and the cheap fabric ensures they are all sweating when they get to the cool sanctuary of the dressing room.

Royle's message is a simple one. As a teenager for Everton, he appeared at Wembley, hardly had any touches of the ball and vowed to learn from his experience. 'Make sure you enjoy it,' he tells his players. 'Settle quickly. Enjoy it. This is an experience you may never have again.'

Not everyone thinks his side are underdogs. In *The Times*, Stuart Jones has them down as marginal favourites. Forest have only won one in 10 and Brian Clough joked in the build-up that the coach driver was the only person he knew would be making the trip. But they are a fine side. Their ranks feature three England internationals who played against Czechoslavakia in midweek. In Des Walker and Stuart Pearce, they boast two of the finest defenders on the planet. Nigel Clough, the manager's son, is a smart striker who has inherited his father's eye for goal.

The players line-up in the tunnel. Pearce tries to throw his weight around, aggressively shouting to anyone who will listen about what he is going to do. Barlow's mind again returns to that schoolboy rugby match. Royle leads his team out into the bright sunshine alongside Clough Sr and savours the moment. This is what it is all about.

* * * * *

The national anthem is sung, the Duchess of Kent is greeted, and Forest kick-off. As they have done so many times, Oldham start quickly. Irwin, on the right, passes forward to Ritchie who, with one touch, flicks it to Adams. The little winger knocks the ball past his marker, Pearce, who stumbles, wrongfooted, and he is away up the touchline, to a huge roar. Cover comes over but instead of crossing, Adams sees keeper Steve Sutton off his line and tries to chip him. The shot, hit with power, is too quick for Sutton and his outstretched arm but it drops over the bar and onto the roof of the net. So close to a perfect start.

Forest stir, and Rhodes gets some confidence when he palms away a header from winger Franz Carr. It is a frantic opening.

At the other end, Holden finds room on the left and crosses for Adams, who is free at the far post, but he rushes his header and it drifts wide before Ritchie stings Sutton's palms from distance. The breakthrough will not arrive. Forest look ominously fresh and dangerous on the break. Rhodes, who is justifying his selection, pushes a Garry Parker shot around the post. As the break approaches, Milligan beautifully sets up Adams but his shot is wild and wide, while Carr does similar at the other end. Royle, on the Oldham bench, is in a shirt and tie for the occasion along with aviator shades. He chews his nails. Perhaps for the first time this year he looks nervous.

Half-time comes and there is an issue. As Milligan wrenches his boot off in the dressing room he is in agony. A roll down of the sock reveals multiple blisters. His team-mates report the same issue. New boots and a bone-dry surface do not mix well. Oldham have shaded the opening 45 but, after an entertaining start, it has become a cagey affair.

Up in the commentary booth the compliments keep coming. 'If you didn't know, you wouldn't think they were the Second Division side,' Liverpool legend Ian St John explains.

A marching band clears the famous field and Oldham kick-off and again attack. Irwin blasts a free-kick into the wall before Bunn, who has been quiet, hits one on the half-volley miles over the bar. It is not like him. 'Forest can't get out of their own half at the moment,' says Brian Moore for ITV.

Sutton sends the resulting goal-kick deep and Nigel Jemson, the small Forest striker, somehow nips in front of Barrett to win the header. Jemson's flick finds Clough, who turns and runs towards the Oldham area, taking Warhurst with him. The speed of the counter has caught those in blue by surprise. Jemson has continued his run and Clough slides it inside Warhurst. Barrett is not there to cover. The pass is timed to perfection. Jemson has a clean run at Rhodes. He sidefoots at goal and the keeper stops it brilliantly with his legs. At this point, the ball could rebound anywhere, but it rolls back to the striker who taps it into the open goal. The cheers of the Forest fans are drowned out with anguished cries of 'Come on Oldham' but the First Division team has a precious lead, against the run of play.

Suddenly, Oldham are ragged. Rhodes is forced to handle outside the area and from the resulting free-kick Earl Barrett gets his head in the way of a ferocious Pearce piledriver and collapses to the floor. Following his concussion at Portsmouth, it will be his second headache of the week. 'Incredibly brave,' says Jimmy Greaves.

Bunn is not right. He has not been the same since his injury and Royle decides to act. He takes him off and replaces him with Palmer. When the chants of 'Ooh Roger Palmer,' the Chaddy End staple, are belted out at the national stadium, it is almost surreal.

Forest have grown in confidence. The goal is priceless. They are at their best on the counter and now they have a lead to hold onto against a team in its 61st match which may be on the verge of wilting in the North London sunshine.

Twenty minutes remain when Warhurst sends a free-kick long into the Forest box. Ritchie flicks it on towards Palmer, who contorts his body and guides his header towards the far corner. It is beyond Sutton and it is heading into the goal. Oldham are attacking their own end of the stadium and the fans are on their feet, in the early throes of celebration. All that is left is for it to hit the back of the net. It does not. Sutton, somehow and with the ball behind him, has performed an almost-backwards dive and, one-handed, has managed to claw the ball away from its joyous destiny. Instead there is agony.

Oldham pile on the pressure. The attacks almost always end with the intervention of the magnificent Walker. Warhurst, perhaps playing his best game of the season, blasts one just the wrong side of Sutton's post while Henry's touch deserts him just yards from goal.

Ten minutes remain but Oldham are visibly shattered. Forest are snuffing out every attack and are now looking the more likely scorers. Walker is righty named man-of-the-match. Two minutes. Not a sniff. Every cross is being cleared. Into the last minute. 'It looks as though poor old Joe Royle and Oldham will go away empty handed with the one consolation, and a big one it is, that they have given a lot of people such a lot of pleasure up and down the country this season,' says Moore. One final attack. Holden's cross. This time Pearce volleys clear. The whistle blows. It is over. Again, the blue shirts sink to their knees. There is to be no Littlewoods Cup. No major silverware. This incredible season will not produce a trophy.

Royle heads on to the pitch. 'Well done, lad,' he says to Irwin, patting the defender on the head. A similar message is delivered to the rest of what is a devastated group. 'We love you Oldham, we do' is sung by the thousands in blue and white. 'They have to be proud of their team,' says Moore, and they are. There may not be a trophy but nobody imagined this. If anyone, at the start of the season, would have promised a Wembley final they would have been laughed out of a town that scarcely cared for its football team. And now this. 33,000 decked in club colours. Husbands, wives, children, grandparents, all on Latics' big day out.

Milligan sprints up the steps to get his losers' medal. He wants to get this out of the way. It is the quickest losers' parade in history. Ian Stott, enjoying his day next to royalty, shakes hands but the players want to be anywhere but there.

Forest head up and lift the trophy. Royle, on the pitch, gets a tap on the shoulder. It is Clough, in his famous green jumper. 'Come on, young man,' the legendary Forest boss says. 'Let's you and me go and get a drink.'

The players, still disconsolate, head towards their fans. It is only then that the penny drops. There is nothing to be ashamed of. There is a sea of smiling faces. A population that wants to give thanks for what they have received.

Not so long ago, Oldham were lucky to get 5,000 braving the elements at Boundary Park. This group, with its swashbuckling, no limits, beautiful football, has filled half of Wembley stadium. They are the toast of not only Oldham, but the nation. They have illuminated a town, they have won an army of new followers. The applause is for them.

In the tunnel, before they can get that drink, Clough and Royle are stopped for an interview. 'I couldn't believe how well Oldham played,' the Forest boss says. 'But I did warn everybody beforehand.'

'I'm very proud of them,' says Royle. 'A little bit tired in one or two positions but over the competition we've been great.'

'I hope it's not going to be a season where you dip out on everything,' interviewer Gary Newbon asks.

'Let's get today out of the way,' Royle responds. 'We'll recharge the batteries and then go again Tuesday, Thursday, Saturday, Monday.' Four games in seven days to save a season.

The managers eventually shake hands and head to the dressing rooms. Clough, who has bizarrely been blanking match-winner Jemson, jumps in the Forest bath, while down the corridor it is a more sombre atmosphere in Oldham's.

There is silence. It is broken when Andy Holden, who has watched the match with his wife, enters the room. 'I want to tell you all how proud I am,' he says. 'Each and every one of you. For what you have done out there and for what you have done this season. I am proud of all of you. What you've achieved has been unbelievable.'

One man who has had a better afternoon than most is Marshall. With his head in bits, he had headed straight for the bar in the executive section of the stadium before kick-off. Inside, he had heard the familiar booming tones of Neil Kinnock, leader of the opposition Labour Party. Marshall, never one for being backwards about coming forwards, made a beeline for the bald Welshman. 'My dad loves you,' he told him. The pair immediately hit it off, before drinking the bar dry for the rest of the afternoon.

After showering and changing, the players head to the coach. But it will not be taking them straight home. Before the match, in what had seemed like a good idea, a reception dinner had been organised with families at a pub and restaurant in Northampton. None of the players are in the mood for it.

After arriving, they head to the bar before being called into the restaurant for their meals. Marshall takes some convincing. He had been under the impression that they would be going straight back to Oldham. 'I just want to fucking go home,' he says, loudly. Eventually, after kicking down a toilet door, he enters the main room and, thanks to his late arrival, there are no seats left on the tables with his fellow players so he has to sit on a table of directors and their wives. One of the wives, with no ill-will intended, can see he is upset and asks him what the matter is. 'What's the matter?' he says, loudly, attracting the attention of others including his manager. 'None of us wants to fucking be here! We want to go back to our town. We want to go home.'

With that he storms out, sending his chair skidding across the floor. There is an uneasy silence. Marshall heads back to the bar. Rick Holden follows him and tries to settle things down.

Perhaps it is the weight of the occasion, the emotion of defeat, or the effect of a day spent under a blazing sun. For whatever reason, something in Royle snaps. He has seen enough. To the amazement of those present, Royle charges out of his own chair and heads to the bar. 'What the fuck do you think you are doing?' he roars when he confronts his striker. Marshall gives it back to his manager. 'Fucking shut up, horse head' is his less than subtle retort. By this time, other players have gathered.

The red mist has descended. Royle, a big man, grabs hold of the nearest object he can find, which happens to be a bar stool. The players are stunned. He is not, is he? He is. As if he was picking up a pebble, Royle holds the stool above his head. He is going to throw a bar stool at one of his players. Ritchie and Adams react the quickest and hurl themselves in between the pair. They are joined by Willie Donachie. 'Whoa, whoa,' someone shouts, as a melee ensues. Ritchie manages to grab the furniture and disaster is averted.

Royle walks off in disgust. He knows Marshall can be a pain in the arse and he often loves him for it, but this was a bridge too far. Emotions are running high. It was not meant to be like this.

The following night, an open-top bus tour takes place. The streets of a previously indifferent town are packed for the homecoming. Local television and radio are there. 'I want you to turn up to tomorrow's game,' says Royle. 'We're going to get promotion for you instead.' As he gazes out from the balcony of the Civic Centre to thousands of smiling faces, Royle is reminded of a conversation he had with a stayaway in his early years. 'We've never had any glamour, any cup runs,' he was told. 'If that happens, the crowds will come.'

'We kept our part,' he tells the masses. 'And you kept yours.'

Around the same time Royle addresses his adoring masses, the Inspirals are due to see theirs. The group are backstage for the latest date on their tour at Nottingham Rock City, a grand old venue known for its raucous acoustics. From their dressing room they can hear another packed house being whipped into a frenzy ahead of their arrival on stage in what has become a continuously euphoric moment. Tonight, however, is different. Tonight, as they walk into the light, the familiar, deafening cheers, are absent. Instead, 2,000 Nottinghamshire voices greet them with boisterous, cheeky chants of 'Brian Clough's red and white army!' The group laugh. Lead singer Tom Hingley fires back with an 'Ooh Roger Palmer' and they launch into their set.

CHAPTER TWENTY-SEVEN

Four Games, Seven Days

THIS is the equation: Oldham are eight points away from a play-off place with two games in hand. They have four games to play in a week. The first, on Tuesday, is the visit of lowly Oxford United to Boundary Park. Following the civic reception, Royle's men are again greeted like heroes when they emerge from the tunnel by a crowd of close to 13,000. They will not be deserted now. Incredibly, they summon more energy. A Rick Holden hat-trick helps them to a 4-1 win in an utterly dominant display. Oxford do not have a shot on target until the final 15 minutes.

But Sunderland, who occupy the final play-off place, win at Port Vale. The Wearsiders' victory means Oldham have to beat Wolves, two days later, to keep their slim hopes alive. In the 63rd game of their season, they are leggy. The visitors, themselves with an outside chance of promotion, squander a host of chances. On 39 minutes, Oldham take the lead against the run of play when Roger Palmer stabs home after Willie Donachie – now in the squad and playing thanks to the injury crisis – flicks on a corner.

At half-time, Milligan succumbs to the problem that has been plaguing him for months. This is the bare bones. Oldham hang on, but with two minutes to play a slip from Paul Warhurst opens a gap and substitute Tim Steele equalises. With that, hopes of promotion pretty much vanish. While it is mathematically possible, Oldham need to win their last two matches and hope that Blackburn lose their final game of the season. Royle tells Bob Young in the *Chron* that Warhurst's mistake is not what has cost them promotion.

'I have my own theories and we'll be making every effort to rectify the problem,' he says. The problem does not take a rocket scientist to solve. It is the inability to win matches away from the fortress. Oldham have lost 13 times in the league and 12 of those defeats have come on the road.

By the time they make the journey to the north-east on Saturday, Sunderland have now assured themselves of that play-off spot.

For the trip to Roker Park, Royle is without Ian Marshall, Andy Holden, Denis Irwin, Mike Milligan, Nick Henry and Frank Bunn. Donachie, at 38, starts again. To make matters worse, Warhurst limps off with a hamstring strain. But something strange happens. The makeshift side not only win, but they score three goals through Adams, Ritchie and Palmer, with Sunderland managing two in response. News, however, filters through that Blackburn have drawn and there will be no promotion this season. Their fate is sealed.

At the final whistle there is another strange occurrence. The Sunderland supporters swarm onto the pitch and make their way towards the terrace where the 2,000 Oldham fans are stood. There is concern that trouble is about to rear its ugly head but there does not need to be. Those in the red and white striped shirts are passionate, decent, football-loving people. Like the rest of the nation, they have watched this team in front of them in blue on their televisions all winter. They have no intention of causing trouble. They want to show their appreciation. In almost surreal scenes, the Sunderland supporters shake hands with Oldham's players before applauding those who have made their way to the north-east.

The final leg on this incredible 65-game marathon is a Bank Holiday Monday trip across the Pennines to relegated Bradford City. Oldham are so stretched that Andy Barlow plays in central defence. The curtain comes down on the most inspiring season in the club's history with a nondescript 1-1 draw.

After the match, the travelling party stops off at a pub close to the M62. The manager and directors gather in the lounge, while the players head to the pool room. That pool room looks like a war zone. Track-suited bodies are sprawled across chairs and tables. They can give no more. They can barely summon the strength to get to the bar.

Back in the lounge, the directors tell Royle that they would like to take him and Donachie out for dinner, later in the week, and that they both must come. Royle tells Donachie, who is his usual guarded self. 'Na,' he says. 'You go, you're the manager.' Royle insists. 'They've said you have to. It'll be nice, come on.' Reluctantly, Donachie agrees. The meal is at La Pergola, high in the Saddleworth hills. As Royle promised, it is an evening of fine food and fine company.

Following desserts, one of the directors delivers a speech of appreciation for what the two men have achieved. He then produces two small boxes. Inside each is an engraved Rolex. On the back, they are engraved with a message. 'Thanks for a memorable season. OAFC.' Donachie, from the Gorbals, has never even had a stopwatch before. He now has a Rolex.

At the end of the week, Royle attends an end-of-season Manager of the Year awards ceremony in London. He knows that he has not won, but it is nice to be invited. During the evening Brian Moore, who commentated on the Littlewoods Cup final, delivers a speech. He talks about 'the team which warmed the whole country throughout the winter months'.

Behind him, a giant screen starts to show highlights of Oldham's season, the giant killings of Arsenal and Everton, the massacre of West Ham. While they have not won promotion, or a trophy, the gravity of what Royle and his squad has achieved dawns on him, as he sits in his tuxedo, and a lump appears in his throat. Oldham's crowds have improved to a barely believable average of more than 11,000 but, given by the postmarks on the letters Royle receives, his team has made an impact right across the world.

CHAPTER TWENTY-EIGHT

Florida

MANCHESTER Airport, Departures. A group of excited young men are gathered waiting for the rest of their party to arrive before checking in. Walking towards them is a sight that has to be seen to be believed. The face is familiar but the attire is not. The late arrival is wearing lime green Lycra shorts. He is also sporting a cowboy-style tan leather jacket, complete with tassels that bounce from side to side as he walks.

On his head there is a novelty hat, which has two cans of Budweiser attached to each side and two plastic tubes that go from the cans to the wearer's mouth. To complete the look, the man is also carrying what looks like a tiny accountant's briefcase.

'What the fuck is that?' asks one of the group. That is Rick Holden, and he intends to enjoy himself.

The players and coaching staff have been treated to an 11-day trip to Clearwater, Florida, by a grateful board who are stunned at the returns their efforts have yielded. The club's bank balance has never looked better and it is only right that they are rewarded.

The group that heads across the Atlantic does not include Nick Henry, who has had to stay behind for a knee operation. What was always going to be a boozy trip started in a taxi carrying

Holden and Ian Marshall in the early hours of the morning and it goes steadily downhill from there. When quizzed over where his actual suitcase is, rather than the comedy one he is carrying, Holden tells his team-mates that this one contains everything he needs. 'Three pairs of underpants, three pairs of socks, three t-shirts.' Once a student, always a student.

Once checked in at the hotel, the players head to the beach, via the bar. They are told that if they are drinking in public, they will have to put their cans and bottles in a brown paper bag, so they are not on display in accordance with local laws.

And so a group of professional footballers, who got to Wembley and an FA Cup final just weeks before, head to the sands clutching little brown bags like a bunch of hobos.

The Floridian heat at this time of year is intense. Andy Ritchie, of pale complexion, is sunbathing at the side of his pal, Frank Bunn, who tends to turn brown. Ritchie has buried his feet in the sand and is quickly asking when they can head back to the cool, air-conditioned rooms of the hotel. What Ritchie has not realised is that the sand will offer little protection from the blazing rays. When they finally leave, he realises, but it is too late. His feet are lobster-red and have swollen considerably. When they go out later that night, Ritchie has to borrow a pair of shoes from Bunn, who is two sizes larger than him.

A hotel close to theirs has a nightclub underneath and quickly becomes a favourite haunt. That is, until Mike Milligan risks the wrath of the American police. Twelve months after their brush with the law in Magaluf, they are at it again. A 21st birthday party is being held in the club for a local girl and the venue is filled with helium balloons for the occasion. Milligan thinks it will be a good idea to deflate one of the balloons and sets about the task. It slips from his grasp, rises upwards towards one of the many rotating fans in the club and it explodes with a loud bang, taking out the power at the same time. It triggers hysteria and before long, the police arrive. The club is shut down for the evening amid initial suspicions that there has been some kind of gang shooting.

The swimming pool becomes the centre of activity in the daytime. One of the group has had to put his passport out to dry after being thrown in fully clothed. Milligan hatches another plan, and this time Jon Hallworth is his target. The goalkeeper has been drinking bottles of Budweiser like they have been going out of fashion and has already sunk a few when Milligan approaches the bar. He has taken half a dozen empties and filled them with pool water.

He asks the barmaid to put them in the fridge and hand them to Hallworth whenever he asks for a drink. She thinks that the English soccer players are funny and duly obliges. Hallworth, throat numbed by heavy drinking, is on his fourth doctored bottle before he realises something is amiss.

The shenanigans continue. Bill Urmson has come on the trip and is quickly at the centre of Milligan's next plan. Each night, he heads to bed at around midnight. On one of the evenings, Milligan and Andy Rhodes go to reception and claim that Mr Urmson, in their group, has lost his room key. The trusting receptionist duly hands one over. Clutching a bucket filled with ice-cold water they have found from somewhere, the sniggering footballers let themselves in and find the youth coach in a coma-like sleep. They drench him. Urmson awakes with a start, spots Milligan and chases after him.

Rhodes has escaped into the bathroom but cannot get out because Urmson, shaking his head and shivering, has come back into the room. The goalkeeper can hardly contain himself when the coach plants himself down on the loo, just on the other side of the shower curtain, behind which he is hiding. 'Fucking Milligan,' he is muttering to himself, 'I'll fucking have him.' Rhodes yanks the curtain back and makes a horrendous, banshee-like scream. Urmson, still on the toilet, jumps out of his skin for the second time in as many minutes.

The next morning at breakfast, Royle has the pair around his table. 'I'm not having that,' he says. 'You could have killed him, you're going back.'

The pair beg for forgiveness and are ultimately successful. The bollocking does not deter them, on another night, breaking into Urmson's room again and stealing all his clothes.

Royle again summons a meeting. 'Has anyone got anything to say?' All eyes go to the floor. 'Right,' Royle adds. 'If Bill's clothes aren't back in five minutes you're all going on the next flight home.'

Milligan manages to hoodwink the receptionist for a key again and swiftly replaces the missing items. In the corridor he passes Royle and utters what has become his catchphrase. 'It weren't me, gaffer.'

Gary Williams, the veteran squad man who has made a few substitute appearances, is next. Some of the players think he is spending too much time in his room so one of the group finds a newspaper, sticks half of it under his door and sets the other half on fire. Quickly, the smoke alarm sounds and security, brandishing guns, are on the scene.

It is the final straw and there are no more high-jinks, other than Milligan taking Urmson's new Casio watch, which he has not figured out how to use properly yet, and setting the alarm for 3am. When it goes off, he cannot figure out how to stop it.

'Nice night, Bill?' asks Milligan, the next morning.

The final two highlights of the trip concern Ritchie. All week, the players have been moaning about how tight he is. 'Always last to the bar,' the consensus. They have been taking it in turns to buy rounds. Twelve draft Buds at $2 each. Eventually, they drink the bar dry and all that is left are cans, which are half the size and twice the price. It is Ritchie's round and the group insist that he has to buy each player two cans, to make up for the lack of size.

Ritchie gets his own back, however, as they go for a walk down Clearwater's main street. They have been relatively anonymous throughout the trip, given America is yet to fall in love with soccer. But one local approaches the group. 'Hey,' he says to Ritchie. 'Are you that famous Andy Ritchie guy?' Ritchie, delighted, stops to have a chat with his trans-Atlantic fan. Anybody but him, is the consensus from the rest of the group. Andy Famous, the nickname Rhodes had bestowed on him, sticks.

PART THREE:

HISTORY BOYS
1990-91

CHAPTER TWENTY-NINE

Keeping The Dream Alive

OLD Trafford, one of world football's iconic landmarks, is looking a picture. The bright, warm sunshine reflects off the tens of thousands of bright red seats and the freshly-mowed green grass glistens after a drenching from the sprinklers. Even empty, its giant, wraparound two-tiered stands and towering Stretford End are an impressive sight.

Down on the pitch, Denis Irwin is being shown around. It is a little different from Boundary Park. Alex Ferguson is leading the charm offensive but the reality is that there is little need for it. From the moment he heard that Manchester United were interested in him, he was sold. At Oldham the players used to nip into the office before each match to have a look at the list of 'Brussels' set to attend. 'Brussels' was the term they used for scouts. The previous season had seen United's representative attend on a number of occasions. Before one midweek match, Irwin had noticed Ferguson at the top of the tunnel steps, deep in conversation with Royle.

A fee of £625,000 has been agreed between the two clubs. Ferguson impresses Irwin. He tells him about his plan to awaken the slumbering giant. He tells him that his performances against his own side in the two semi-finals were magnificent, and that he would expect more of the same. There is a spring in his step. After eventually defeating Oldham, United had gone on to lift the FA Cup after Crystal Palace took them to a replay. The trophy is Ferguson's first silverware and it has strengthened what was a precarious position and he believes it could kickstart an era of success at the club. The Scot tells the Irishman that, with the veteran Viv Anderson not far from retirement, there is a ready-made place in his side waiting for him.

Ferguson does not need to do anything else. Personal terms are agreed. Irwin, who Leeds United sent packing on a free transfer, who was set to drop into the Fourth Division until Joe Royle twisted Ian Stott's arm, becomes one of the most expensive full-backs in English football.

He is not the only departure. Despite the fact that their players tried to kick him off the park in the second instalment of the trilogy, despite the fact that Norman Whiteside was sent off for booting him in the air, Everton want Mike Milligan. If you cannot beat them, buy them. Milligan's central role in Oldham's exploits has led many to view him as the best midfielder outside the First Division. After some negotiations, Ian Stott gets his price. Oldham, for the first time, are to sell a player for £1m.

Milligan has reservations. He has been at Boundary Park for half a decade and he feels that there is unfinished business, with the club still in the Second Division. But he is also restless. He wants to play at the top and he wants to do it now. Terms are agreed. The mouthy kid who looked lost to the game, who was working in a Manchester sports department and on a building site, is on his way to one of the biggest clubs in the country. Oldham have banked £1.625m on two players who cost them nothing. Stott is a happy man.

Now, Royle's acumen will be tested like never before. He

believes Paul Warhurst can step in for Irwin at right-back. Neil Redfearn can come in from the right and partner Nick Henry in midfield.

Instead, he turns his attention to other parts of the field. Despite his late-season return, patience with Andy Rhodes's off-field antics has expired and he is sold to Dunfermline Athletic, in Scotland's Premier Division. It leaves Jon Hallworth as his only recognised goalkeeper. Royle has known for a long time who he wants. He remembers the performances of John Keeley, the Brighton keeper who has repeatedly prevented a cricket score when the two sides have met on the plastic.

The difference now is that he has the money to sign him. A fee of £240,000 is agreed. Keeley is on a flight to Romania with his Brighton team-mates when his agent, also on the trip, comes down to his seat and whispers that the deal is done. After a miserable few days on what has become a pointless pre-season tour, he heads to Boundary Park to discuss terms. Everything is quickly agreed. 'Anything else, gents?' asks Royle. 'Well,' says the agent. 'There is one thing. At Brighton, it was written in John's contract that the club would pay for his contact lenses.'

Royle thinks that the man is joking. He is not. For a moment, he ponders the merits of signing a goalkeeper with eyesight issues but Keeley has a superb record with Brighton, which Royle has seen for himself on more than one occasion, and the deal – including contact lenses – is done.

He also needs a striker. To universal dismay, Frank Bunn continues to struggle with his knee. Operations have not worked. Royle has long-admired David Currie, who was prolific for Darlington and Barnsley. Currie has struggled after a £1m move to Forest in January. Royle calls his old pal Brian Clough and for a fee of less than half of that, Currie – who has a look of the Queen frontman Freddie Mercury – has broken free of the City Ground and is on his way to Boundary Park. With a dry sense of humour and northern wit, he quickly fits in, despite a love for double denim which is relentlessly ridiculed.

While there is sadness at the losses of Irwin and Milligan, the Oldham public are not about to walk away. Royle has broken the club record transfer fees paid twice in weeks and the bulk of the squad that thrilled them every week has been retained. Season ticket sales double, to 5,000, and 5,000 more sign up as members. The four-year loan Hardy agreed for Latique has been repaid in one year. Another floor is added.

When he learns that the bookmakers, unconvinced, are offering 25-1 to win the title, Royle has an idea. He tells his board to back them, as insurance against bonus payments they would have to make to the players should they do so. The idea is met with nervous pessimism. 'You'll put the mockers on it!' the manager is told.

'This is too good to miss,' he tells them. 'For a start we've got a plastic pitch. Everyone hates it and we ain't going to lose many here. We need to improve our away form and we'll do that. You have to do it.' Eventually, they agree.

The theme of the forthcoming season will be Keeping the Dream Alive. A German pop band, Freiheit, released a song with the same title a couple of years ago and it plays while Royle is having dinner in a restaurant with directors. They agree that it is a fitting anthem.

The signs are good. The players have returned fit and in-shape. There is an unspoken desire to right the wrongs of the previous season. Royle gathers them in the players' lounge on their first day back. He also asks all the staff to join them. Office workers, tea ladies. Everyone is there. The message is clear – we are all in this together. He tells them that while last season was magnificent, they did not win anything. He urges them to remember those feelings – on that traumatic wet Wednesday night at Maine Road and under the baking Wembley Sunday sun – and use them as motivation.

'You should have been promoted,' he says. 'You will be promoted this year.' He tells them to forget the past. That they are good enough to be playing the top sides in the country every week, not just in cup competitions. Royle is not one for Churchillian speeches but his words, spoken quietly, are inspiring. He refers to the First Division as the 'promised land'. It is time to get down to business.

A Friday night pre-season trip to Halifax has captured the imagination. Rick Holden has arranged for a rare weekend outing of The Tuesday Club. Following the match on his old stomping ground, they will be making the short trip to the Golden Fleece. After a 3-0 victory, the group arrives and are greeted by Phil Brown, who is currently having a competition with Holden to see who can grow their hair the longest.

The Oldham winger remains a devotee of Mario Kempes and his team-mates believe he is modelling his look on the Argentina great's shoulder-length style. The beers flow. It has been a long day and at one point Holden, sat at the end of the bar, nods off, with his head resting against the wall. From somewhere an electric razor appears. With Holden still asleep, half of his flowing locks fall to the floor. Eventually, he stirs. On the other side of the bar he catches sight of himself in a mirror and does a double take. He turns his head to the side and the extent of the damage is revealed. After recovering from the initial shock, he turns to his team-mates and demands the identity of the culprit. Unsurprisingly, nobody steps forward.

There is now another issue, aside from the obvious. The players have to be at Boundary Park for a warm down training session at 9am the following morning. There is no time for Holden to get to a barber to even out his new do.

The cackle of laughter starts in the players' lounge. Holden is half bald, half flowing locks. The comparison is quickly made with Phil Oakey, the lead singer of 80s new romantic act The Human League. Holden walks around the group, stopping in front of those who were in the pub at the time of the crime. 'You're owed,' he says to each suspect, before moving onto the next. 'You're owed.'

The group head out onto the Astroturf where Royle catches his first glimpse. 'Fucking hell,' is his initial reaction. He cannot believe what he is seeing. The session, which was always going to be a light affair, rapidly deteriorates into a farce. The players cannot do anything other than collapse in laughter. Each sight of Holden triggers another fit of giggles. Royle has seen enough. After about 15 minutes he calls for the group's attention. 'Right you lot,' he says. 'Piss off home. I'll see you on Monday.'

Holden wisely uses the time to head to the barber's shop. When they return on Monday, both sides of his head are matching. There is more laughter.

While the serious business of promotion dominates the agenda, the humour remains. The team photo is a case in point. It is a substantial operation to get the whole of the squad together and in place. Finally, with everyone in position, they are ready but it is a typically windy day at Boundary Park and the ball in front of them will not stay still. Gordon Lawton, all 25-stone of him, has to get on his hands and knees and place some double-sided tape on the bottom of it, to much hilarity. Finally, they are ready, but a fraction of a second before the camera clicks and in a pre-planned move, Neil Redfearn and Nick Henry put one of their hands on each other's knee, instead of their own, and a glimpse of the squad's mischievous streak is captured for eternity.

Lawton has already been the butt of jokes. He had treated himself to a three-week summer trip around large parts of the world, finishing in the US. His journey home featured a four-hour gap at Boston's Logan Airport. The stop prompted an idea. *Cheers*, the sitcom about life in a Boston bar, is a big favourite of the players. Lawton looked at a map and saw that Logan was very close to the city itself. With his bags safely checked through to Manchester, he got a taxi to the real-life bar the film is based on, which cost a fortune. With the clock ticking he bought some souvenirs – bar towels emblazoned with the *Cheers* crest before making it back to the airport for his flight home. When the players returned for pre-season he generously handed them out, proud of his achievement. Proud until one of the players called him. 'Hey Gordy,' he says. 'These towels – have you seen what it says in the corner?' Lawton has not. 'Made in Rochdale!'

CHAPTER THIRTY

Flyer

IT has been agreed. Following barstoolgate and clear-the-air-talks, Ian Marshall will be playing as a striker this season. For the first game of the season, at Wolves, he will be alongside Andy Ritchie. On the bench will be Roger Palmer and Paul Moulden. Action has been taken to address the lack of goals on the road.

A glorious afternoon and a packed Molineux greet the two sides. The ground is filled with 21,000 supporters and with optimism. In the summer, England's surprise run to the semi-finals of the World Cup in Italy has made football cool again after the traumatic, hooligan-dominated 1980s. It feels like a new dawn, Wolves fancy their own chances of promotion and those in old gold shirts make a strong start, taking the lead when Steve Bull beats a rusty offside trap and hammers past Hallworth.

The keeper is in the side because John Keeley, in the final training session before the big kick-off, has broken a finger saving a shot in a freak occurrence.

Oldham respond, and equalise when Andy Ritchie tees up Marshall, who miskicks his shot from his left foot onto his right from close range. Wolves keeper Mike Stowell dives to his left in anticipation and can only watch from the floor as the ball, which has ballooned into the air, drops into his net. It is fortuitous but Marshall does not care. He is already vindicated. Number nine on his back, he runs to the celebrating Oldham fans, arm aloft.

Following the break, Wolves continue to press and go in front when Bull, who looks offside, controls a cross that has sailed over the head of Barrett and, for the second time, smashes past Hallworth.

Oldham have not been at their best and it looks like their away day issues have followed them into the new season.

Then it clicks. First, Ritchie crosses to the far post and Marshall powers a looping header into the far corner. Bizarrely, it is disallowed for an offside. It is a warning. Moments later Hallworth boots one downfield. Marshall flicks it on and it hits the back of Ritchie, who is running towards goal. For the second time, luck is on Marshall's side. Having cannoned off his unsuspecting team-mate, the ball sits up for him. Thirty-five yards out, Marshall does not think twice. He swings his right boot and connects on the volley. It sails over the head of Stowell and drops into his net. A screamer.

Oldham are not done. Before a minute has passed, they are back on the attack. Ritchie, on the right, expertly finds room and sends in a low cross. Wolves cannot clear. It falls for Marshall who turns and hits another volley, this time from the edge of the area. For the second time in 60 seconds, a white object is hurtling towards Stowell's goal at speed. For the second time in 60 seconds he can do nothing about it. Oldham lead, Marshall, who has a hat-trick, is rugby tackled to the floor by Rick Holden.

Wolves' gloriously biased in-house commentator has gone from delight to despair. 'I don't think he can believe it,' he says in the gantry. 'The ball's fallen to him twice, he's hit it twice and twice it's gone past Mike Stowell.' Oldham win. It is a big statement.

'He's been mithering me to play there since the day I signed him,' Royle tells reporters. 'There'll be no living with him this weekend.'

There is also no living with Oldham. After Wolves they win again. And again and again and again. Five games, five victories. Fifteen points. It is their best start to a season since 1930. The only negative is another knee injury to Andy Holden, in the first home match of the season, a 2-0 stroll over Leicester City which is watched by 13,000. Mr Chairman no longer needs much persuading. The cheque book comes out again and the transfer record is broken again. Royle goes to Hull City for their commanding, calm centre-half Richard Jobson. The fee, £460,000, is another statement of intent. Oldham mean business.

The football has not been as flowing as it was the previous season, but there is a steely edge. More than 5,000 – a number higher than home gates in the not-too-distant past, made the short journey to Barnsley for the second road trip where, despite an under-par performance, a 1-0 victory was secured. 'If we can play shit and win,' Marshall told his team-mates, 'we've got a chance'.

A disappointing home draw against Charlton breaks the streak but the Addicks manager Lennie Lawrence is delighted with a point. 'Not many teams will come away from here with something,' he tells reporters. 'In fact, some of them will be beaten before they step on the artificial pitch.'

They roll on. At Middlesbrough, a Roger Palmer special grabs a 1-0 win. Oldham have won their first three away matches, equalling last season's total before September is over. They are top of the league. From 21 points, they have 19. Runaway leaders. Redfearn has adopted well to his new role in the middle. Henry is Henry. His incredible work-rate has increased since Milligan's departure. He has had to curb his attacking instinct to accommodate Redfearn but he has also adopted seamlessly. The only issue is his knee, which has developed a worrying habit of swelling up after each match following his operation.

In goal, Jon Hallworth has risen to the challenge. In a 0-0 draw at West Brom, he is outstanding. One save sticks out. After a rush of blood to the head, he races from his area to reach a through ball with his feet, but his clearance falls to an Albion player. Hallworth starts sprinting back to his goal in a state of panic. When the shot comes in he, at full stretch diving backwards, manages to claw it to safety. Not that he gets much appreciation. 'What the fuck were you doing?' he is asked in the dressing room by his incredulous team-mates after full-time.

Hallworth's form is just as well. In his first training session back after returning from injury, John Keeley breaks a finger in his other hand. The odds are millions to one. The number one jersey remains in the possession of the suddenly-assured captain.

CHAPTER THIRTY-ONE

The Day-To-Day

DESPITE Oldham's elevation to serious promotion contenders, despite average gates tripling and despite the money they have made, some things remain the same. Royle still does his Sunday drive-bys to make sure no enterprising local kids have broken into Little Wembley. Every penny still counts, and when kit starts going missing, the manager is called in to address the situation.

The likely offender will be from the youth team, and Royle calls the club's youngsters into a meeting. They know why they are there. Ever since Ian Marshall's boots went missing, prompting an inevitable response, the thief within the ranks has been the talk of the dressing room.

'Listen,' he tells them. 'It's got to stop. I know some of you may see it as a perk but it is not. If it does not stop, I'll get the police in and they'll start fingerprinting the place and I don't want that. In the meantime, if anyone knows who it is, tell Billy Urmson or put a note under my door. I'm not looking to name and shame.'

The reality is that Royle has a good idea who is responsible. There is an overseas trialist at the club who has been spotted leaving the ground with someone else's boots. Ian Liversedge has also had one of his precious going-out shirts – which he leaves at the club so his wife only sees him packing his tracksuits for away matches – stolen from the physios' room. The Soss loves his clothes, and stealing his prized shirt is a hanging offence.

Royle calls the youngster in. 'Listen,' he says. 'Ian Marshall's boots...' The player cuts him off. 'No boss,' he says. 'He's finished with them – they're his old ones.'

'No,' says Royle. 'They're his match boots.'

The boy is unrepentant. 'Son, your trial is finished,' Royle tells him. 'We can't go on like this and, by the way, I'm going to ring your mum and dad.'

Royle, himself the father of three sons, is true to his word. He calls the parents overseas and tells him what has happened. The response is not what he is expecting. 'Oh,' says the father. 'He's not been at that again, has he?' The parent then pleads with Royle to give his boy a second chance. He promises him it will not happen again. Royle, from one father to another, obliges. The thefts stop. But after a short while, more items go missing.

The youngster, called into the manager's office again, swears blind that it is not him. He is emphatic. 'Honestly,' he says, 'I wouldn't do that.'

Royle wants to believe him but he has an idea. He grabs Urmson and the pair drive to a pub in Chadderton, which has an upstairs room that serves as the youngster's digs. They walk through the front door and the first thing they notice is that the two bar staff are wearing full Oldham Athletic tracksuits, with the initials of players etched onto them.

It is all Royle can do not to burst into laughter. The landlady, also wearing a nicked Oldham tracksuit top, sees her visitors. 'You're going to send him home, aren't you?' she says. 'Yes,' responds Royle. 'And the tops,' he adds, pointing at the three of them. 'Get them off – we need them.' He then walks upstairs to the youngster's room. 'Bill,' he says, with wonder in his voice. 'It's like Aladdin's bloody cave in here.' There are piles of club clothes spread out across the floor. Even worse, there are kitbags, medical bags, and the Soss's missing shirt. There is even one of the long, warm Umbro coats that Royle wears on matchdays in the winter, complete with the initials 'JR'. The pair walk out with two bin bags full of stolen goods and have to go back in to pick up what is remaining. When they get to the sanctuary of the car they erupt in laughter.

Later, the boy's stricken mother calls and tells Royle that this is a cry for attention and asks him to give her son another chance. 'I'm sorry,' he says, 'but aside from the stealing, he's just not good enough.'

The smiles keep coming. In the midst of the unbeaten start comes a rare weekend without a game. In Alan Hardy's commercial office, Gordon Lawton has a plan. He is missing Andy Rhodes and it just so happens that Dunfermline are hosting Rangers, who will have Andy Goram in goal following his move from Hibs, on the spare Saturday. He calls Rhodes and asks him if he can get him a ticket. 'No problem, Gordy,' is the immediate response. 'It'll be good to see you.'

Lawton gets to East End Park early, and heads to the ticket office. He tells the woman working there that there should be a ticket under the name of Gordon Lawton. She returns with an envelope that is around six-inches thick and is bursting at the seams, which strikes him as a little odd.

He opens it, and there are around 50 tickets inside. Lawton thinks there must be some kind of error, when he sees the envelope also contains a handwritten note in Rhodes's unmistakable scrawl. 'Will this be enough room for you, you fat cunt?' his old pal has written. Lawton starts laughing. 'The cheeky bastard,' he thinks. When Rhodes emerges from the tunnel for the game he turns around to the main stand and spots his guest. The goalkeeper rolls his hand over his belly and mouths 'you fat bastard' at him.

Lawton, however, has the last laugh. Rhodes ends up getting sent off early in the game and they spend the rest of the afternoon in the pub.

The unbeaten run stretches into November and to a fixture with fellow promotion contenders Sheffield Wednesday, at the South Yorkshire side's cavernous Hillsborough home. Close to 35,000 see Nick Henry and David Currie put Oldham 2-0 up, before the hosts mount a recovery and snatch a point thanks to two penalties. It is a fine advertisement for the Second Division, a match that ebbs and flows in front of a huge crowd, which Wednesday's boss and former Manchester United manager Ron Atkinson describes as 'one of the best I've ever seen'.

But the press are not interested in discussing the ins and outs of the game. Everton, having made a poor start to the season, have sacked Colin Harvey and they want to know if Royle will be his replacement. A breathless Andy Ritchie, leaving the pitch, is ambushed by a TV reporter demanding to know if he thinks his manager is off. Word gets back to Royle, who suffers a rare sense of humour failure. He is not impressed and tells the reporters as much. A television crew, seeking an interview, also gets a mouthful.

The first league defeat of the season, at Port Vale, does little to help, along with a 2-0 loss at Bristol Rovers.

But the reality is that Oldham are never going to lose Royle at this stage. Ian Stott is many things but he is not stupid. A new, three-year contract is signed. Everton re-appoint former boss Howard Kendall and Royle's players respond with a 6-1 thrashing of Brighton, who no longer have John Keeley in their ranks to keep the score down.

After defeating Notts County over two legs, Oldham head to Elland Road in the Rumbelows Cup, the new name for the Littlewoods Cup, but are beaten by Leeds, now in the top flight. They will not be back at Wembley, but the overriding feeling is that concentration this year must lie solely on the league. The memories of the promotion wrecking side-effects of last year's cup runs are still raw.

As November turns into December, there is a distraction of a six-a-side tournament at Manchester's G-Mex centre, where they face American side Baltimore Blast. As Oldham wait in the tunnel, Nottingham Forest's Stuart Pearce, whose side are also in the competition, spots them. 'Here they are, look, it's the People's Champions,' he sneers. Few shed any tears over a 6-1 defeat to the visiting side from overseas, as they don't over a mistake-ridden 7-2 reverse at Sheffield United in the Zenith Data Systems Cup, the new name for the Simod Cup. Defeats of Wolves and Plymouth, which see Oldham score nine goals in two games, put them top of the table as Christmas approaches.

The spirit remains strong. On a Tuesday Club outing into Manchester, the group are walking across Albert Square, in the city centre when Marshall tells them all to stop. The streets are filled with buskers and clearly the Liverpudlian has been inspired. He takes off his coat, throws it on the floor and then starts to breakdance, with no music to accompany him. Passers-by are impressed, and a few coins are thrown into his discarded jacket.

It is a surprise that the striker is in such a good mood. Earlier in the week John Keeley had been at his house when a snow storm descended. It continued when the goalkeeper got into his car to go home.

The next morning, when Keeley walked into the dressing room, Marshall was waiting for him. 'You've killed my fucking cat!' he told him.

Keeley had no idea that he reversed over the pet while on Marshall's drive and is mortified. It is the latest in a series of tales of woe for the London-born keeper, who is having a miserable time. Aside from the injuries, he and his wife have failed to settle in Oldham – for good reason. They bought a detached home on a new estate in an elevated area called Moorside. They are the first people in, with building work continuing on the other houses. What nobody had told them is that Moorside, while a pleasant area inhabited by Andy Barlow, is next to a sprawling council estate called Sholver.

In their first week in the new house, their garage was broken into and their cars were stolen. They brought in a security firm to fit a burglar alarm and went home to Essex for the weekend. The man who installed the alarm could not finish the job and was going to come back on Monday. When Keeley and his wife returned home on Sunday afternoon, they found that the house had been broken into for the second time in a week.

On Boxing Day, Oldham head to West Ham, their main rivals for top spot. They travel down on Christmas Day and the trip, as it always does, features plenty of mickey-taking of Derek

Painter, the driver and proud owner of Mostonian coaches. 'How's that boil on your foot, Derek?' comes the cry from the back of the bus. 'What are you talking about?' is the reply, in squeaky Mancunian.

'The one that's stopping you from pressing the fucking accelerator!'

Oldham are staying overnight at The Swallow Hotel, Waltham Abbey and Royle decides to get in on the act. As they pull into the gates he gets off the vehicle and has a quiet word with the security guard. 'Listen, son,' he says to the guard. 'We're having a bit of a giggle with the driver. Tell him his coach looks nice but it's a bit dated.'

The guard rises to the challenge in fine style. He walks over to Derek's window and asks him to wind it down. They exchange pleasantries and then he does his stuff. 'Nice coach, this,' he says. 'Didn't realise they still made them.' Derek is apopletic, but says nothing. However, when the man asks him if they have solid tyres the coaching staff cannot contain themselves. They burst out laughing and the joke is over.

The following morning they set off for what is an early kick-off. Jon Hallworth, having played in the south for a long time, knows the area well. They head for the M25, the motorway that circles the capital, but start travelling anti-clockwise. 'Derek – you're going the wrong way,' shouts Hallworth.

'Fuck off, goalie, what the fuck do you know?' is the driver's high-pitched reply.

Hallworth laughs. 'Let me know when you get to Tottenham,' he says.

When the penny drops that the goalie is right, alarm bells ring. The Metropolitan Police are called and they provide an escort from North to East London, but the damage is done. Oldham arrive a mere 30 minutes before kick-off. It is hardly ideal preparation.

Despite Hallworth saving a penalty, they lose 2-0 and the Hammers take over at the top of the league. A 0-0 draw at Millwall and a 1-1 stalemate with Newcastle United complete a disappointing festive period.

CHAPTER THIRTY-TWO

Away Days

WITH the rain relentless and the Fratton Park pitch a mess, there is discussion over whether Joe Royle and his squad should make the long journey to Hampshire on the Friday before the game. Given that, as things stand, it remains on, they have little choice.

But when they arrive at their hotel, the rain is still coming down and it continues throughout the evening. At 9pm, the players retire to their rooms. It is an unspoken agreement. At 9pm each Friday a Channel 4 triple-header starts. *Cheers*, followed by *The Golden Girls*, followed by *Whose Line Is It Anyway?* The group's love of *Cheers* is understandable. It tells the story of Sam Malone, a former Boston Red Sox baseball star, and the everyday Joes who frequent his bar. *Whose Line Is It Anyway?* is an entertaining comedy show, where regulars compete in various improv challenges. The squad's love of *The Golden Girls*, a soap based on the japes of a group of middle-aged women who share a Florida home, is slightly more surprising – but they will not miss an episode.

For this trip, Ian Marshall and Neil Adams are sharing a room. Marshall looks out of the window. 'Addo,' he says, 'there's fuck's chance of this game going ahead'.

After checking in, Marshall had spotted a cylindrical machine at the end of the corridor that dispenses cans of soft drink and miniature bottles of the hard stuff.

'Let's have a couple,' he now says. Adams is nervous. The pair agree to phone ClubCall, the telephone news service which serves each club. They tap in the number for the Portsmouth line. The news is as they expected. As it stands, the match is still on, but any overnight rain will make its go-ahead unlikely.

'Fuck it,' says Marshall. He disappears and returns with a bottle of vodka and a can of lemonade. The pair have another six. Eventually, well past midnight and well pissed, they fall asleep.

The following morning arrives. They have slept in and missed the traditional walk. Royle will not be impressed. Marshall draws back the curtains and the rain is nowhere to be seen. 'Fuck,' he says. He hastily calls ClubCall again. The game is on.

When the group arrive at Fratton Park they read the programme as part of the build-up. In it, there is a piece which questions Oldham's ability to play on grass, an argument that Royle and co thought they had put to bed. Royle pins it up on the wall for everyone to see.

What follows is the best away performance of the season. A 4-1 victory in which Marshall scores twice. The first of his brace comes courtesy of an assist from Adams, who also performs well. As they walk off the boggy pitch, Marshall puts his arm around his team-mate. 'Same again next away match?' he jokes.

Back at Boundary Park, Barnsley are seen off 2-0 in front of another crowd north of 13,000. Then comes a bizarre 5-1 defeat at Oxford where Rick Holden, furious at being substituted, lies on a wall in front of the visiting fans, rather than taking a seat in the dugout. From there, he barracks Jon Hallworth.

Defeat at Notts County in the FA Cup removes any further distractions from the league campaign. With the final third of the season approaching, Royle feels he needs fresh blood to carry his side over the line. He signs right-back Gunnar Halle from Norwegians Lillestrom for £280,000 and Scottish midfielder Paul Kane from Hibs for £350,000. They will not run out of bodies again.

* * * * *

Another long trip arrives in the shape of a visit to Brighton. As they often do, a game of cards is arranged to pass the time. The contest starts outside Boundary Park and the final two who remain in the game are Gordon Lawton and Royle. Lawton is confident of victory and makes a fatal mistake. 'If I lose with this hand,' he tells the rest of the group, 'I will check in at the hotel naked.' He should know better. Inspired by his promise, the players surreptitiously begin to pass Royle cards under the table. Finally, it is time to show hands. Lawton goes first. Four of a kind. Then it is Royle's turn. A straight flush. The manager wins. There are loud cheers. 'Off you go, Gordy,' he says.

Lawton, in shock, takes off his clothes. He is handed the check-in documentation. He goes through the revolving doors of what is a high-quality hotel and approaches the horrified woman on reception. Lawton does not flinch. 'Party of 24, Oldham Athletic,' he says. The woman has already hit the panic button. She pressed it when she caught sight of Lawton grappling with the revolving doors. Security suddenly appear on the scene. At the same time, Royle runs in and tells them that it is a wind-up and the situation is calmed.

As he always does on away trips, Royle and his staff wait until the players are safely tucked up in bed and head out for a meal later that night. On the way back to the hotel, they are walking down Brighton's famous Lanes when a bouncer outside a club recognises the Oldham manager. 'Hey Joe,' he says. 'Do you think you're going to win tomorrow?'

'Yes lads,' the manager replies. 'Put some money on it.'

'I wouldn't be so sure,' the doorman responds. 'They're all on the fucking dancefloor in here.'

Royle sends Ian Liversedge and Ronnie Evans in to identify the culprits. They are told to get their backsides back to the hotel and they are subsequently fined. The following day, thanks to an Andy Ritchie screamer, Oldham win 2-1. Royle tells the press: 'The real reason we are doing so well is that little Oldham probably has the biggest squad in the second division. The chairman pointed out to me that we fielded £1.3m worth of players in a reserve match last week.' Following a subsequent 2-0 home win over Bristol Rovers, the biggest squad in the division goes back to the top of the league.

The mood in the group is buoyant, but one player is frustrated. Neil Adams is sick of being substituted. When Oldham are leading matches deep into the second half, he is often the man taken off as the manager looks to make a defensive move to protect the three points. The players know that he is annoyed because he has told them. 'That number seven board,' he says, 'it's like toast – always popping up.' He feels that he could be having a world class game but that it will make no difference. His team-mates take great pleasure in his pain. They have even started sniggering on the pitch when number seven is told to come in.

A few weeks ago he decided that enough was enough. He knew that the boards were kept in a satchel in the boot room. One afternoon, he sneaked in, opened the bag and quietly removed the number seven board and put it in the boot of his car. On Saturday, as was the norm, Oldham lead going into the final 15 minutes and there was inevitable activity in the dugout.

Up went the number seven. They had found a spare. Before the next match, Adams sneaked into the room again and took out the spare seven. This time, just to make sure, he set fire to it and threw it into a skip outside a house on Sheepfoot Lane. Next game, again, Oldham lead and it was time for him to come off. He noticed Liversedge run up the steps to the tunnel and come back down, shrugging his shoulders and holding his palms out to the side. Eventually, two numbers were held up – three and four. A bemused Richard Jobson (four) and Andy Barlow (three) headed towards the touchline. 'No!' Soss shouted. 'Three plus four – seven! Addo! You're coming off.'

Adams was furious. After the 2-2 draw at Swindon, which follows the Brighton victory, the players gather for a pint in the Horton Arms, in Chadderton. Adams has his back to the door and cannot see that his manager has entered the building and is within earshot. Hallworth quickly changes the conversation to him being taken off all the time. 'It's a joke,' says Adams. 'I'm going to knock on his door and I'm going to tell him. He can run but he can't hide. I'll show him!'

Not long later, Royle leans into view. 'Evening, Neil,' he says, with a smile.

Adams turns back to his team-mates, who are roaring with laughter.

'You bastards,' he says.

Royle likes Adams, knows he has a point and cuts him some slack. But his patience has been stretched beyond breaking point by another player.

In the mid-80s, a young goalkeeper by the name of Andy Gorton was the back-up to Andy Goram. While not blessed with height, Gorton had incredible reflexes and some saw him as a better prospect than Goram, which was some call. On the occasions he was called upon, he was little short of magnificent. But Gorton hailed from a notorious, crime ridden area of nearby Salford, and there were always nagging concerns about the company he kept.

Reluctantly, Royle had released him, but with Keeley suffering from continuing injuries, he needed back-up for Hallworth and Gorton had been winning favourable reviews at non-league Glossop North End. Royle took a gamble and paid the local side £3,000. But within weeks, a landlord accused Gorton of hurling a Molotov cocktail at his pub after he had earlier refused to serve him. When word reached the training ground, the players joked that Gorton should tell the court at his impending case that he intended to drink the cocktail, rather than launch it. The gag was funny, but Royle knews that the situation was no laughing matter. He is prepared to cut his players some slack but there has to be limits and Gorton was shown the door.

A win over West Brom is followed by the visit of lowly Hull City. Aided by a poor refereeing performance, the visitors have a shock lead. At half-time, the players gather in the tunnel for the second half and the man in the middle appears. 'Ref,' says Ian Marshall, attracting his attention. 'What would happen if I called you a twat?' Ritchie, ever-sensible, attempts to intervene. 'Come on, Marshy,' he says.

'No,' says Marshall. 'Come on, what would happen?' The referee tells him that he would send him off. 'OK, what would happen if I thought you were a twat?' To his credit, the referee engages. 'Well, Ian,' he says. 'Everyone is entitled to their opinion and there's nothing I can do about that.'

'Right then,' Marshall responds. 'Ref, I think you're a twat.' The official smiles but a 2-1 defeat is no laughing matter. Neither is the 2-0 reverse at Blackburn which follows. West Ham arrive for a Good Friday showdown and, thanks to an incredible performance from Ludek Miklosko in goal, look set for a huge win before a last-gasp Ritchie penalty grabs a point. A win at Plymouth is followed by a disappointing home draw with Millwall. The Hammers take over at the top and their position is strengthened when Oldham miss a host of chances to draw 0-0 at Leicester, lose 3-2 at Newcastle and draw 1-1 at Charlton, where Paul Warhurst is sent off.

Royle is alleged to have thrown a bucket of water over a photographer on an ill-tempered night. But the feeling is that the hard work has been done. After a 2-1 home win over Bristol City they know that three points on the road at Ipswich, the following Saturday, will take them back to the First Division after a 68-year absence.

CHAPTER THIRTY-THREE

Up

IN the Portman Road dressing room, the time has come. Joe Royle enters, to address his players. Win today and they will earn promotion to the top flight of English football. Little Oldham will be in with the big boys. For him, this should be the culmination of nine years of work. It will also be justice. Justice for last season's heartache. Justice for the anguish that descended 12 months ago.

He approaches the front of the room, with a serious expression. The players have rarely seen their manager like this. 'You've all done incredibly well and you know that I am proud of you,' he tells them. 'But this is it. This is the game that changes your life. This is your destiny. You have worked fucking hard for this and you deserve it. You will be playing against the best players, you will be getting more money. But if you want that, you have to get out there and do it.'

It is powerful. Nick Henry feels the hairs stand up on the back of his neck. Then, to the amazement of most, Rick Holden steps forward. The previous night, at the Moat House Hotel where the squad had stayed, he had been unable to sleep and had watched television into the early hours, much to the annoyance of room-mate Jon Hallworth. In the morning he had gone for a walk around the grounds of the hotel, which was a rarity, given he usually stayed in bed while Hallworth fetched him his *Daily Telegraph* and a coffee. While out, he bumped into Royle and Willie Donachie and told them his thoughts. Royle had asked him if he would repeat them to the squad and now is the time.

Holden, sporting the early signs of a beard (he has vowed not to shave until promotion was secured), steps forward and addresses the group. His message is similar to that of his manager, and he adds that they will become Oldham Athletic legends. It goes down well. They know that when Rick Holden is delivering a speech, it is time to get serious.

It works. The players are fired up. In the case of Andy Barlow, the hometown boy, perhaps too fired up. With the game less than a minute old, mid-table Ipswich's manager, John Lyall, has not even got to the dugout from the tunnel when his Dutch playmaker Romeo Zondervan lands on top of it. Barlow has gone in hard, in an attempt to set the tone, and is lucky to receive a yellow, rather than red, card.

Oldham set the early pace. Two long throws from Barlow create havoc in the home side's defence and Ipswich suffer another blow when midfielder Simon Milton unwittingly boots team-mate Steve Palmer in the head in what is a freak accident. The influential Palmer has to be substituted.

Royle, as creative as ever, has moved Barrett into midfield to partner Henry and the pair get a vice-like grip on the contest. It is his latest masterstroke.

Chances, however, are elusive. The closest to an opener is when Neil Thompson hammers a 25-yard free-kick towards the top corner. Hallworth, back at his previous club, dives to his right and manages to get a faint touch which diverts the ball on to the crossbar.

Then, on 38 minutes, it happens. Barlow, proving to be a menace on the left, sends over a booming cross that Rick Holden would be proud of. Marshall, on the corner of the six-yard box, is surrounded by two Ipswich defenders. It does not matter. The big man positions himself between his markers. As the ball drops he times his jump to perfection. The connection is clean. Marshall's forehead sends it across Craig Forrest in the Ipswich goal, and into the back of the net. The goal is scored where the 3,000 Oldham fans who have made the four-hour, 250-mile round trip, and who sense history, are stood. There is wild celebration. They know that there is a mean streak to this side that did not exist last season. Few will come from behind. Promotion is on.

Following the break, Oldham, in their all-red away kit, remain in control. Henry, who has excelled in the absence of Mike Milligan, is everywhere, harassing the hosts. When sub Tony Humes dallies on the ball, midway inside his own half, he nips in front of him and dinks the ball behind the defence.

It goes from one Liverpudlian to another. The ever-alert Marshall has set off and he is in. His first touch, with his right foot, is a good one, and he arrows in on goal. Forrest races off his line to narrow the angle. This is a time for cool heads and Marshall has one. He opens his body, as if to shoot, but instead touches the ball to his left. Forrest is fooled. He has committed himself to the shot and is left grasping at thin air.

Having rounded the goalkeeper, the angle Marshall has is tight, and there is an Ipswich defender sliding along the ground to block his shot. With his left foot, Marshall clips towards goal. He is aware of his environment and it is the right move. The ball sails over the outstretched boot of the defender, creeps inside the far post and nestles in the back of the net. Sixty-eight minutes have gone and it is 2-0.

Marshall wheels away in a celebration that is now familiar. This. Is. It. On the terrace at the other end, it is pandemonium. There is time left but surely, surely, Oldham are up.

In the main stand, Ian Stott can barely contain himself. Neither can the bench.

With 10 minutes to play, striker Chris Kiwomya beats Oldham's offside trap, steers past Hallworth and the lead is halved. But even now, there is a belief that the home side will not score again. As the minutes tick down, the noise gets louder from the raucous corner. Oldham will not be breached again, will not be denied again. An Ipswich throw-in is cleared on the edge of the box and referee Gary Willard's whistle confirms it. Oldham are promoted. They have done it. Royle has done it.

In the main stand, Donachie stands and shakes the hand of a beaming Stott, who is surveying the scenes to his left and may well have a tear in his eye. A lone police officer tries valiantly to keep delirious fans on the terrace but he has no chance. They have waited a lifetime for this. Dozens clamber over the fences to greet their heroes. Royle calmly walks onto the surface. He knew this was coming. Rick Holden almost immediately takes a running jump into his arms. Henry is raised aloft on the shoulders of one of the invaders.

In the dressing room, champagne is being sprayed by all bar Holden, who refuses to waste it and instead swigs from the bottle. Lyall enters and graciously congratulates the celebrating players.

'We intend to make a few pub landlords happy on our way home tonight,' Royle tells the press.

'Staying up will be the hard part,' he adds, looking ahead. 'But we already have the players to do it. They deserve the chance to show what they can do in the First Division. Last season we gained friends, money, respect and esteem, but this is the first time we have won anything.'

Royle can also not resist a dig at the doubters. 'It was nice to clinch promotion on grass,' he says. 'And we are looking forward to playing on it all the time next season. Other teams have only had to play on our plastic once a season, but my lads have had to adjust from one to the other every week.'

Three matches remain to overtake West Ham. 'We want the title now,' Royle adds.

But first, it is time to party. The coach journey back to Oldham on the Mostonian is one to remember. Even Derek is smiling. The beers are flowing, along with songs. Notts County, a rough-and-tumble team managed by an equally aggressive manager in Neil Warnock, for whom the players have little time, are the ones who will have to settle for the play-offs. The group, to the tune of MC Hammer's *Can't Touch This*, begin to sing 'Warnock can't touch us'.

The coach drops them off in Oldham town centre where they join hordes of celebrating fans. Some head for a nightclub named Henry Afrikas, a favourite of Marshall's thanks to its unique acts and potty-mouthed transgender DJ.

The mood is surreal. Oldham's town hall steps are an iconic landmark throughout the borough. During his time as one of the town's MPs, Winston Churchill had addressed crowds from them. They are now the scene of an equally fervent but slightly less measured gathering. Fans are queuing to bare their backsides, having vowed to do so if Latics ever made the top flight. Rick

Holden ends up walking back to his flat in Springhead, around two miles from the town centre. On his way home, he passes an Indian restaurant and sees Royle and Donachie sat at a table at the window. They have not seen him. He bangs on the glass and frightens the life out of the pair of them. Even now, on this historic day, he cannot resist. It earns him a bollocking on the Monday morning but it is of little importance. For now, on this beautiful evening, it is April 27, 1991, and Oldham Athletic are in the First Division.

CHAPTER THIRTY-FOUR

'Redfearn, Right-Footed...'

'THAT was fucking abysmal.' Joe Royle is not happy. The first of Oldham's final three matches has ended in a limp 2-0 surrender at Neil Warnock's hated Notts County. He is furious and he is letting his players know as much. It is a far cry from the previous weekend. 'You should be embarrassed,' he adds. 'That's not you.'

While promotion, the priority, has already been achieved, Royle wants the title. What he has just seen at Meadow Lane is unacceptable. He singles out five of his players for credit and tells the rest that they should be ashamed of themselves. 'I'll remember this when some of you come knocking on my door for new contracts next season,' he ends.

'So much for Ipswich being the game that changes our lives,' is the consensus of the group at the back of the Mostonian.

For the midweek visit of Middlesbrough, Royle hands a debut to 17-year-old midfielder Paul Bernard, who plays well in a 2-0 win. Bernard takes the place of Redfearn, one of those Royle has had words with. The midfielder, who has scored 16 goals, was not impressed. A transfer request followed. 'We are not in the business of keeping unsettled players,' was Royle's retort.

The picture is now clear. Sheffield Wednesday arrive on Saturday. To win the league, Oldham need a victory and they need West Ham to lose at home to Notts County, an unlikely prospect. Should the Yorkshire side, who have also already been promoted, leave Boundary Park with three points, Oldham will end the season in third place, having spent most of it in the top two.

The day arrives, sunny and blustery. In the press box, Stuart Pyke goes through his notes. A commentator for Piccadilly Radio, the Manchester-based station that is first port of call for the region's football fans on Saturday afternoons, he is almost part of the furniture at the club and is well-liked by the staff and players.

On away trips, he – and other members of the press – will often travel on the coach. Born in St Helens, Pyke is an Evertonian, but he is unashamedly in Oldham's corner. As he looks out across the soon-to-be-packed stadium, he reflects on how far the club has come since he arrived on the scene in the mid-80s and almost got himself banned before he had even started.

New to the job and keen to impress, he watched the limp FA Cup defeat to Orient in 1986, attended by 3,604. It was the nadir of Royle's reign and those who could be bothered turning up were not happy. Pyke quickly made his way into the Chaddy End and carried out a vox pop, where the disgruntled few made their feelings towards the manager perfectly clear. Their frank comments were broadcast, and on Monday morning young Pyke got a call from Royle. 'My office, now,' he was told.

What followed was the biggest rollicking of his life. Pyke was told in no uncertain terms that if he was to succeed in his role then he would need to alter his approach. That he would need to understand who he had to keep onside. At the time he felt he was just doing his job, but kept quiet and took his fellow Merseysider's words on the chin. Now, he knows he made the right move. Royle and his team have provided some incredible moments in a blossoming career. As the gates open and fans begin to pour in, he hopes that Oldham can provide the perfect ending to what is already a fairytale.

Beneath him, in Royle's office, Ron Atkinson – the Wednesday manager – appears to be on fine form. The laughter can be heard down the corridor. Royle and Atkinson have a long history. While at Old Trafford, Atkinson had a five-a-side team that would play at their training ground, The Cliff. When he was sacked, the team was subsequently made homeless and quickly relocated to the Boundary Park plastic. Royle often makes guest appearances for them, and they are good friends.

'Come on, Joe,' says Atkinson, all charm and geniality. 'Let's me and you leave the boys to it and go and have a glass of wine. Let them play the game, we'll just stay here and enjoy ourselves. We're both promoted, what does it matter?'

Close to 19,000 greet the teams as they walk down the steps. Oldham are in their new kit, which is again all-blue. Wednesday, who weeks ago defeated Manchester United to win the League Cup, which is now known as the Rumbelows Cup, at Wembley. They are a side packed with talent, with the lethal, local striker David Hirst a formidable opponent.

There is a party atmosphere. *Fanfare For The Common Man* sounds on the Tannoy for the final time this season and the volume rises in anticipation. The players jog down the steps, dodging balloons, and head onto the plastic, which will be hosting its final match. The much-debated surface has been outlawed. Unlike Oldham, it will have no place in the First

Division next season. The game is also significant because it is the last time that there will be terracing in the Chaddy End. As part of the shift to all-seater stadia following the Hillsborough Disaster, seats will be installed over the summer. It is a big job, and already the roof covering has been removed in preparation. Underneath rusted, exposed framework, 5,000 are packed in together for the final time.

Ahead of kick-off, club sponsors Lookers' player of the season is announced. Andy Barlow runs across to pick up a giant cheque for the princely sum of £500.

The atmosphere initially seems relaxed. Even if Oldham win, and that is far from a foregone conclusion, the chances of West Ham slipping up at Upton Park are remote, even if they are facing Warnock's savvy, physical Magpies.

Everything changes before two minutes has elapsed. After an Oldham attack ends, the visitors head straight down to the Chaddy End and take the lead when Hirst nods beyond Hallworth into the corner for his 32nd goal of the season. At the front of the stand, around 100 Wednesday supporters celebrate exuberantly, barging into the young children who frequent that part of the stadium and sending many sprawling. The Wednesday fans should not be there but somehow have managed to get tickets. Their presence incenses. At first there is a chant of 'Get them out'. Then, with seemingly no police involvement, some of the home supporters decide to take matters into their own hands.

It happens quickly. All of a sudden the invaders are surrounded. Fists begin to fly. It is an ugly scene. Many scramble over the advertisement boards and onto the pitch to escape. As a result, the game has to be stopped. Finally the police, whose numbers had been at the Rochdale Road End, segregating Oldham and Wednesday fans across three pens, arrive. They surround the Wednesday supporters, who are now all on the pitch, and take them to the away end amid chants of 'You dirty Yorkshire bastards'. One, however, will not be seeing the rest of the match. He is grabbed around the neck by an officer and taken up the steps towards the playing tunnel. The unfortunate soul is pelted with missiles as he is dragged towards the exit.

Finally, he reaches the top of the steps and what would appear to be sanctuary. However, Alan Hardy, who watches matches from that vantage point and who presumably thinks that the cameras will be on the pitch, swiftly and craftily boots him in the shin, one more for his troubles.

The atmosphere has changed. The game restarts and Bernard, who has kept his place, glances a header which Kevin Pressman, the Wednesday keeper, does well to hold. Oldham keep up the pressure but this is a super Wednesday side and they repeatedly threaten on the counter-attack. Gunnar Halle pulls up injured and Redfearn is sent on with a point to prove, but the pattern of the game fails to change. Oldham have had chances but at half-time, the hosts are lucky that the score remains 1-0. Hirst alone could have had a hat-trick.

The only positive has been the score from Upton Park, which Hardy has repeatedly asked Mark Gorey to flash on the scoreboard. He gladly obliges. West Ham went 1-0 down after 17 minutes. Ten minutes later it was 2-0. Each update is greeted with roars of encouragement.

The second-half starts with Marshall missing a glorious chance from a Rick Holden cross, but a relaxed and composed

Wednesday then pick up where they left off. A cross from full-back Nigel Worthington is headed away by Richard Jobson but it falls to midfielder Danny Wilson, who strikes it beautifully on the half volley and it zooms past Hallworth. This was never going to be an easy task, but at 2-0 it looks near impossible.

Roger Palmer, not in the squad, has seen enough. He calls a taxi to take him to his mother's house in Sale and is picked up outside the main entrance.

Oldham do what only they can do, what they are programmed to do. They dust themselves down and begin to exert more pressure. Barlow takes matters into his own hands, barging opposition full-back Roland Nilsson to the floor as he tries to shield the ball out for a goal-kick. A free-kick is not given and the newly-crowned player of the season crosses for Marshall, at the near post. The big man controls and jabs a shot at goal but Pressman saves with his legs. The rebound bounces back at the striker and he stabs it above the keeper and into the back of the net. Finally, there is something to cheer. An hour has gone. West Ham are still losing. There is faint hope.

Palmer's taxi is at the bottom of Broadway and the driver is listening to Piccadilly. '2-1, Roger,' he says. Palmer, in the back seat, nods.

Wednesday retain their shape. John Sheridan, whose brilliant strike defeated United, is played in by Hirst and Hallworth, magnificent all season, dives at his feet to pinch the ball. Had he not done so, it would be game over. But it is not.

Chances are, however, getting slimmer with every passing second. To not win the title will be a shame, but to finish third will be an outrage.

Wednesday begin to drop deeper. Oldham accept the invite.

Pressman denies Rick Holden from almost point-blank range with a terrific block. It will not happen.

Ten minutes to go. Hallworth bangs one downfield. Marshall flicks on but Paul Moulden's shot is blocked. The yellow wall continues to do its job. Redfearn, the most advanced full-back the game has seen, races after the loose ball. He expertly cuts inside his marker and crosses to the far post. Marshall heads it back towards the centre but Carlton Palmer clears with his chest. The giant Wednesday midfielder chases after the ball to complete the clearance but the bounce, on the plastic, means it is out of reach. Bernard, on the edge of the area, hits it on the turn, goalwards. Pressman has it covered but it cannons off the outstretched boot of Nilsson, wrongfoots the goalkeeper and Oldham have equalised.

It is too much. Hundreds of fans invade the pitch. Bernard disappears underneath them. On the Tannoy, the announcer pleads with them to get back into the Chaddy End. They oblige.

* * * * *

The Radio Cars taxi is now close to Manchester city centre. 'Roger,' says the driver, an Oldham fan who has unfortunately not been able to swap his shift. There has, unsurprisingly, been few takers. 'It's 2-2!' Again, the striker nods, almost dismissively. This is now an onslaught. There have been incredible moments to savour in the last two seasons but there has never been noise like this. In the commentary box, Pyke is relaying the action to his listeners. He feels like the ground is wrapped in a bubble. Everything is looking inwards. The pressure is intense. It has to burst.

Oldham are leaving themselves exposed in the pursuit of glory. Hirst, on the break, strikes one inches wide of goal.

Redfearn heads another Rick Holden cross over the bar. Injury time. West Ham are still losing in East London. Ron Atkinson, shades on, is in front of his bench, biting his nails. Any thoughts of a glass of wine are long gone. Another Rick Holden cross finds Moulden. The striker turns. He has a sight of goal. He shoots and his shot hits defender Viv Anderson on his arm. 17,000 voices scream 'handball!'. Referee Vic Callow is unmoved. There are howls of anguish.

Anderson clears to Barlow. The full-back smashes a hopeful volley which Sheridan, now in defence, stops and controls. An artistic player, the Mancunian Ireland international does not hammer the ball clear. Instead, he takes it past Moulden towards the edge of the area.

Barlow sees the ball rolling across. 'I can get that,' he thinks. He can see Sheridan in the corner of his eye advancing to clear it. It is a race. Whoever gets there first will win. Barlow, born and raised in Oldham, a man who has seen decades of failure, who knows what this means, is not going to lose. He gets a toe to the ball a fraction of a second before Sheridan, who has not seen him coming from a crowd of players. The Wednesday man has committed to the clearance but the ball has gone and he connects with Barlow, who crashes to the turf.

'Penalty! Oldham have got a penalty in injury time!' screams Pyke, whose voice breaks under the strain. And they have. 'I don't believe this!' the commentator adds, now close to screaming. 'We have played two minutes of injury time and Oldham have a penalty that can win them the Second Division title!'

Another pitch invasion holds up the game. Wednesday's

players protest, furiously. They think Barlow has dived. Wilson is booked. 'It all adds to the pressure,' adds Pyke. 'They can't look in the main stand at Boundary Park.'

The Radio Cars cab is now on the M56. It is too much for the driver, who pulls onto the hard shoulder and gets out, leaving Palmer in the back seat. He drops to his knees. He cannot listen.

Amid the mayhem, Redfearn steps forward and picks the ball up. He does not understand what all the fuss is about. Having seen the pitch invasion for the equaliser, he is, incredibly, under the mistaken impression that a draw will be enough to clinch the title.

The midfielder is the son of Brian, himself a player for the likes of Bradford Park Avenue and Darlington. The pair spent hours on playing fields when he was a child, father passing down the skills he picked up during his own career to the son.

There is one which he is about to repeat. With hysteria all around him, Redfearn is the coolest man in Oldham, because he knows exactly what to do.

The trick with penalties is to perform your run-up at a certain angle which allows you to decide which direction you are going to put the ball at the last moment. Before connection, you then hesitate slightly, glance up and examine the goalkeeper to see if they have provided a tell-tale sign of which way they are going to dive. Often, they have. While the legs often remain static, a slight shift in the upper body almost always gives the game away.

He repeats the process. 'Redfearn, comes up, right-footed,' relays a breathless Pyke. The moment has come. Time stands still. Redfearn gets to the ball, pauses, and glances up. Pressman's upper body has moved. Pressman has moved. He is going to his right. He has given the game away. Redfearn sidefoots low in the opposite direction. It rolls gently into the bottom corner.

'It's there!' shouts Pyke, deafening listeners in homes across Greater Manchester. And it is. 'It's there!,' he repeats. 'Neil Redfearn, the hero of Oldham.'

A sea of baggy denim invades the pitch. The noise is incredible. It is a noise this old ground has never heard before. The sound of success. Moulden tries to grab Redfearn, who is racing back to his own half to avoid being mobbed. He grabs a piece of shirt and is sent flying.

At the side of the M56 the Radio Cars driver glances nervously back at his car. In the back seat Palmer is smiling. He gives the thumbs up. 'Are we going back then, Roger?' he asks. 'No,' is the deadpan response. 'Take me to my mum's.'

Back at Boundary Park, hundreds have poured onto the pitch. 'Oldham fans think it's all over,' says Pyke. 'And I wish I could have said, in the immortal words, that it is now, but it isn't.'

On the Tannoy, the announcer pleads with fans to get back into the stands. The scoreboard flashes up the final score from Upton Park. The place erupts again.

Wednesday have kicked off and are attempting to attack. Barlow gets to a loose ball and wallops it out of the ground.

Pyke sounds like he is having an on-air breakdown. 'Still we play on,' he bemoans. 'We are top of the league,' is belted out by the believers.

'Five minutes of injury time have been played at Boundary Park,' says the commentator, whose emotion fits the occasion. 'Sensational scenes here. They are off the Oldham bench. They're ready to celebrate. Some people can hardly look.'

The whistles are deafening.

Barrett heads clear, Jobson heads clear, Kane passes to Redfearn, Redfearn passes to Moulden. Callow blows his whistle. For the second time in three minutes, the roof is lifted. It is done. Oldham have won something. They have landed silverware. They are the champions.

'Celebration time!' Pyke bellows. 'Oldham Athletic have won the Second Division title on the last day of the season, in injury time of the last match of the season. Absolutely amazing scenes here at Boundary Park.'

The players race for the tunnel, where a dozen police officers are trying to keep a clear path. This time, thousands sprint onto the pitch. Hordes of joyous punters. This is history.

It starts at the back of the Chaddy End, and within seconds three-quarters of the ground is singing it. 'One Joe Royle, there's only one Joe Royle.'

Marshall has not made it off in time and is mobbed, before being carried on shoulders across the pitch. Barlow has also suffered the same fate. He is stripped of his jersey and has to keep his hands on his shorts to stop them from going the same way.

Police on horseback head towards a seething away end. Back on the Tannoy, a call is sent out for the fans to head back into the stands so the players can do a lap of honour. The area clears, but there is no trophy. The league, in its wisdom, has sent it to Upton Park and there is no replica. Amid the confusion in East London, it has already been engraved with West Ham's name. Instead, Barrett has to wave a silver eagle, hastily provided by sponsors Barclays, to the sky.

The players head down the steps for a lap of honour but it is futile. Another invasion ensues. Amid the mayhem, Marshall and Rick Holden are hoisted aloft. Elsewhere in the madness a fan has somehow ended up with the number seven, which he joyously raises above his head. At the top of the tunnel steps Royle studies the scene and a grin spreads across his face. Finally, they make it back to the dressing room and the champagne. Gordon Lawton is manhandled and launched into the bath, fully clothed.

Marshall grabs Redfearn. 'It's a fucking good job you scored,' he tells his team-mate. 'You'd have been lynched if you'd missed.' Redfearn asks him what he means. 'Cos we've won the fucking title,' Marshall tells him, incredulously. The magnitude of what he has just done finally dawns on Redfearn, who wisely decides to keep quiet about his failure to recognise the importance of his spot-kick.

Outside the Wednesday dressing room, Atkinson is furious. He feels his team has been robbed and is criticising the referee and the pitch. Even the scoreboard comes in for some stick, for having the temerity of flashing up score updates from Upton Park. He enters Royle's office, where the party is getting started and his old friend, wary of his pre-kick-off glass of wine comment, smiles when he sees him with a face he thinks resembles that of a robber's dog.

In East Germany, where the Inspirals are touring, Graham Lambert is oblivious to what has happened in front of his old spot in the Chaddy End. He managed to get a half-time update and was dismayed to hear that Oldham were losing 2-0. Believing that they had no hope of overcoming the deficit, he turned his thoughts elsewhere, happy, at least, that his team had been promoted.

At around 6pm CET, Noel Gallagher, the band's cocksure, Manchester City-supporting roadie, wanders over and looks at him. 'By the way,' he says, 'your cunts have won the league', and wanders off. Lambert is stunned.

Back in Oldham, fans head to pubs and to the town. John Battye goes to the Queens, a no-nonsense watering hole within walking distance of the emptying ground. The landlord thrusts a bottle of Moet and Chandon towards him. 'I didn't know you knew what this was!' he tells him.

The players head down the road to the Horton Arms, which is packed to the rafters. Jon Hallworth arrives, still dressed in his kit.

From there they head to the town centre. Even Barlow goes with them. Marshall brings his parents along for the ride. They go to Henry Afrikas, where they are invited on stage. The DJ plays Tina Turner's *Simply The Best* and everyone in the ramshackle venue sings it.

Later in this momentous evening, police are called to Mumps roundabout, the entrance to the town centre. A group of 13 fans, well-oiled, have lain down in the road to spell out 'OAFC' and are refusing to move. An after-party of sorts is held at Monty's, nearby. Many do not leave until 7am.

Royle has held a party at his own house, and is congratulated there by Alex Ferguson. The drinks are flowing.

At some point in the evening, he reflects on what he has witnessed, what he has masterminded. Not even a decade has passed since he was on the hard shoulder of the M62 with his thumb out. Less than 10 years since he insisted on a one-year contract, unsure of how this was to work out on a day when bailiffs would later size up his office furniture. Since he was buying cut-price towels for his players and stencilling their initials on to training kit in the garage of his home.

It has been a long journey but Oldham Athletic, little Oldham Athletic, are in the First Division. In three months, they will take their place with the likes of United, Liverpool and Arsenal. Already, some are predicting a fight against relegation. It should be a season of struggle. But Royle is Royle. He has achieved miracles and he is ready for more. He is confident in this group. Never one to rest on his laurels, he has already made discreet enquiries and believes he can get Mike Milligan back from Everton. He believes his team, with a couple of acquisitions, can challenge for Europe. He smiles and heads back to the party. He thinks of Europe.

ACKNOWLEDGEMENTS

The idea for this book came from the late Gordon Lawton. While covering Oldham for the *Manchester Evening News*, unfortunately in more barren times than those featured within these pages, I got to know the big man very well. He would often recall the 'glory days' and have me and the other hacks in stitches with some of his tales as we waited for the latest manager to arrive in the press conference room with his trusty sidekick Roy Butterworth, who continues to look after the media for the club into his 80s.

Gordy told me I should write a book about what happened on the field as well as off it. He sent me an email with a list of names and numbers of my heroes. Andy Ritchie, Ian Marshall, Mike Milligan ... it went on. I didn't really know what to expect. Would there be a reluctance to reminisce? Suspicions over a journalist and his motives?

What I found was a series of open doors. Those I contacted were happy to speak and generous with their time. Over the next six years, on days off and holidays, I went through the list, travelling the country to speak to those involved. Joe and Jan Royle must have been sick of me turning up at their Ormskirk home, Dictaphone in hand, but they were always welcoming hosts. I had a memorable lunch with Ian Marshall at the Hilton in Leicester. Mike Milligan, back in town for an event at the club, gave me four hours of sheer gold at the hotel in the shadows of Boundary Park and Neil Redfearn told me the story of THAT penalty at a Starbuck's in a retail outlet in Pontefract. Earl Barrett reflected on his Rochdale childhood in a video call from Houston, Texas, where he now coaches. If I could have transported myself back to a 12-year-old me in 1990 and told him what I would be doing 30 years later I am not sure he would have believed me.

In 2017, Gordy sadly passed away while on holiday and it gave me a kick up the backside to crack on. The 30th anniversary of the Sheffield Wednesday game seemed like a good time to aim for and, thanks to the help of all at Reach Sport, we are not a million miles away.

Gordy is not here to read it, but I like to think that he would have approved. God bless you, sir.

As I write, the Oldham Athletic of today could not be more removed from the one you have just read about. The promotion secured by Marshall at Ipswich remains the last we have enjoyed. The club now sits in the bottom tier of professional football. Fans have formed a protest group against its owners. There are grave concerns that liquidation may not be a million miles away.

But enough of that. I am one of the lucky ones who witnessed the miracle, albeit at a young age. Generations born just after me have had no such good fortune. They have been served a diet of mediocrity – and this book is as much for them as it is for anyone else.

ACKNOWLEDGEMENTS

Once upon a time, it was not like this. The idea seems laughable now but we feared nobody. We took on the best this country had to offer and more often than not left them trailing in our wake.

That is the message to those who were not there – This Is How It Feels.

Mike Keegan,
Bundoza Café Bar,
Tokyo, July 2021.

The vast majority of this book came from interviews I carried out with many of the characters involved and my thanks goes to them for their time. I am also grateful for the detail found in the following works:

Joe Royle, The Autobiography, Joe Royle
Pinch Me Not, Tony Bugby
Keeping The Dream Alive, Stewart W. Beckett
14 Great Games: Oldham Athletic,
Rick Holden and Dave Moore
Football – It's A Minging Life:
Rick Holden The Autobiography, Rick Holden
Pine Villa & Oldham Athletic:
A 100 Year Journey,
Stewart W. Beckett

Thanks, Mike

The Neil Redfearn penalty, Oldham v Sheffield Wednesday, May 11, 1991.

Courtesy of Paul Town (Stadium Portraits) and Andrew Mellor.